The first-ever publication of the prestigious annual Jacek Woroniecki Memorial Lectures!

How to Listen & How to Speak

Standing on the Shoulders of Giants to Renew Commonsense and Uncommonsense Wisdom in the Contemporary World

Peter A. Redpath

En Route Books and Media, LLC
St. Louis, MO

⊕ENROUTE
Make the time

En Route Books and Media, LLC
5705 Rhodes Avenue
St. Louis, MO 63109

Cover credit: Sebastian Mahfood

Copyright © 2021 Peter A. Redpath

ISBN-13: 978-1-952464-83-6
Library of Congress Control Number: 2021940397

AQUINAS SCHOOL OF LEADERSHIP, LLC
Volume One

No part of this book may be reproduced, stored in a retrieval system, or transmitted in any form, or by any means, electronic, mechanical, photocopying, or otherwise, without the prior written permission of the author.

Dedication

*Dedicated to Jerome Meric Pessagno,
for introducing me to the teachings of Saint Thomas Aquinas,*

to a group of dedicated high school religious brothers and secular faculty who, together with Meric, introduced me to the uncommon commonsense wisdom tradition of Western civilization;

and to Charles Bonaventure Crowley, O.P.—a Grand Master among those who understand

"Give me a lever long enough
and a fulcrum on which to place it,
and I shall move the world!"

Archimedes of Syracuse (c. 287–c. 212 B.C.)

Author's Statement about Notes and Bibliography:

To make this book as reader friendly as possible, I will use no footnotes or endnotes. All notes, page numbers, and annotation will refer to passages cited from bibliographical works below, or comments about these passages; and appear in the body of the text, following the passage(s) they cite.

Bibliography

Adler, Mortimer J. *Aristotle for Everybody*: *Difficult Thought Made Easy.* New York: Touchstone, 1977.

———. "The Bodyguards of Truth," in *Proceedings of the American Catholic Philosophical Association* (1976), 125.

———. *How to Speak. How to Listen.* Collier Books: Macmillan Publishing Co., 1983.

———. *Philosopher at Large*: An Intellectual Autobiography. New York: Collier Books: Macmillan Publishing Co., 1977.

———. *A Second Look in the Rearview Mirror.* New York: Macmillan Publishing Company, 1992.

———. *How to Read a Book.* London: Jarrold Publishers, Ltd., 1949.

Aristotle. *On the Heavens.* Trans. J.L. Stocks. In Richard McKeon (ed). *The Basic Works of Aristotle.* New York: Random House, 1968.

---. *Metaphysics*. Trans. W.D. Ross. In Richard McKeon (ed). *The Basic Works of Aristotle*. New York: Random House, 1968.

---. *Nicomachean Ethics*. Trans. W.D. Ross. In Richard McKeon (ed). *The Basic Works of Aristotle*. New York: Random House, 1968.

---. *Physics*. R.P. Hardie and R.K. Gaye. In Richard McKeon (ed). *The Basic Works of Aristotle*. New York: Random House, 1968.

---. *Politics*. Trans. Benjamin Jowett. In Richard McKeon (ed). *The Basic Works of Aristotle*. New York: Random House, 1968.

Diodorus Siculus. *Bibliotheca historica*: available online at https://mythagora.com/bios/muses.html

Galileo Galilei, *Assayer*. In *The Scientific Background of Modern Philosophy*. Ed. Michael R. Matthews. Indianapolis and Cambridge, Mass.: Hackett Publishing Company, Ltd., 1989.

---. *Dialogues Concerning the Two Chief World Systems*. In *The Scientific Background of Modern Philosophy*. Ed. Michael R. Matthews. Indianapolis and Cambridge, Mass.: Hackett Publishing Company, Ltd., 1989.

Gilson, Étienne, *History of Christian Philosophy in the Middle Ages*. New York, Random House, 1954.

---. *Painting and Reality*. New York; Pantheon Books. Published for the Bollingen Foundation, Inc., Bollingen Series 35, 1957.

Plato. *Apology*. Trans. Hugh Treddenick. In Edith Hamilton and Huntington Cairns *The Collected Dialogues of Plato: Including the Letters*. Published for the Bollingen Foundation, Inc., Bollingen Series 71, 1966.

Phaedo. Trans. Hugh Treddenick. In Edith Hamilton and Huntington Cairns *The Collected Dialogues of Plato: Including the Letters*. Published for the Bollingen Foundation, Inc., Bollingen Series 71, 1966.

———. *Meno*. Trans. W.K.C. Guthrie. In Edith Hamilton and Huntington Cairns *The Collected Dialogues of Plato: Including the Letters*. Published for the Bollingen Foundation, Inc., Bollingen Series 71, 1966.

———. *Republic*. Trans. Paul Shorey. In Edith Hamilton and Huntington Cairns *The Collected Dialogues of Plato: Including the Letters*. Published for the Bollingen Foundation, Inc., Bollingen Series 71, 1966.

———. *Theaetetus*. Trans. F.M. Cornford. In Edith Hamilton and Huntington Cairns *The Collected Dialogues of Plato: Including the Letters*. Published for the Bollingen Foundation, Inc., Bollingen Series 71, 1966.

Redpath, Peter A. *An Introduction to Ragamuffin Ethics*. En Route Books & Media. St. Louis, Mo., 2017.

Sandstrom, Gregory. Laws of Media—The Four Effects: A McLuhan contribution to social epistemology. *In Social Epistemology Review and Reply Collective* 1 (12): 1–6 http://wp.me/p1Bfg0-uc, 2012.

Thomas Aquinas. *Commentary on the Metaphysics of Aristotle*. Trans. John P. Rowan. Chicago: Henry Regnery. Co., Inc. 1961.

———. *Commentary on the Nicomachean Ethics of Aristotle*. Trans. C.I. Litzinger. Notre Dame, Ind.: Dumb Ox Books, 1993.

———. *Commentary on the Posterior Analytics of Aristotle*. Trans. F.R. Larcher, based on the Leonine text. Albany, NY: Magi Books, 1970.

———. *Summa theologiae*. Ed. Commisio Piana. Ottawa, 1953.

Contents

Author's Introduction i

Acknowledgments vii

ONE 1
    Lesson 1—General Introduction: The Chief Aim of This Course, How We Will Realize It, and Division of Mortimer J. Adler's Text: *How to Speak. How to Listen.*

TWO 49
    Lesson 2—Distinguishing Solitary and Social Language Arts

THREE 69
    Lesson 3—Uninterrupted Speech as The Amiable, Good-will, Gateway to Friendly Conversation

FOUR 115
    Lesson 4—Analysis of "The 'Sales Talk' and Other Forms of Persuasive Speech"

FIVE 147
    Lesson 5—Understanding Lectures and Other Forms of Instructive Speech

SIX 175
> Lesson 6—Commonsense Rules for Composing and Delivering a Speech

SEVEN 191
> Lesson 7—Silent Listening as a Commonsense Liberal Art Activity

EIGHT 203
> Lesson 8—How to Apply the Commonsense Liberal Art of Listening to Taking Lecture Notes

NINE 219
> Lesson 9—How to Use Question and Answer Forums to Learn to Excel at All Forms of Social Talk

TEN 241
> Lesson 10—How to Use Some Commonsense Principles of Two-Way Talk to Excel at Both Playful and Serious Conversations

ELEVEN 249
> Lesson 11—Some Commonsense Rules Applicable to Making Every Kind of Conversation Pleasurable and Profitable

TWELVE 267
    Lesson 12—Commonsense Gateways to Achieving
    Partial and Total Agreement in Two-Way Talks

THIRTEEN 287
    Lesson 13—Commonsense Advice for Understanding
    How to Succeed at the 3 Species of Teaching and
    Learning

FOURTEEN 297
    Lesson 14—The Crucial Importance of Two-Way
    Conversation for Achieving Human Happiness and
    Global Peace

FIFTEEN 327
    Lesson 15—Common sense: The Personal Meeting
    Point in and through which Providence First Touches
    an Animal Soul as that of a Human Person

Author's Introduction

As the title and subtitle of this book clearly indicate, while its subject is chiefly human communication in the form of listening and speaking, I consider this subject in subordinate relation to its being a chief means for enabling contemporary readers to come into contact with common and uncommon commonsense wisdom of past intellectual giants. In addition, I do this for the chief goal of fostering world peace by enabling my readers to enrich their own lives and that of others by acquiring some of this wisdom and putting it to use on a daily basis.

I have not written this book because I am chiefly interested in understanding the nature of human communication, listening and speaking, or the teachings of the intellectual giants to which I mainly refer within this work: Thales, Socrates, Plato, Aristotle, St. Thomas Aquinas, and Mortimer J. Adler. I have written it because, like many contemporary human beings, I am mainly concerned about the glaring loss of common sense and commonsense wisdom from the West and globally—and the terrible damage this loss is causing to human, and other forms of, life on a global scale.

Author's Introduction

Like many of our contemporaries, I consider loss of common sense the chief cause of all contemporary world problems. Unlike many of them, however, through decades of reading authors renowned for their common sense, I do not think understanding its nature is difficult to comprehend. Because all somewhat healthy human beings are born with some measure of common sense as part of a specific and individual human nature as an innate, imperfectly possessed habit and virtue, all such individuals *cannot not* understand what is common sense. Just like we immediately induce the nature of a whole and a part, we immediately understand what is common sense.

However, its evident familiarity to us *as a first principle of understanding*—a something-we-know-best that *stands under* and makes intelligible (helps us to define and explain to ourselves and to others)—everything else we know makes understanding it initially difficult for us. Because we use it to define everything else, strictly speaking, we cannot define it. At best, we imperfectly define it negatively and relationally to subjects we can and do, more strictly speaking, define. We do the same thing when imperfectly defining a whole and a part as causes that, when harmoniously related, bring organizations into being; or a unit as an undivided multitude and a multitude as a divided unit.

Related to the work of Adler—*How to Speak. How to Listen.*—to which I refer more than to any other in my monograph, a chief reason for using this is because, more than any other I have found, I consider it to be an easily readable means through which to transmit to a contemporary, popular audience a tradition of wealth that encompasses immeasurable amounts of commonsense and uncommon commonsense wisdom. At first glance, Adler's book might appear to be simply a handbook for teaching the classical rhetoric of Aristotle. In actuality, while anyone who reads it for the chief aim of learning that subject may likely find pleasure and profit in so doing, the work's content and main goal is much richer than that. *Adler's monograph is an introduction to a tradition of the uncommon commonsense metaphysical wisdom and moral prudence started by the Ancient Greeks.*

Historically in the West, students of Aristotle's philosophy often refer to it as *the philosophy of common sense*. Adler was one of these students. At times, he referred to Aristotle's philosophy as *the philosophy of uncommon common sense*, meaning that, more than other species of philosophy, it contained a greater wealth of common sense—all philosophy properly-so-called (and especially the Ancient Greek philosophical tradition going back through Socrates to Thales) being *a cultural enterprise tradition* in uncommon common sense wisdom. One reason he did so was because Adler had thought that, in the teachings of Aristotle, the uncommon commonsense principles of philosophy as the Ancient Greek philosophers had understood it were most completely contained, expressed, and defended.

Beyond this, Adler had maintained that, mainly through their reading of Aristotle, the late Medieval Scholastic philosophers who had taught at the Medieval universities (especially St. Thomas Aquinas) had inherited this understanding of philosophy as an uncommon commonsense enterprise in wisdom in the form of a Great Conversation. They had also passed on this inheritance to modernity—until this tradition became sundered, and largely abandoned, through the teachings chiefly of the *Father or Modern Philosophy*, René Descartes (b. 1596; d. 1650), and those of the Enlightenment thinkers, Immanuel Kant (b. 1724; d. 1804) and Georg Hegel (b. 1770; d. 1831) and their historical descendants.

My chief interest in writing my monograph, How to Listen and How to Speak, *is not as a commentary on Adler's book.* It is not to teach readers classical rhetoric, or Adler's understanding of this subject. It is to use some topics Adler discusses in his monograph to transcend his book as an introduction to the tradition of the uncommon commonsense metaphysical wisdom and moral prudence of the Ancient Greeks; and, thereby, hopefully contribute to his work to help foster establishment of future global peace.

In writing his work, I contend that Adler had stood on the metaphysical and moral teachings of Aristotle and St. Thomas Aquinas to convey to his readers an understanding of the nature of Aristotle's rhetoric as an essential means for conveying to readers of his time and to posterity a specific understanding of philosophy as an essential humanistic, educational tool that might, someday, be able to issue in global peace! Thus understood, rhetoric enables teachers to convey a living tradition of uncommon commonsense wisdom and promotion of peace among human beings from one generation to another. In so doing, it trans-generationally conveys uncommon commonsense metaphysical wisdom and moral prudence in the form of a cultural heritage as a traditional enterprise (team effort) that fosters trans-generational improvement of individual and social life, and peaceful and cooperative living together.

For this reason, I have composed the chapters of my monograph in the form of lessons that can be used as part of an academic course of instruction in commonsense wisdom and leadership coaching out of which I hope a future commonsense wisdom academy and post-Enlightenment uncommon commonsense wisdom university will naturally eventually grow.

Peter A. Redpath
CEO, Aquinas School of Leadership, LLC
Providentially completed and published on:
06 June 2021

In solemn memory and gratitude for the gallant soldiers who gave their lives on D-Day to save Western Civilization.

Acknowledgments

I wish to thank my friend and colleague Dr. Sebastian Mahfood, OP, founder and publisher of En Route Books & Media, for accepting this monograph for publication. I hope he finds its sales pleasurable and profitable.

I also want to thank three colleagues and friends—Professors Bob Ginsberg, Richard T. Hull (R.I.P.), and Jorge J. E. Gracia—for, several decades ago, schooling me in commonsense research and editing practices that have served me well during my academic career and have helped me understand and appreciate the nature of philosophy as a commonsense cultural enterprise.

I want to thank my colleague and friend Marvin B. Daniel Peláez for the terrific proofreading and editing work he did to help get this monograph into publishable form. Any remaining typos and editorial errors within it are my responsibility.

Finally, I wish to thank my colleagues at the John Paul II Catholic University of Lublin, Prof. dr. hab. Piotr Jaroszyński and Prof. dr. hab. Imelda Chłodna-Błach for inviting, and assisting, me to give the prestigious 2021 Jacek Woroniecki Memorial Lectures. In so doing, with the help of the students participating, they enabled me analogously to compare and articulate the historical, cultural, and civilizational magnitude of these Lectures and my current monograph to that of the celebrated 'Father of Modern Philosophy' René Descartes first presenting his work, *Meditations on First Philosophy*, to "The Most Wise and Illustrious The Dean and Doctors of the Sacred Faculty of Theology in Paris" at the University of Paris in 1641. They did so, particularly, by allowing me, for a first time publicly, in detail, at a prestigious international university, to show how the contents of this book and these Lectures contain the main philosophical, psychological, and social science remedy to counteract the widespread cultural and civilizational damage that, unwittingly on his part, Descartes's misunderstanding of the nature of philosophy—especially of the human person, metaphysics, wisdom, prudence, and common sense—unleashed on future generations of human beings in the West and globally.

—CHAPTER ONE—

Lesson 1—General Introduction: The Chief Aim of This Course, How We Will Realize It, and Division of Mortimer J. Adler's Text: *How to Speak. How to Listen.*

Hello, my name is Dr. Peter Redpath. Welcome to the first lesson of this 15-lesson educational project to use topics from Mortimer J. Adler's classic book in the art of communicating commonsense wisdom—*How to Speak. How to Listen.*—to: 1) stand on the shoulders of classical intellectual giants; 2) hopefully, see deeply into and beyond their understanding of such wisdom and uncommonsense wisdom; and 3) use this more penetrating understanding to communicate and renew all forms of common sense in the contemporary world.

Each lesson in this investigation is based upon topics discussed within division of Adler's book into 5 parts comprised of 14 chapters, and 1 set of 3 appendices. This set of appendices is simply a 15th chapter divided into 3 parts.

Part 1 of Adler's monograph is entitled "Prologue." Part 2 is called "Uninterrupted Speech." Part 3 has the title "Silent Listening." Adler names Part 4 "Two-way Talk." And he calls Part 5 "Epilogue."

The Prologue contained in Part 1 consists of 2 chapters. Chapter 1, which I will consider in this first lesson, has the title, "The Untaught Skills." Chapter 2 is entitled, "The Solitary and the Social."

Specific Introduction, Part 1, Chapter 1: Human communication as the main means by which human beings share a single understanding and, with it, common sense.

Part 1, Chapter 1, about untaught skills, considers two questions: 1) "How do you make contact with a mind of another person?"; and 2) "In what way should that other person respond to your effort?" While Adler does not explicitly state in this Chapter precisely what he means when he entitles it "Untaught Skills," what he says explicitly on the last page of Part 4, Chapter 8, and what he makes evident in his Chapter 1, clarify why he does so.

In Chapter 8, (p. 112) he states that, whether or not human beings agree or disagree about some subject of discussion, "the ultimate purpose of (human/my addition) communication . . . is the meeting of minds in such a way that they share a common understanding." According to Adler, the chief aim of human communication is to convey knowledge of some subject in such a way that the parties communicating possess exactly the same understanding of it, whether this understanding be generic, specific, or individual. Both parties understand precisely what they are talking about and precisely the way they are talking about it. For example, if two medical doctors are talking about the human heart and one is a cancer specialist while the other is a heart surgeon, they both understand precisely that they are talking about the human heart in relationship to cancer or to some other heart-related issue. In short, people who reach a meeting of minds about something possess the exact same commonsense understanding of it, one that needs no explanation to the parties involved! They immediately know precisely what the other is thinking about and the way he or she is thinking about it. To them, what they are saying and the way they are saying it just makes common sense.

A caution about a major mistake to avoid in order to use conversations to achieve successful, shared understanding and common sense: Be on the same page!

Adler is well known to have been mainly a self-professed student of Aristotle, to have applied Aristotle's teachings to try to help resolve contemporary problems. And Adler well understood that, according to Aristotle (*On the Heavens*, bk, 1, ch. 5), small mistakes about first principles in the beginning of an investigation tend greatly to multiply as an inquiry continues. This observation applies to ordinary conversations just as much as it does to scientific investigations.

Conversations tend to make no intellectually beneficial advancement unless the people involved in them are talking about the same subject (what Aristotle called a *genus*) in more or less the same way. Knowledge that two people are doing this does not come from reasoning or scientific demonstration. It comes from immediate commonsense understanding, induction prior to reasoning or scientific demonstration.

A first principle, necessary condition, of profitable conversation, one that contains some intellectual richness, wealth, common sense is that the people involved in it understand precisely what they are talking about and how they are talking about it. This means that the people themselves and what they are talking about are among the chief first principles of the conversations. While logical premises are first principles of logical reasoning, not every principle, or first principle, is a principle of logic. Before we can reason about anything logically or not logically, we must first know something without having to reason about it. We can only reason about what, in some way, we know.

Following Aristotle, Adler calls what we know through immediate induction, without the need to reason about it to make it intelligible to us, *understanding*. Because what we reason about necessarily involves immediately knowing some subject without needing to reason about it, Adler considers what we know in such a way to be a matter of *common understanding*, or *common sense*.

Apparent from what Adler says about common understanding is that he considers this to be more or less identical with what most human beings appear always and everywhere to call *common sense*: immediately understanding what anyone and everyone familiar with the subject knows to be so true about it that it is a commonly assumed starting point for any intelligible, and especially, profitable, conversation. Today, in the United States, we would say that people who do not engage in conversation starting in this way *are not on the same page*. Aristotle would say they are not talking about the same subject in the same way, or they do not belong to the same genus.

Why and how all somewhat physically and psychologically healthy human beings are born, naturally endowed, with some measure of commonsense ability.

Aristotle was convinced that, to some extent, all somewhat healthy human beings are born with physical and psychological qualities/dispositions that incline us to be more or less physically and psychologically healthy. Regarding psychological health these qualities incline us to be more or less emotionally disposed to: 1) be sensitive to pleasure or pain/temperate or intemperate; 2) be fearful or daring/courageous or cowardly; 3) be easygoing or irascible; 4) be shy or gregarious; 5) be just or unjust/friendly or unfriendly, or 6) be prudent or imprudent.

And they also incline us to be more or less intellectually talented or endowed. Hence, some children are born with a greater or lesser facility to learn music or mathematics; think productively or practically, concretely or abstractly; immediately to understand first principles, have strong psychological induction faculties; or *possess some common sense considered in general or in relation to this or that subject.*

Why and how philosophy/science is essentially *uncommon* commonsense organizational psychology.

Aristotle considered a person especially strong in native endowment and/or native endowment and some acquired experience in such an ability to possess *some wisdom in understanding* (*commonsense wisdom*) about it: some understanding about evident principles an organizational whole contains that proximately cause it to exist as a harmonious unity of parts that generate some unique organizational act. He also thought that this organizational act (effect generated by harmonious unity of action of the parts of an organizational whole) exists as a sign (*sign vehicle*, to use a term coined by Adler's one-time assistant, John N. Deely) of a real relation that causes its organizational unity. He maintained that this organizational unity can be expressed in terms of a real definition (a relation of a real genus [which expresses, signifies, the harmonious unity of the parts of the organizational whole] and species [which expresses the organizational action; the harmonious action that an organizational whole, through harmonious cooperation of its parts, aims to, and unless, in some way frustrated, does generate]).

Analogous to such a person would be a person more scientifically advanced in this or that subject. Such a person would be inclined to be wiser in understanding and reasoning about this subject. That is, he or she would be qualitatively more intensely, strongly, perfectly possessed of commonsense: richer, wealthier, in it and its application. Having qualitatively more of what Medieval scholastic philosophers called a *virtus* (strength/virtue) in having and exercising it, such a person, being stronger in induction ability, would be qualitatively wiser at least in relation to that subject.

At least implicitly, such being how Adler understood common sense in the way I have just described it, he maintained that, for any human being to be able to engage in profitable conversation, one somewhat qualitatively rich in understanding related to a subject, that person must have some measure of common sense, be *somewhat* wise by natural endowment alone or natural endowment plus acquired experience related to it. Scientific/philosophical advancement related to that subject, therefore, is simply becoming qualitatively more wise, more perfect in possessing/having commonsense wisdom—in specifically and individually understanding what someone already generically and implicitly understands about it.

Since, by its nature, understanding some subject contains within it some measure of endowed wisdom upon which wise reasoning essentially depends and flows from as from a proximate first principle, cause, and measure, for Adler, philosophy is simply qualitatively more perfect, *uncommon* intellectual understanding and reasoning (*uncommon* commonsense wisdom) reflecting upon qualitatively less perfect, commonsense wisdom. And he maintains that this is chiefly what the leading Ancient Greek philosophers, especially Aristotle, understood philosophy to be. For this reason, within Western philosophical history the philosophy of Aristotle has often been referred to as "the philosophy of common sense."

Why, in maintaining that philosophy is *uncommon* common sense, Adler was standing on the shoulders of Ancient Greek philosophical giants, including Thales.

In adopting this understanding of philosophy, Adler was doing nothing more than following in the great Gadfly-tradition of the stonemason Socrates when, in Plato's *Meno* (82a–86c), Socrates worked with Menon's servant's commonsense understanding (understanding that contained some wisdom by natural endowment and prior experience) of geometrical figures to introduce him to and teach him *The Pythagorean Theorem* related to the hypotenuse of a triangle. Therein, Socrates shows Menon's servant that philosophy involves understanding the nature of principles/causes that, when applied to knowing a subject, puts interlocutors on the same page about it and its behavior as an organizational whole. Philosophy starts to cause in them a common understanding, enabling them to share a meeting of minds when they talk about some subject, its unity, and the way it acts. And, while Adler does not explicitly say so, he is also indicating that, since philosophy and science are identical for Aristotle, this is also the philosophical/scientific disposition of human psychology considered in general: *The psychological habit of generically and/or specifically and/or individually wondering about organizational existence, unity, and behavior.*

How Thales was a master of common and *uncommon* common sense.

That this was the case among the Ancient Greek philosophers was not something that started with Socrates. It was present in the very first beginnings of philosophy among the ancient physicists, including the reputed Father of Western Philosophy: Thales. Well known to anyone who has studied Ancient Greek philosophy is the story told by Plato (in his *Theaetetus*, 174a–174b) and Aristotle (in his *Politics*, bk. 1, ch. 11, 1259a 1–36).

In Plato's account, Thales is portrayed as intellectually wise (having uncommon common sense) but lacking in ordinary common sense. According to this tale attributed in origin to a Thracian servant-girl, the well-known astronomer and reputed wise man Thales was so lacking in ordinary (common) common sense that, while he was intellectually absorbed with his head up in the clouds contemplating the movement of the stars, he could not see what was in front of him and fell into a well.

In Aristotle's version, tired of being ridiculed for his poverty due to his lack of ordinary common sense (for which Socrates is repeatedly mocked, especially by sophists, in Plato's dialogues), by *using* his knowledge of astronomy to make himself rich, Thales decided to teach his critics a lesson about the worth of philosophy. Somehow, due to his observation of the winter movement of stars, Thales had concluded that the next spring and summer would produce a bumper crop of olives. Foreseeing with financial common sense that this would be the case, he put down a deposit at a low price for use of all the local olive presses. When the harvest time came, Aristotle tells us he then rented them out at any amount he wanted and quickly became rich.

How Aristotle explained Thales' financial common sense.

While some people attributed Thales' success to an uncommon, scientific/philosophical wisdom (*uncommon* commonsense wisdom/common-knowledge perfection in understanding) on his part, Aristotle maintains it was nothing of the sort. It was based upon common financial knowledge (commonsense financial understanding and wisdom) universal to anybody who understands the nature of *monopolies* and how to use them to: 1) acquire wealth as a kind of *self-sufficiency* and, thereby, 2) become a *self-provider*. Aristotle adds that the knowledge Thales had applied was simply commonsense financial wisdom/common financial understanding (*meeting of minds*) for many an Ancient Greek.

As indicative or this commonsense financial wisdom, Aristotle gives the example of a Sicilian merchant who had analogously applied the monopolistic financial practice Thales had used. The merchant did so by buying up all the iron from local iron mines and became the only seller of iron in Syracuse. Without increasing his price much, Aristotle reports that this man was quickly able to make a 200% profit on his initial investment. In addition, he says that, when the ruler of Syracuse, the tyrant Dionysius, had heard about what had happened, thinking that this man had discovered some secret way of making money that could hurt his political interests and career, he told the merchant he could keep his money, but only if he agreed to leave Syracuse.

Aristotle adds that, when they lack money, like households, city-states often monopolize, stock up on, necessary goods/*provisions* (*prudently see ahead*, create an abundance or storehouse [like a bank or treasury] of wealth) to sell them at a later date at a higher price. He even recommends this practice to rulers of city-states because, since a city-state is an organization of households, like an ordinary household, a city-state often lacks money. For this reason, *prudent* (commonsense) rulers need to have their cities master the practice of being self-providers, learn how to achieve a monopoly, and even have public officials devote themselves to the study of its use related to finance in general. (*Politics*, bk. 1, ch. 11, 1259a 1–36)

How Aristotle missed a *Eureka!-moment* related to the essential connection among liberal arts education, the nature of monopolies, and philosophy/science as a form of psychological wealth.

Aristotle glosses over the profundity of his observation regarding Thales' understanding the nature of monopolies and how skillfully to practice them. While he does not treat this observation as a *Eureka!-moment* like that of Archimedes, he had every right to do so—as, standing on Aristotle's shoulders and those of Thales, I will now, especially in light of what Aristotle says about understanding the benefit that liberal arts education adds to acquisition of wealth.

According to Aristotle, work that is *most* an art and free (liberal) is the kind that *least* depends upon chance, uncertainty, contingency, and indeterminacy (like understanding *how to use* monopoly to make work as financially beneficial, productive, and enriching as actually possible [actually doable]). In contrast, work that is *least artistic, free/ liberal,* and *most servile* is bodily work that lacks direction by human understanding (common sense): the one that most depends

Chapter 1: General Introduction

upon all the aforementioned obstacles. Aristotle maintained that, for a human being, the most free, masterly, liberal art is the one that is least servile and most *common-sensical*: the one that *is most humanly useful/humanistic.*

Such work most involves use of human understanding (taking advantage of, leveraging, commonsense and uncommon commonsense wisdom) and least involves use of the body, while the most servile least depends upon human understanding (taking advantage of, leveraging, commonsense and uncommon commonsense wisdom) and most on a mindless body. What makes the arts to be arts and liberal is not simply understanding. It is right/beneficial, or virtuous, *use* of understanding—one that, in a way, enables a person to take advantage of personal talent/skill to become like a sole-proprietor monopoly when exercising a human behavior: become someone better at doing/producing something humanly beneficial than anyone or almost anyone else.

Arts that are most truly liberal are those that *stretch* (extend in qualitative strength, width, and depth) *the human imagination so as to enable the human understanding to acquire and improve command and control over bodily movements and inculcate them with intellectual and moral virtue/ common sense.* This is precisely what the arts of Thales and the Sicilian merchant, both of whom saw an essential connection to wealth-increase by *stretching* (educating) *their imaginations* to synthesize three of their talents: 1) applying some uncommon commonsense understanding related to the *use (application) of the financial art of money making and* 2) *the liberal, rhetorical art of negotiating skills to reap great wealth from their understanding of* 3) physics (such as the movement of the stars and where to find [discover] iron).

According to Aristotle *arts are chiefly psychological habits of excellent use* (habitual use of common sense) that generate human wealth: human habits that make virtuous use of human understanding to remove the element of chance from beneficial, humanly enriching, action—action that truly improves, liberates, human life in the form of healthy organizational being and behavior: human greatness! Because they are as good as they can be without the addition of intellectual assistance, servile arts, those that are the least truly liberal and humanly enriching, involve little endowed or acquired, virtuous human understanding (endowed or acquired common sense/virtue) rightly to direct them. Naturally endowed virtue (commonsense wisdom), excellence, and a little intellectual experience (acquired commonsense wisdom) is enough for them analogously to be called *arts*. (Aristotle, *Politics*, bk. 1, ch. 11, 1258a 35–38)

Nevertheless, adding acquired virtue (commonsense wisdom/common understanding wisdom) that makes human action certain/sure to succeed, lacking in contingency and chance, predictable and fixed, predetermined in outcome to already-existing, endowed virtue (commonsense wisdom/common understanding wisdom) adds a qualitatively higher form of liberty, human wealth/capital, and common sense (*a monopolistic quality of sole proprietorship*) to physical and psychological health and action that is a necessary condition for exercising free human life (and especially that of political life of a citizen), not of a slave or serf.

Furthermore, right (commonsense) use of monopoly (being a mono-polis, a city-state unto oneself, self-sufficient/ determined/reliant) as a sole proprietor of one's own virtues/ talents is a necessary [naturally endowed and acquired resource] form of wealth that is a necessary condition for acquisition of all other species of wealth. Wealth chiefly consists in having and being able to put some resource/good to beneficial personal use. Essentially, human wealth is abundance of greatness in strength in *having and being able wisely to put to use* a human good/perfection in health, whether that be physical or psychological. In so doing, an abundance of acquired intellectual and moral virtue causes an individual human being to become analogous to a healthy household or city-state: self-reliant, a bank-vault of talent.

Why and how widely-distributed, de-centralized, monopolies within a culture are individually and socially good, not evil: storehouses, bank-vaults of individual and cultural common and uncommon sense.

When virtuously applied, and especially when widely distributed, monopoly is not something evil. It is something good, a necessary condition for storing up (having a treasury/thesaurus) of different forms of physical and psychological wealth: storehouses of individual and social common sense. It consists in becoming perfectly self-possessed, a self-master, or something akin to these: exercising self-ownership of the necessary means for producing perfectly healthy human action and a happy individual and social human life.

What else is a talented vocalist like Andrea Bocelli but a sole-proprietor monopolist of a fine art? Precisely because he has a monopoly on a talent, he advances beneficial social communication and exchange of human goods, including financial, psychological, and physical health! What healthy societies have is not a lack of monopoly. They have widely and deeply distributed, decentralized, monopolies in the form of talented sole proprietors freely exchanging talentedly produced and humanly healthy products/goods.

They do not have one or a few centralized monopolies such as those that exist in contemporary Enlightenment socialist utopias and Enlightenment colleges and universities (which attempt at every turn to transform talented people into serfs/employees servicing and sustaining in existence centralized administrative/bureaucratic monopolies) that often unwittingly traffic in promoting slavery, serfdom, and other forms of humanly destructive behavior among their faculty and students.

Mortimer J. Adler understood very well the points I have just made about the way in which endowed and acquired virtue/talent (commonsense, and *uncommon* commonsense wisdom), especially widely distributed, decentralized, natural and acquired philosophical ability as a cultural enterprise, tends to liberate human beings from poverty, slavery, and other forms of unhealthy human lifestyles. Like Aristotle, according to Adler, unless a person has some wisdom, common sense, already, philosophy is worthless. As he was fond of saying, "Philosophy bakes no cakes and builds no bridges."

As he tells us in *Aristotle for Everybody: Difficult Thought Made Easy*, philosophy is *useful*, wealth-enabling/generating only to people who already have some common sense (common understanding knowledge of, familiarity with) something. To such people, like Thales and Socrates, the practice of philosophy should give *uncommon* wealth-enabling/generating common sense of the subject they already know. (xiv) Like Socrates, Adler tells us philosophy will enable such people in a qualitatively better, more perfect, way to understand things they already know. (ix) That is, it will enable a person who already has been able to recognize principles at work causing organizations to exist and behave the way they do more precisely to understand: 1) the nature of these principles/causes and 2) why precisely applying, executing, these principles (like Thales) in this or that situation in this or that way causes these organizations to exist and behave the way they do.

Recall that, in the *Apology*, according to Socrates, what got him into trouble in Athens was what he called his *ordinary human wisdom* (commonsense wisdom), which was unlike (*really uncommon* in contrast to) the *reputedly uncommon* wisdom of the professional *wise-men* (sophists) of his time (including some politicians, poets, and craftsmen) who had a reputation for having a monopoly on all wisdom but were not really wise in a philosophical (*uncommon*) sense. All these had a s*erious and hubristic psychological flaw* of claiming to know what they knew and what they did not know. (Plato, *Apology*, 20d–23b)

Unlike the fake wisdom of these individuals, who could not explain how they knew what they knew (if they actually knew anything at all) by being able to identify the principles and causes that enabled things of which they claimed to have a professional expertise to exist as organizational wholes and behave the way they did, Socrates' uncommon, commonsense wisdom consisted in only claiming to know those subjects that he could explain, like an organizational behavioral psychologist (which is what all the leading Ancient Greek philosophers considered themselves to be), in terms of the principles and causes of their behavior. Adler's attempt to revive philosophy in this tradition of the uncommon common sense (sole-proprietorship behavioral psychology) of the Gadfly Socrates caused Adler to be hated by many of the same sort of sophists that, in ancient Greece, hated Socrates for exposing them as fakes, claiming scientifically/philosophically to know what they did not know in that way, or often in any way at all. A chief aim of this current study is to do the same thing to revive philosophical/scientific education in our time in the West and globally.

A more specific consideration of philosophical/scientific (uncommon common sense) education: Having the ability to stretch the imagination to think outside the box and avoid having tunnel vision and a beltway mentality.

To consider more specifically this quest of reviving philosophical/scientific (uncommon common sense) education in the West and globally, I need to return to Part 1, Chapter 1, of Adler's book *How to Speak. How to Listen*, in which he considers the two questions: 1) "How do you make contact with a mind of another person?" and 2) "In what way should that other person respond to your effort?"

To answer these questions, as Adler has told us, we have to understand that "the ultimate purpose of (human/my addition) communication . . . is the meeting of the minds in such a way that they share a common understanding." We actually have to do more than this. We have to share the same personal psychology as the person or persons with whom we seek to communicate. In a sense, we have to share the same desire to communicate, exchange understanding, more or less in the same way and to do so using the same images. We actually have to want to communicate with, understand, what another person is understanding the way he or she is understanding it. This is what is actually involved in reaching *commonsense agreement*!

And to do this we must first have some natural or acquired talent, enriching-principle, perfecting quality of naturally endowed wealth in personal communications ability: personal likability as a kind of behavioral psychologist. To some extent, we must be a resource, thesaurus, of personal understanding of and in common-sense wisdom simply to be able to imagine the way another person imagines. If we cannot first personally imagine what another person is thinking, engage in personal common-sense imagining (not simply have a meeting of minds), we cannot understand what he or she is understanding/thinking *and the way he or she is understanding/thinking it*. The individual human person, not a mind, is the individual that understands, thinks, imagines. Looking at another person as another mind is too impersonal, *Cartesian*, to be right.

But how can we do this? Many people might think doing this is impossible. In actuality, because we do it all the time, it is not impossible at all. If something is actual, it cannot be impossible.

To understand how this *meeting of personal psychologies* actually occurs is also simple. Many people throughout the world are familiar with psychological dispositions that incline people not to be able to communicate, or not to *be on the same page (achieve commonsense agreement)* with another person. In the United States today, we use three common images to communicate this psychological disability. We refer to it as: 1) the inability to think outside the box; 2) having tunnel vision; and 3) having a beltway mentality.

In each case, these images convey the psychology of a person who is a specialist, even over-specialized, someone with an understanding so narrow that he or she cannot even imagine, much less understand, how another person understands something: what is the genus (organizational whole) within which another person is locating (defining) and imagining what he or she is thinking about (genera, species, and individuals) so as initially to make them intelligible to himself or herself.

Such a person is like someone who lives life in a box, cut off from the outside world. In Washington, D.C., because so many politicians tend to have this mentality and Washington is surrounded by an automobile beltway, Americans tend to refer to this as *having a beltway mentality*. Those inside the beltway (the *Elites*) tend to be unable to imagine, much less understand, the way *people* (individual persons) outside the beltway (*the Deplorables*) imagine and understand; and vice versa.

In Book 7 of his *Republic* (514a–519c), Plato gives his famous *Myth of the Cave* example to provide an image to make understandable to his readers the narrow psychological disposition that some people tend to have that prevents them from being able to acquire the uncommon common sense (sole-proprietorship/monopolistic-like wisdom) of someone like Socrates. Their narrow way of imagining people and things inclines them to view everything like prisoners chained together would do: only to be able to look ahead to viewing images being projected onto the wall of a cave from sunlight entering into the cave from outside (somewhat like listening to contemporary-media, political talking-points). To get them out of this narrow understanding, Plato maintained that some prisoner would have to escape from the cave and later return to it and start to try to convey (at first, largely unsuccessfully) to those still present within it what actually exists and goes on in reality.

Over many decades, I have found that academicians in general, and especially logicians (who tend to be generally unable psychologically to distinguish between conceptual and behavioral contradictions), tend to have this mentality. When I was young, my mother used to say, "Sometimes the smartest people are the dumbest." As a youth, I could not understand precisely what she meant, how this conceptual contradiction could possibly be true. As I got older, I understood that she was referring to this psychological disability of over-specialized knowledge, having common sense in one area of understanding that acted as an obstacle to having common sense in another. Adler maintained that a "specialization in generalization" is needed to overcome this disability of over-specialized knowledge which acts as a kind of ignorance.

Why Adler should have entitled his book *How to Listen and How to Speak.*

As many academicians recognize, the beginning of specialization in generalized knowledge starts with *a stretching of the human imagination* that only a liberal arts education can cause. As Adler well understood, liberal arts education is simply the beginning of an uncommon, sole-proprietorship, acquired common sense understanding that is somewhat philosophical and, more precisely, metaphysical in nature.

In every area of specialized understanding, people who possess this knowledge do so because they have some talent, form of common sense, that enables them to imagine, understand, *induce* the principles/causes (the generic and specific parts signified through real definitions) that are involved in generating organizational wholes and how they are put together (synthesized) and separated (analyzed) into the parts that harmonize to cause their activity. Unique to sole-proprietor metaphysicians like Adler (who practiced metaphysics in the tradition of Socrates, Plato, and Aristotle) is that classical Western metaphysicians chiefly, behaviorally—not logically—*first induce and then*, only afterwards, *investigate* the principles and causes involved in proximately generating any and every kind of organizational whole. They do this to make more precisely intelligible, understandable, to themselves and to others how organizations in general and in precise detail come to be and operate the way they do.

For this reason, the Ancient Greeks called this psychological habit "first philosophy." By this they meant *the qualitatively highest science*, the most highly intellectual of the sciences, a science that only one or a few human beings appear ever to be able to master, become sole-proprietor monopolists in.

The Ancient Greeks valued the liberal arts precisely because they saw them as imaginative and intellectual starting points of free human action and *gateways* to highest human freedom: the godlike uncommon commonsense science of metaphysics. They considered the liberal arts to be essential enabling means, the first imaginative and intellectual steps, *gateways*, to acquiring the qualitatively higher commonsense abilities they needed to know so as to transcend the slavery that ignorance tends to cause and become free like a god should be free.

Given his uncommon commonsense wisdom, Aristotle, in turn, understood the gateway to the liberal arts to reside in the psychological disposition of "teachability." During the Latin Middle Ages, Scholastic thinkers used the term *docilitas* (docility) to convey an understanding of what Aristotle meant by this psychological quality/educational virtue. *Saint Thomas Aquinas maintained that docility is a part of prudence.* (*Summa theologiae*, 2–2, q. 49, a. 2 respondeo)

In the tradition of Aristotle, Mortimer Adler, in turn, was of the opinion that personal psychological receptivity to the common understanding/common sense desire to communicate/share understanding with other people must precede a person's ability actually to achieve a meeting of minds so as to acquire uncommon common sense, or any common-sense understanding at all. And, he understood the *gateway* to such personal receptivity to understanding to lie chiefly in the desire (disposition of having good will) and ability to be a good listener, really to want to listen to and understand what another person has to say. For this reason, Adler should have entitled his book *How to Listen and How to Speak* (which is the title to which I have given this study in which I am presently engaged) and not *How to Speak. How to Listen.*

The four uses of language and why the art of listening well is the *gateway* to all the other communications arts and higher forms of common sense.

Briefly pausing discussion about which is the better title for such a work like this essentially devoted to communications arts, I return to the first question of Adler's first chapter regarding untaught skills of communicating with the mind of another human being by maintaining that, while we can make contact with the mind of another person in many ways (such as crying, gesturing, using bodily, or facial, signs), generally we do so through use of verbal or written language:

speaking or listening, writing or reading, which Adler calls, "The four uses of language." (3)

From there he goes on to note that these four uses consist of two complementary pairs that are intellectually useless without each other. More than this, however, these are somewhat analogously opposing species existing within the genus of human communication. Writing and reading, speaking and listening, are opposingly related forms of linguistic communication. The first two in each pair are active, while the second two are passive, in relation to the other member of the respective pairs. Yet, in and of themselves, in a way, each is active.

To be a good listener or reader, for example, as Adler notes, a person must be more than a passive recipient of information coming from a speaker or writer. He or she must be a skilled, *attentive*, listener or reader.

Analogously, a good writer or speaker must also be an attentive reader or listener. Every skilled writer is a skilled editor, and every skilled editor is a skilled reader—listens attentively to, is able skillfully to take in, imagine, conceive, and understand what he or she has written. Every skilled editor, in turn, is a skilled reader, attentively listens to, reads, what he, she, or someone has written to try to imagine, conceive, and comprehend how it will sound when read by, or spoken to, a member of an audience. Through talent, training, or both, as Adler remarks, some people are better (that is, qualitatively more rich, psychologically wealthier in having the enabling means of being) readers and writers/listeners and speakers than are others; and to be fully appreciated by others their respective opposites must be proportionately skilled/rich in all four skills. As he says, "Even the most skilled writing remains ineffective when it falls into the hands of unskilled readers." (3)

As Adler remarks, these four acts are the essentially commonsense enabling means, *gateways*, in and through which the psyche of one human person, in a way, reaches out to make contact with the psyche of another in a single act of understanding; and each requires exceptional skill (wealth of commonsense ability) to apply commonsense understanding to be exceptionally effective, and some natural and acquired skill to be effective at all.

How does an act of understanding existing in the intellect of one person touch the understanding existing in the intellect of another person and, in so doing, combine to form a single understanding that both are understanding each other? While Adler does not ask this precise question, I need to answer it to explain the simpler question he does ask about how the mind of one person is able to reach out to and make contact with the mind of another.

Because of the complexity of answering such metaphysical questions, reasonable to understand is why not many people have been trained to attempt to do so. Not so reasonable to understand, however, is why, given their crucial importance to effective human communication and social life in general, so few human beings are taught in school to become effective readers and writers, listeners and speakers?

In 1940 (eighty years before the day I started composing this book and these Lessons), Adler had written a bestseller-work entitled *How to Read a Book*. It has gone through many re-printings since then and is still in publication today. In that work, he referred to different, then-current, academic studies which had indicated that, by the time he or she reached college- and university-level instruction, the average reading comprehension ability of a typical American student tended to be on a sixth-grade level. (39)

While attempts at improving writing continued to exist after the elementary level in American high schools, colleges, and universities, Adler noted that no corresponding attempts widely existed during the twentieth century to improve listening, speaking, and reading comprehension skills. (3–4) And, while Adler could not have specifically noted this, contemporary attempts to improve writing often tend to fail on higher educational levels because the means often used to effect this even today are chiefly through improvement in use of grammar and punctuation.

Regarding speaking well, Adler remarked that elementary school students are rarely taught this as an effective means for helping to improve reading and writing. And regarding listening he says:

What about listening? Is anyone anywhere taught how to listen? How utterly amazing is the general assumption that the ability to listen well is a natural gift for which no training is required. How extraordinary is the fact that no effort is made anywhere in the whole educational process to help individuals learn how to listen well—at least well enough to close the circuit and make speech effective as a means of communication.

What makes these things so amazing and extraordinary is the fact that the two generally untaught skills, speaking and listening, are much more difficult to acquire and more difficult to teach than the parallel skills of writing and reading. (5)

Adler explains the reason this is so to be that, while complaints about the lower level of skill that American elementary, high school, and college graduates attain in writing and reading is widespread and indignant, few, if any, complaints tend to be raised about the low level of skill they attain in speaking and listening. Nonetheless, he observes that, "however low the level of writing and reading is today among those who have the advantages of twelve or more years of schooling, much lower still is the level of skill in speaking that most people possess, and lowest of all is skill in listening." (5)

Clearly, since listening is still currently the lowest of all the language comprehension arts taught in schools in the

West and globally (and the one most crucial for being in touch with reality, and, therefore, common sense, in general, and the intellectual *understanding* of other human beings), it must also be the most crucial and currently lowest comprehension skill in the United States, the West, and world in general, for having and advancing in and surpassing ordinary commonsense wisdom!

Such being so, Adler really should have entitled his masterful companion to his 1940 bestseller *How to Listen. How to Speak.* From personal experience of 52 years of college and university teaching, I can attest with no doubt that listening with one's intellect and senses, as a whole person (*especially active, or attentively, as a seriously-interested observer*), is the educational skill most lacking in students everywhere today, the one out of which, as Aristotle and Saint Thomas Aquinas had observed, through teaching, all learning, including ordinary commonsense wisdom, grows—just as all sense faculties grow out of the sense of touch.

Why the Ancient Greek, Roman, and Medieval students tended to be better listeners and speakers than are most students today.

While many readers or people who might hear about the immediately above claim might consider it to be ridiculous, as Adler rightly observes, in the period prior to the Gutenberg press, people in the West in general, and those educated by private tutors or in academic institutions, tended to be better listeners and speakers than we are today. They "had to be," he states, "because, in the absence of the printed page and with written books available only to the very few, those who had some kind of schooling," if they really wanted to learn, students who were learning from teachers "were compelled to learn by listening to what the teacher said." (6)

The Western practice of teaching by lecturing, as the introductory form of learning for all students, largely started, in part, at Medieval universities because this form of teaching was centered on rediscovered writings of Aristotle that had been largely lost since the decline of Rome around the year 400 A.D. During the eleventh and twelfth centuries, these had started to return to the West through Spain and Sicily in the form of translations from Arabic. These works had to be translated into Latin so that Western students could learn from them. In addition, at the time, other works of traditional Western learning had only existed in Latin in manuscript form. Not even the Bible had existed in a widespread fashion. Hence, the tradition in Medieval churches to have scenes from Scripture depicted in stained-glass windows.

Even in earlier cathedral and monastic schools in the Latin West, these, too, had to be taught initially by means of lecturing. As Adler notes, in the great Medieval universities like Padua, Paris, Cologne, Oxford, and Cambridge, teachers were lecturers in a different sense of the word *lecture* than the one now generally in use. (6) As the Latin term *lectio* (from which the English term *lecture* is derived) indicates, lecturing in a Medieval university and cathedral and monastic schools "consisted in reading a text aloud, accompanied by a running commentary on the text read. Whatever the students learned, they learned by listening, and the better they were able to listen, the more they were able to learn." (6) By necessity, just to get by, and even more to succeed at higher learning, students had to be exceptionally good listeners: better, more attentive, than mostly all Western college and university students and professors are today!

And centuries before that, in Ancient Greece, in the Agora in Athens, they had to be exceptionally good/attentive listeners *to hear and understand* what someone like Socrates was saying to his interlocutors. Most people who learned at that time did so through speaking and listening (conversation), not through reading and writing.

Socrates himself never wrote down any of his philosophy for popular consumption. Well known to anyone who has any familiarity with Ancient Greek philosophy is that Socrates refused to do so because he said he thought doing so to be an inferior way of communicating knowledge, and it would weaken the strength of human memory. He thought that face-to-face conversation by means of direct speaking and listening was the most effective way to learn.

The Ancient Greek method of learning in general was through memorization by means of song (meter and rhyme): music. The epic poets themselves, who were the first chief educators among the Ancient Greeks, were essentially musicians, wandering minstrels. For this reason, they tended to be treated like contemporary Rock Stars when they visited a city. And when the Ancient Greeks eventually developed what later became known as the *liberal arts*, generically they called these subjects of study *music* and claimed that their origin lay in *inspiration* (uncommon common sense) by the Muses (nine goddesses of arts like poetry, literature, song and dance, comedy and tragedy, history, and romance).

Eventually, in the Latin West, because, as Aristotle has already told us, such subjects of study tend to: 1) develop in human beings rich imaginations needed for human beings to become highly intellectual self-providers liberated from the vicissitudes of chance, doubt, and drudgery of largely unproductive, hard, serf-like, slavish, bodily labor and 2) individuals who first came to be educated by means of teachers were free men, not slaves, these subjects started to become referred to as *liberal arts* (liberating arts that chiefly aimed at intellectual understanding and acts of leisure, not productive or practical activity).

To preserve their property, free men in Ancient Greece and Rome had to be skilled at public speaking in law courts and in the Forum. For this reason, they were attracted to study among the Ancient rhetoricians who early on had been generically called "sophists," some of whom had claimed to be teachers of the science of politics (political scientists) when, in reality, all they tended to do was to take money to train people how to lecture in a convincing way to an ignorant audience.

At first in the Latin West, the liberal arts were chiefly limited to the arts of speaking and listening of grammar, rhetoric, and logic (the famous Latin *trivium* [three ways, or means] of liberating a person from the slavery, servile work, drudgery that ignorance tends to produce). However, these three generic arts included different species, and these were sometimes conflated in Medieval education. For example, the art of letter writing (*ars dictaninis*)—which was even widely taught in American elementary, grammar schools up through the mid-twentieth century—was, during the Latin Middle Ages and Italian Renaissance (and wherever, and whenever it is taught, tends to be), a conflation of grammar and rhetoric. In addition, for much of the Medieval period, the whole of philosophy (which was then considered by scholars to be identical with science) tended to be identified with the liberal arts, and the liberal arts tended to be reduced to the *trivium*.

Nonetheless, during the entire Latin Middle Ages, four other subjects of study were considered to be essential parts of liberal arts education: the *quadrivium* of arithmetic, astronomy, geometry, and music. Despite the fact that the liberal arts appeared to be arts that liberate human beings from ignorance through development of the skills of listening and speaking, this is only the case because human beings chiefly *use* these skills to master control of and to direct the operations of the human imagination, through which, with assistance of the human sense memory, the human intellect initially and habitually moves the parts of the human body.

Liberal arts are intellectual command and control arts through which the human intellect, *using/applying* the human imagination and sense memory as intellectual tools, embeds and directs the operations of the human body with commonsense, and uncommonsense wisdom in the form of intellectual principles of right understanding and right reason: know-what and know-how!

Any art that is laborsaving, which saves a human being from the need to engage in the drudgery of servile work, and obstacles produced by the contingencies generated by chance, indeterminacy, and different forms of human physical and psychological weakness (such as physical illness, doubt, ignorance, moral turpitude, lack of docility, and so on) is a liberal art. The term *liberal art* is applied analogously. During the Italian Renaissance, since the thinkers of the time were very much interested in productive and practical activities that required the invention of new labor-saving devices, they extended the subjects included within the traditional liberal (*or humanizing because liberating*) arts to include history and ethics; and, during the eighteenth century the name of these traditional subjects became changed to the more currently used one today: *humanities*.

Around the same time the concepts of philosophy and science increasingly started to become separated. So, too, began a separation between the essential connection of philosophy/science to wisdom. Science became largely reduced to mathematical physics, philosophy became largely identified with systematic logic, and both became increasingly separated from any essential to pursuit, or acquisition of wisdom.

One reason Italian Renaissance humanists had started to extend the understanding of a liberal art to be more culturally inclusive was because they understood that liberal arts and science are more than an individual psychological habit. It is a cultural enterprise/habit essentially depending upon cultural educational supports that transmit historical and social/cultural commonsense and uncommonsense wisdom from one generation to another. They recognized that this *thesaurus of commonsense and uncommonsense wisdom* facilitates cooperative social behavior (*docilitas*: receptivity to listening and learning) in the form of justly and prudentially, courageously, and temperately free human behavior cooperating with other people as team-member parts of an organizational/cultural whole.

Shipbuilders, homebuilders, engineers, sailors, pilots, military leaders, real politicians, merchants, financiers, business people, and so on, essentially employ labor-saving knowledge in a teamwork-form of a commonsense and uncommonsense wisdom, knowhow, of a Thales. To be able to do so they need cultural supports in the form of transgenerational, educational institutions of commonsense and uncommonsense wisdom-monopolies and socio-political conversation: a cultural humanism in the form of a transgenerational cultural enterprise/transgenerational cultural teamwork requiring leisure time to do research and study.

Why the ability to stretch the human imagination is crucial to transgenerational transmission of common and uncommon, common sense.

During the Italian Renaissance, to acquire such common sense and uncommon sense wisdom-monopolies and socio-political, cultural conversation skills unavailable to him at the dull-witted, educational institutions of his time, the genius, mathematical-physicist Galileo Galilei abandoned the universities of his day and started to converse face-to-face with Venetian shipbuilders. He did so because, as he says in his brilliant works, the *Assayer* (56) and *Dialogues Concerning the Two Chief World Systems* (63–68), he had recognized that to acquire the commonsense wisdom he needed to advance uncommon commonsense wisdom in physics, first he had to stretch his commonsense imagination to a more abstract, uncommon, *innovative* level. To stretch commonsense in the intellect and turn experiential common sense into intellectual uncommon commonsense wisdom and understanding, a person must first have uncommon commonsense wisdom and understanding in his or her imagination.

A person with a dull, impoverished, poor imagination (like academics and Enlightenment intellectuals who tend to be unable to distinguish between conceptual and behavioral contradictions and non-contradictions) is a person lacking in imaginative *and innovative* common sense and uncommon commonsense understanding/wisdom. He or she can never *induce* the principles, evident common understandings, that are needed to be intellectually applied in an individual situation to: 1) save himself or herself from unnecessary, slavish work, and avoid the drudgery caused by ignorance and foolishness, uncontrollable and unexpected events; or 2) develop a science as a cultural, trans-generational, enterprise from essentially uncooperative work with equally dull, impoverished, imaginations.

How the Ancient liberal arts first developed and evolved.

After the decline of the Western Roman Empire around the year 400 A. D.—and the attempt to restore the skills of reading and writing, speaking and listening, within the West—with the start of the ninth-century Carolingian Renaissance, primacy of educational focus at the time related to restoring the liberal arts chiefly concentrated on reviving the skill of grammar, followed about a century later by logic; and then on rhetoric, within which were included the studies of poetry and letter writing. Stress on the study of mathematics (arithmetic and geometry) did not happen until they became of interest within the Cathedral School of Chartres (which emphasized studies in mathematics and physics) around the eleventh and twelfth centuries.

This historical turn of events is radically different from the historical origin of the liberal arts within the *quadrivium*, not the *trivium*, in Egypt (where Aristotle reports they began among religious schools which were apparently subsidized by the pharaohs). Paradoxically perhaps to some readers is to learn that the first of the liberal arts was not listening to, nor reading, literary works. It was the study of mathematics, chiefly that of geometry where, prior to Aristotle and Thales, Egyptian politicians (pharaohs) understood the commonsense use of geometry could serve for land-measuring purposes as a means for collecting taxes.

While a consensus exists among Western intellectual historians that the Muses of the Ancient Greeks and Romans were nine in number and were thought to be the daughters of Zeus and Memory, different versions of their origins exist. Homer (fl. 8th century B. C.) reports them to be nine in number, and Hesiod (fl. 750–650 B. C.) reportedly was the first person to give them individual names. Later writers, like the Ancient Greek historian Diodorus Siculus (Diodorus of

Sicily [b. 91 B.C.; d. 30 B.C)]), in his monumental *Bibliotheca historica*:

> suggested that the Greeks incorporated the Muses into their pantheon from a group of Egyptian goddesses with similar attributes. According to that line of reasoning, the Egyptian god Osiris took nine talented maidens with him on his travels because of his fondness for song and dance. The maidens eventually became Egyptian goddesses and were then adopted by the Greeks to become the Muses. That claim is further supported by the fact that the leader of Osiris's Egyptian maidens was called the '*hegetes*,' which was said to be the basis for the name Musegetes, an alias for Apollon as Leader of the Muses. (https://mythagora.com/bios/muses.html)

Since Aristotle was the tutor of Alexander the Great, and Alexander, along with Homer and Hesiod, is a likely source of Aristotle's report that the liberal arts started in Egypt as part of a religious community, Aristotle's claim that study of the liberal arts (which was, from its inception, considered identical with music [inspiration by the Muses]) started with mathematics, suggests that the reason music traditionally has been included within the Ancient *quadrivium*, and not the *trivium*, is because, as the first and entire genus of the liberal arts, it was the first principle of all the other species.

In a way, the others grew out of it as a proximate and generating cause.

The first subjects that had grown out of the liberal art of music (the art of the Muses) were arithmetic and geometry, and both of these were first applied as *measuring principles* of uncommon commonsense wisdom in Egypt for taxation purposes to farms and for farming and navigation purposes to the study of the heavens. Historically, the *trivium* appears to have broken off from the *quadrivium, not the other way around*. And it appears to have done so chiefly to become a separate division within the liberal arts that focused more generally on listening and speaking, reading and writing as freedom-enhancing qualities (qualities that help develop the life and culture of a free people and free society) to perfect these arts as more fully liberal, liberating from slave-like existence.

That this is a reasonable account of the historical origin and initial development of the liberal arts is, also, supported by the fact that *principles are measures* and, according to Aristotle, the idea of being a measure is first derived by inducing the idea of unity from sensing a continuous quantity (like time) being indivisible. (*Metaphysics*, bk. 10, ch. 1, 1052b19–1053b8 and Saint Thomas Aquinas, *Commentary on the Metaphysics of Aristotle*, bk. 5, l. 2, nn. 1937—1960) *The principles of the liberal arts are intellectual measures of intelligibility* (indivisible intelligibles) that escape the notice of the external senses. They are causes that an intellectual art enables some human beings (either through a limited natural or acquired virtue [*quantitatis virtutis*], or both, to recognize to make some plurality intelligible as a one, a unit of intelligibility [*intelligibilis indivisibilis*]). For example, a geometrician walking across a courtyard might notice a triangle where someone else only sees a roof.

In addition, in his *Nicomachean Ethics*, Aristotle maintains the first of the virtues that human beings recognize are not speculative sciences. They are the productive virtues of the arts of making and doing (like sailing and shipbuilding) and the practical, cardinal moral virtues that enable human beings to operate as organization units, especially the first of the social moral virtues, justice, and the form of all moral virtue: prudence. In his *Physics* (bk. 2., ch. 2, 194b1–8), Aristotle maintains that the arts of use (practical activity) must pre-exist arts of making (production, such as manufacturing and tool making). He says, for example, that the art of sailing governs the art of shipbuilding (how sailors sail determines how shipbuilders build ships).

Special note should be made that Aristotle's claim is true only up to the historical point of artistic development in which, as Marshall McLuhan has keenly observed, by incorporating them into itself, intellectually-developed and applied technologies (note that, etymologically, a technology is a *wordsmith*) replace the art of doing (such as sailing) by technologically incorporating this art into the art of making (shipbuilding). (See, Gregory, Sandstrom, "Laws of Media," 3-6) When shipbuilding technology, for example, incorporates computerized controls and, as much as possible, commonsense-like/robotic reactions (similar to those a slave as a living technology could perform) into the art of sailing, to that extent, through what we commonly call today *Artificial Intelligence (AI)*, by incorporating the art of sailing into a part of manufacturing a ship, the art of shipbuilding replaces/obsolesces the art of sailing. When this happens, this once-living, vibrant art (Muse) tends to become a largely lost, mostly forgotten, one (often relegated to a Museum, retirement home for Muses).

Recall, too, that, for Aristotle, we derive an understanding of the moral virtue of justice through the ideas of numerical and geometrical equality, and especially through geometrical equality when we are dealing with contributive and distributive justice.

This, also, helps to explain why both the Ancient Greeks and Egyptians would have included astronomy along with music among the arts of the *quadrivium*, and why both would have included astronomy within the *quadrivium* at all. Being more or less identical with astrology, Ancient Greek and Egyptian astronomy was the original source of the Ancients' knowledge of the gods in terms of mythopoeic metaphysics/mythology, the origin of all epic poetry; and the chief source of all education by listening and teaching for the Ancient Egyptians and the Greeks.

In addition, knowledge of astronomy and mathematics was crucial for financial well-being of these societies for both navigation via seafaring and producing food through farming. The value of these arts for advancement of practical and productive knowledge largely escaped the notice of the early and middle Medieval periods during which, due to the need to restore literacy to continental Europe, the whole of philosophy/science was largely, if not entirely, reduced to the *trivium*, or one of its divisions. And it remained there until after the investigations in physical science by thinkers like Galileo and Sir Isaac Newton. After them, in Western education, the *trivium* became largely reduced to *trivia* and the whole of philosophy/science became largely conflated with the *quadrivium*.

How the modern liberal arts, especially those of listening and speaking, tended to develop within American education since the eighteenth century.

The above abbreviated history of the nature and development of the liberal arts in the West that I have just given extends from the Ancient Egyptians and Greeks up to approximately the eighteenth century. Around this time, as Adler says, "Anyone who looks up the curriculums of the educational institutions in this country (United States of America/my addition) in the eighteenth century will find that it included instruction and grammar, rhetoric, and logic, still conceived as arts or skills in the use of language—skills in writing and speaking and also reading, if not in listening." (7)

Toward the start of the twentieth century, however, Adler reports a remarkable difference:

> By the end of the 19th century, grammar still remains, but rhetoric and logic were no longer part of basic schooling, and in our own century (the twentieth), instruction in grammar has dwindled away, though vestiges of it still remain here and there.
>
> The liberal arts as recognized elements in basic schooling have been replaced by instruction in English. It is this so-called English teacher who gives elementary instruction in reading and elementary and more advanced instruction in composition. Unfortunately, the latter usually lays much more stress on what is called 'creative writing' than it does on writing that tries to convey thought—ideas, knowledge, or understanding. Some students receive instruction in public speaking, but this falls far short of training in all the skills required for effective speech. None, as I have said before, receives any instruction in listening. (7–8)

And, as a result, Adler should have noted a student is given no instruction at all in advancing in common sense or uncommon common sense. In the contemporary West, formal educational instruction in common sense through school teaching has pretty much entirely ceased to exist and is being largely replaced by technology, especially by Artificial Intelligence (AI)!

Evident to Adler while he was alive was that the then-current, impoverished situation in higher education could not be improved simply by increasing instruction in listening. He said to assume that, if deficiencies in listening were remedied, reading and writing ability would automatically increase, is a mistake. This is no more true than to assume that if a person knows how to read and write well he or she will know how to listen and speak well. (6)

The reason he gives for this is that speaking and listening, reading and writing, are remarkably different. Both sets of opposites require acquiring qualitatively different skills. While all four activities involve use of language in which at least two people reach out and respond to one another, the wide variety of contingencies related to speaking and listening well in different situations make then much more demanding and difficult to do well than reading and writing. (9)

Reading and writing abstract more from the vagaries of time and place essentially involved in oral discourse. By repeatedly re-reading or re-writing something, a person is able to revise and improve upon what he or she has written or read before passing this along into written or oral form (such as in the form of an audio of video) to the psyche of another human being. Both give a person the luxury of self-editing before verbally or in written form passing along something one has written or read to someone else to listen to or read. (9)

From the standpoint of the opportunity to correct mistakes before communicating with someone else, speaking and listening—especially those that are impromptu in nature—are much more qualitatively demanding skills flawlessly to execute. According to Adler, they more resemble performing arts like music and dance (or one might say competitive sports), which "are unamendable" to perfect execution at an individual time and place (in which they must coincide) than are reading and writing (which essentially lend themselves to future correction if, at first, not perfectly executed). For this reason, among many others, Adler compares reading and writing more to productive arts like painting and sculpture, to which one might add building and on-site engineering. (9–10)

The complexity of excelling in the skills of listening and speaking so far exceed those of reading and writing that Adler refers to them as the reason why he put off "for more than forty years" after he had written his bestseller *How to Read a Book* composing his masterful monograph *How to Speak. How to Listen.* (10)

Part of this complexity involves the fact that, as Adler notes, setting forth rules and directions for reading well is possible without setting forth those for writing well. For this reason, this tends to be the way they are universally taught in schools, everywhere and always. Because speaking and listening considered as a simultaneous act essentially involve what Adler calls *two-way conversation*, or *two-way talk*, teaching their rules and directions separately is not possible. Of course, because they lack this essential element, Adler maintains that the rules and directions for what he calls the *arts of silent reading* and delivering an *uninterrupted speech* are, to some extent, teachable without reference to their opposites. (11) Precisely what are the similarities and differences among these diverse modes of linguistic communication is a subject to which I will now turn my attention, starting with Lesson 2, which Adler devotes to solitary and social listening and speaking and reading and writing in Chapter 2 of *How to Speak. How to Listen.*

—CHAPTER TWO—

Lesson 2—Distinguishing Solitary and Social Language Arts.

Mortimer Adler starts his second chapter (entitled "The Solitary and the Social") related to the language arts of communication by noting that just as use of free time for the pursuits of leisure can be "solitary or social" so "dealing with the minds of others can be" similarly divided. (12) Once again, to stand upon Adler's shoulders and stretch our individual imaginations and understandings beyond his, we need to recall that, strictly speaking, as Adler well knew, unlike angels, the mind, or intellect, of a human being never directly communicates with the mind, or intellect, of another human being. Human beings communicate to each other as psychosomatic persons, individual soul/body time-bound persons having, or not having, free time for pursuits of leisure. Crucial to note about the way Adler begins this chapter is that, unlike many of us today, strictly speaking, he does not identify leisure with free time and free time with having time off from the everyday workaday world. For Adler, *having free time* is not identical with *having leisure;* nor is it identical with *being free,* having endowed or endowed-and-acquired freedom (such as political liberty). At best, the contemporary notion *of having free time* is identical to having a species of circumstantial freedom; and, according to Adler's understanding of the nature of human freedom, a person with circumstantial freedom can have loads of free time and still be a slave and have no leisure.

These reminders being made, a main point Adler appears to want to make at the start of his Chapter 2 is that *use* of human intellect to engage with and react to (communicate with) the intellect of another human being (for example, through direct verbal communication: speech) appears always to be social, not solitary. Solitary use of a human intellect appears to be reserved for ways human beings communicate with non-humans, or alone, communicating with oneself. Considered as such, it appears to be lacking in at least part of the complete quality of liberal arts communication, the type of communication species-specifically human.

At the same time, Adler is not ruling out communicating with a non-human person like the Second Person of the Christian Trinity (the Holy Spirit) through prayer being a form of social communication. Nor is he ruling out communicating with a pet being non-social. It is simply not social in the sense of human communication between two human persons capable of speaking to each other. Human communication (communication between two human beings considered as human persons) is not the same kind of communication between one angel and another, one brute animal and another, or between a human being and God in prayer.

As an example of solitary communication, Adler mentions reading and writing, which he says, "can be done in a solitary fashion, and they usually are—in the solitude of one's study, at one's desk, or in one's armchair." (12) Clearly, when talking about social communication, Adler is chiefly talking about some form of direct (such as face-to-face or by phone) human conversation between at least two human persons capable of talking *with, not at, to, or over,* each other—and doing so mainly, at least in part, for the aim of understanding each other. (12)

Hence he says:

> In contrast to writing and reading, which are usually solitary undertakings, speaking and listening are always social and cannot be otherwise. They always involve human confrontations (that is, physical presence to each other/my addition). They usually involve the physical presence of other persons, the speaker speaking to listeners who are present while he or she speaks, the listener listening to a speaker who is right there. This is one of the things that makes speaking and listening more complex than writing and reading—and more difficult to control for the sake of rendering them more effective. (13)

While, in the above respect, speaking and listening are always social, Adler keenly observes that these opposite extremes of one social act within a real genus of verbal communication can be aborted in one instant and re-engaged in another: "It is aborted when the confrontation of speaker and listener involves the suppression of one or the other. When that happens, you have uninterrupted speech and silent listening. It's something like a one-way street, with all the traffic going in one direction." (13)

Distinguishing interrupted and uninterrupted speech, silent listening, and no listening at all: Why conversational monopolies tend to be socially deadly.

Unhappily, upon first hearing it, what Adler says immediately above might appear to make no common sense. Indeed, precisely speaking, it might appear to convey no intelligible sense/understanding at all. When a conversation becomes interrupted, strictly speaking, what exists is interrupted speech and no listening at all. The social aspect of the speech ends. And what exists appears to be two one-way streets, going in opposite directions: one person, at best and analogously, talking to himself or herself; and another person, at best, analogously listening to himself or herself.

Nonetheless, the point Adler appears to have been trying to make is good. The way he expressed himself, however, could have been better. Adler's point appears to be that conversations as species of social, or two-way street, speech do happen. Contemporary boring lectures—which are actually species of uninterrupted, one-way speech and silent, one-way listening (actually no listening at all, except to the speaker to himself or herself)—resemble bad (aborted) attempts at social speech, real conversation.

No matter what species they take (teachers giving boring lectures to students, politicians giving boring speeches to constituents, committee people giving boring reports to company executives), nor what medium they use (television, radio, internet, or in person), Adler maintains that the result is always the same: someone "monopolizing everyone's attention for a time. These are all varieties of the one-way street." (13) They are also excellent examples of bad use of monopoly.

According to Adler, precisely because they are no conversations at all, conversational monopolies are socially deadly. "Without communication, there can be no community." (15); and without community, communication has no social aspect, is no communication at all.

Distinguishing among 'talk,' 'discussion,' 'conversation,' and 'communication'; and why such distinctions are crucial to make.

For this reason, Adler says: "The social aspect of speaking and listening is consummated rather than aborted when uninterrupted speech and silent listening are replaced by talk, discussion, or conversation. All three of the words I have used—'talk,' 'discussion,' and 'conversation'—have enough common meaning to be almost interchangeable. What is common to all three is the two-way traffic in which individuals are both speakers and listeners, alternating from one role to the other." (14)

While Adler recognizes that 'talk,' 'discussion,' and 'conversation,' are generically the same, he admits that they are specifically different forms of linguistic communication. (14) He starts to explain the difference among them by referring to his initial thought about the title of his book *How to Speak. How to Listen*. He had planned to call it *How to Talk. How to Listen*, until he had realized that, while talking always requires speaking, speaking does not always involve talking.

This led him to a subsequent realization that *speaking to* someone is different from *speaking with* someone. The first mode of communication suggests the one-way street species of communication of speaking-without-listening. The second suggests the two-way street species of communicating: interchangeably speaking and listening together.

In addition, Adler notes that, while many of us use the words *talk* and *speech* synonymously (especially when using the phrases 'giving a talk' and 'giving a speech'), strictly speaking, they are not synonymous. Regarding their difference, he states, "Strictly speaking, you cannot give a talk. You can have one, but only if someone else talks with you. You can give a speech even if the audience that is physically present only appears to be a listening to you." (14)

Regarding the word *discussion*, while Adler admits it always refers to two-way communication, he maintains it is not synonymous in meaning with *conversation*. According to him, a discussion is chiefly a conversation "carried on with a definite and even stated purpose" and "guided or controlled in some way to achieve the goal that has been set"—i.e., a specific means to a specific end. "While all discussions are conversations, not all conversations are discussions." (15) That is, a discussion is a species of conversation.

According to Adler, the difference between a conversation and a discussion lies in the fact that a conversation is a species of linguistic communication in which people often engage for no *specific* (only a general) objective and without considering their speaking together to be an essential means (an essential part of a specific plan) to realize a specific goal. If any specific plan exists, it is simply to share communication, talk with each other. (15)

Because the word 'conversation' conveys a wider meaning than a talk or a discussion—one that can be applied to *informal, idle,* or *small talk* (like that which occurs at a cocktail party) and contrary opposite *formal, major speaking events* (like public debates and disputations)—Adler says he will use the term 'conversation' the most frequently among these three words in his book.

In so doing, Adler states he also prefers use of this term to that of 'communication' because, strictly speaking, *communication* is too wide in meaning and application to convey the unique nature of human conversation:

> There is communication among brute animals in a wide variety of ways, but no conversation. There is even a sense in which any physical thing that sends a signal to another physical thing that receives it and responds to it in some way can be said to be in communication. But the sending and receiving of signals is not conversation, talk, or discussion. Brutes do not talk with one another; they do not carry on discussions.
>
> The one aspect of communication that I wish to preserve in my consideration of conversation is the notion of community that it involves. Without communication, there can be no community. Human beings cannot form a community or share in a common life without communicating with one another. (15)

Precisely because conversation, discussion, and talk are specifically unique forms of social, two-way, human communication—essentially involving the most important, specifically different species of communication in which human beings *listen and speak with one another*—Adler makes special note of their import for enabling human beings to share in a common (that is, specifically human) life.

Chapter 2: Distinguishing Solitary and Social Language Arts   57

He sees these as so crucial that he says, "A lively and flourishing community of human beings (that is, a happy one/my addition) requires that the social aspect of their speaking and listening be consummated rather than aborted." (16)

In addition, he even tells his readers that Parts 2 and 3 of his book naturally flow out of his initial distinction within Part 1 of human communication into the contrary opposite species of social and solitary—social being the most perfect (other-centered and requiring the most leisure time as befits that of a free person/my addition) and solitary being the least perfect in relationship to human perfection and happiness (self-centered and requiring the least leisure time and most befitting that of a slave, not a free person/my addition). (16)

Why understanding the major liberalizing influence Aristotle's *Nicomachean Ethics* had on Adler is crucial to understanding Adler's teachings considered as a whole.

Clearly, as anyone who has ever read the end of Book Four of Aristotle's *Nicomachean Ethics* can recognize, Adler's division of his masterful text on human communication follows Aristotle's understanding in this work of an essential connection within healthy language development that: 1) starts with species of the social virtue of *amiability* (especially in the form of benevolent-like speech: enjoying being with and engaging in two-way talk with other people) that generates healthy communal life (development of the social virtue of benevolence [*good will*], out of which naturally grow the communal moral virtues of justice and friendship); and 2) culminate in maturely-developed human happiness as a life that essentially includes leisurely conversation with wise and prudent friends.

Given the brilliance of these insights, what is sad to see is Adler neglecting the opportunity to emphasize them as an *Archimedes-like Eureka moment*! (similar to Aristotle's failure to do the same thing regarding the brilliant observation he had made related to the nature of monopolies being essential to generating wealth, which I had mentioned in Chapter 1). A chief and essential reason human beings cannot form a community, or share in common life, without directly communicating with one another, is because, without communicating with one another, we cannot share common sense, and especially the commonsense and uncommonsense wisdom and prudence of friends with uncommon commonsense wisdom. And without these being transmitted generationally and trans-generationally, human life (and, with it, human speech) becomes essentially anarchic, sociopathic, slave-like, brutish, and cut off from the enabling means of becoming happy.

Despite failing to take advantage of this opportunity, Adler divides Parts 2, 3, and 4 of his text into topics focused on transmitting progressively socializing liberal arts communications methods of using speaking and listening, reading and writing as means to achieving perfection in conver-

Chapter 2: Distinguishing Solitary and Social Language Arts 59

sation-centered speech. Doing so indicates that his plan in his book was to discuss these topics as essential means to accomplishing this numerically-one end.

For this reason, while Part 2 concentrates on uninterrupted speech in general, it does so chiefly in the form of communication that conforms to the *socially-enriching virtue of amiability* in the form of promoting *docility and truth telling in external acts* through: 1) the art of rhetoric (not sophistry) and 2) different forms of *instructive speech* (talk chiefly aiming at conveying truth, right understanding, common sense) beneficial to *enriching* the social lives of their listeners (not taking advantage of the ignorance of listeners for individual, personal gain).

Operating in this manner, as is clear from the way Adler ends his Chapter 2 (the last chapter in Part 1), therein, following Aristotle's repeated observation that "the end exists in the beginning," Adler expressly states he is returning to the start of this Chapter to indicate that he has divided it according to *talk about* the qualitatively diverse ways human beings can *use* qualitatively more or less perfect species of happiness-promoting leisure time: *free time for leisure (freedom-enriching*, not *spare*, time). In so doing, he begins by dividing such time into solitary and social.

Crucial to note at this point is that, in giving "examples of solitary pursuits," Adler does not first mention, or make any mention of, the *observational empty-time, de-stressing, activity of relaxing* involving some activity like watching a football game and drinking a beer. Instead, he first mentions activities that an Ancient Greek or Medieval Latin would have identified as forms of servile work: cooking, gardening, and carpentry, which he says, "when done for pleasure (the satisfaction of work well done), not for profit"—in the sense of financial gain, or perhaps, psychological or physical health benefit—"are examples of solitary leisure pursuits. So, too," he adds, "are writing and reading, looking at pictures, listening to music, travelling and observing, and above all, thinking." (17)

Hence, Adler would be willing to include as solitary or social acts of *leisure pursuit* (not *relaxing*) and use of *free* (not *empty*) time watching a football game and drinking a beer so long as a person, or persons, did not engage in these chiefly to escape from the drudgery of slave- or serf-like labor in the everyday workaday world. However, he would only do so if the chief aim of these activities was "for the satisfaction of their being personally-enriching" in the sense of strengthening the perfection of freedom-enhancing psychological faculties of human intellect and will.

At this point in his work, even though he does not explicitly say so, Adler goes beyond connecting his study of language arts to Aristotle's social virtue of amiability. He unites it to the topics of the moral psychology of friendship—especially the essential connection among leisurely conversation, friendship, and happiness—about which Aristotle talks in Book Nine of the *Nicomachean Ethics*. For this

Chapter 2: Distinguishing Solitary and Social Language Arts   61

reason, I am convinced that Adler begins the next to last paragraph in his Chapter 2 by saying that the leisure pursuits he considers to be "preeminently social include acts of friendship and, above all, conversation in its many forms."

According to him, good conversation includes the essential qualities of being both psychologically rewarding and enjoyable. He states that engaging in it "is one of the very best uses that human beings can make of their free time. It brings to fruition much that has been gained through other leisure pursuits. It is their true fulfillment." (17)

For this reason, he concludes Chapter 2 and Part 1 by saying, "it is so important for human beings to *enrich* (my emphasis added) their lives by having both the skill that is required for engaging in good conversation and also the will and motivation that impels them to devote much of their free time to it, replacing many of the things that they now resort to in order to fill empty time." (17) Note that, clearly, such conversation is between two human persons, not between two minds!

Some additional information about the way Adler uses insights about the human good from the *Nicomachean Ethics* to transcend *How to Read a Book*.

While Adler had sound reasons for going onto the next part of his text at this point, to make his reasoning about conversation and its commonsense connection to perfecting human life more precisely intelligible, at this point, I need to provide readers with some more information about precisely how Adler is organizing his book *How to Speak. How to Listen.*

At work in the organization of Adler's text is more than his using the social moral virtue of amiability from Aristotle's *Nicomachean Ethics* as a means analogously and progressively to transpose into his book increasingly social (two-way street) forms of human speech and thereby move human communication increasingly from ego-centric one-way, solitary talk to other-centered, social conversation essential to developing and enriching human happiness as a cultural philosophical/scientific enterprise in this life. Essentially connected to the organization and chief aim of the book are three different chief aims for reading that Adler had mentioned forty years before in his masterful *How to Read a Book*.

Like a great painter or sculptor, Adler has principles of harmonious unity, or organization, that he repeatedly applies/uses in all his work to *unify* previously disparate multitudes into essential parts of an organizational whole, or real genus. Among these and readily observable as organizational principles in his *How to Read a Book* and *How to Speak. How to Listen* is Aristotle's threefold division of human good into 1) pleasurable, 2) useful, and 3) perfective and his threefold division of human friendship into 1) enjoyable, 2) utilitarian, and 3) virtuous. Also, readily observable are how both Aristotle and Adler use chief aims for pursuing them as principles to connect these three different forms of good into three distinct forms of conversation that tend to dominate during three different times of human life: 1) youth, 2) middle age, and 3) old age.

For example, in *How to Read a Book*, Adler divides books into specifically three kinds based upon the chief aim a reader has for reading them and the qualitatively different forms of listening they essentially involve: 1) enjoyment, 2) information, or 3) enlightenment. Note that, by 'enjoyment' Adler means pleasure; and by 'enlightenment' he means 'understanding.' Since the only other human good in between these is utility, by 'information' he has to mean a human good that is not chiefly pleasure or enriching in the sense of adding knowledge that perfects the intellect as an intellect: understanding. While, to some extent, some pleasure or enjoyment always accompanies reading for information or enlightenment, both these forms of reading chiefly consist in doing so to increase human knowledge, either: 1) qualitatively to perfect the intellect in its facultative ability to apprehend its natural object: truth; or 2) numerically to increase the content within the intellect to enrich the thesaurus, bank vault, of human knowledge it contains as part of its arsenal of intellectual wealth.

For this reason, to distinguish these three aims of conversing related to reading and learning in general, at times, Adler will say he has read this or that author "for pleasure and profit"; but, in so doing, he has not, in any respect, from this reading increased his understanding by adding to his intellect "a single fundamental truth." For example, in one of his autobiographical works, Adler states:

> To say, as I have said, that I have not learned a single fundamental truth from the writing of modern philosophers is not to say that I have learned nothing at all from them. With the exceptions of Hegel and other post-Kantian German philosophers, I have read their works with both pleasure and profit. The pleasure has come from the perception of errors the serious consequences of which tend to reinforce my hold on the truths I have learned from Aristotle and Aquinas. The profit has come from the perceptions of new but genuine problems, not pseudo-problems, perplexities, and puzzlements invented by therapeutic positivism and by linguistic or analytical philosophy in our own century. In every case the correction of an error or the repair of a deficiency in the philosophy of Aristotle and Aquinas rests on the underlying and controlling principles of Aristotelian and Thomistic thought. In fact, the discovery of such errors or deficiencies almost always springs from close attention and leads to a deeper understanding of those principles. (Mortimer. J. Adler, *A Second Look in the Rearview Mirror*, 241–242)

As another example, at a national philosophical conference at which I had the delight of hearing him deliver a major address that thoroughly captivated his audience, he said the following: "With one or two exceptions, all the fundamental philosophical truths" he had learned over more than fifty years and to which he was then "firmly committed," he had:

> learned from Aristotle, from Aquinas as a student of Aristotle, and from Jacques Maritain as a student of them both. I have searched my mind thoroughly and I cannot find in it a single truth that I have learned from works in modern philosophy written since the beginning of the 17th century. If anyone is outraged by this judgment about almost four hundred years of philosophical thought, let him recover from it by considering the comparable judgment that almost all modern and contemporary philosophers have made about the two thousand years of philosophical thought that preceded the 17th-century. (Mortimer. J. Adler, "The Bodyguards of Truth," 125)

Needless to add—but I will do so anyway—in saying he had not learned a single truth from works in modern philosophy written since the beginning of the seventeenth century, *implicitly*, Adler would have to have included not a single principle of common sense, or commonsense or uncommon commonsense wisdom, the learning of which he had achieved chiefly from the diverse forms of reading, with the help of Aquinas, Aristotle had taught him.

Related to these different species of reading (which is a different way of listening), following Aristotle, Adler essentially relates the three qualitatively different kinds of goods to which I have referred above to three different times of human life: 1) youth, 2) middle age, and 3) old age; and, essentially related to these, three qualitatively and essentially and mainly different kinds of conversation, speaking, and writing: 1) pleasurable, 2) utilitarian, and 3) utilitarian and intellectually and morally virtuous. (17)

For example, because youth tend to be ego-centric and identify all human good with pleasure, they tend to form friendships and think, converse, in different ways chiefly focused upon pleasure—not upon utility or becoming perfected in virtue. In middle age, however, human beings necessarily tend to have to become more conscious of, and preoccupied by, a need to acquire money and other forms of personal wealth through business and other wealth-enriching, self-providing, activities.

Since, in these, friendships tend to require increasing human perfection in possessing socializing intellectual and moral skills/virtues—like language arts and justice and prudence—by necessity, youthful ego-centricity that tends to focus chiefly on personal-pleasure ego-centricity (which, if it must engage in social conversation chiefly aims at doing so to obtain personal pleasure) must give way to at least middle-age utilitarian ego-centricity. When this happens, the topic of utility tends to dominate middle-age conversations and other forms of communications, and obtaining some utility tends to become their chief end.

Because, in turn, old age necessarily has a mixture of all three human goods and contrary opposite evils, all its conversations and other forms of communication tend to have more of a mixture of all three human goods; but because of the need of the elderly increasingly to depend upon others and increasingly to call upon/use others for help, all elderly communications tend to focus on useful and virtuous friendships.

Finally, while Adler tells us that a chief aim, or end, of human life should be for us to engage in conversation, speaking and listening, reading and writing that should be intellectually enriching—as readers hopefully will see as I now turn to examine Part 2, Chapter 1 of Adler's masterful study of human communication—he also maintains that the gateway to all such forms of communication and perfect human socialization and happiness in this life lies in teaching and learning the liberal art of rhetoric, through which students and teachers are chiefly inculcated with the intellectual and prudential moral virtue of docility and, through its prudence, the uncommon common sense wisdom of philosophy.

—CHAPTER THREE—

Lesson 3—Uninterrupted Speech as The Amiable, Goodwill, Gateway to Friendly Conversation

Mortimer Adler's Chapter 3 (entitled "That's Just Rhetoric!") is the first of four chapters in Part 2 of his monograph devoted to the genus of one-way human communication that he names "Uninterrupted Speech." He follows this in Chapter 4 with discussion of a topic he titles "The 'Sales Talk' and Other Forms of Persuasive Speech." Chapter 5 focuses on "Lectures and Other Forms of Instructive Speech"; and he concludes Part 2 by examining the more generic topic of "Preparing and Delivering a Speech."

Evident from the subjects he chose to consider in these chapters is that Adler had modeled his division of Part 2 devoted to speaking after the threefold division of reading he had articulated forty years before in *How to Read a Book*, about which I had spoken in my prior Lesson 2. Therein, Adler had divided reading a book according to three chief purposes, or aims: 1) enjoyment/pleasure, 2) information, and 3) understanding.

In Chapter 3 he is considering speaking chiefly as related to intending to convey pleasure, or to please (talk *nicely*, instead of to inform or enlighten) a listener. He devotes Chapter 4 to speaking to inform, and Chapter 5 to speaking to enlighten, or convey understanding. These two forms of speaking or reading he often refers to as *done for profit* (meaning mainly intellectual utility), in contrast to speaking or reading *for pleasure.*

In addition, crucial to understanding what Adler is doing in this part of his text is recognizing that he evidently has in mind: 1) the distinction he made in the Chapter 2 between "talking *to*" someone and "talking *with*" someone; and 2) that, before a person can transition to and master the liberal art of talking *with* someone—more friendly, conversational speech/two-way talk—a person must first master the gateway, or transitional, *amiable, benevolent-like* habit of talking *to* someone that is not totally monopolistic, solitary, and ego-centric: fake-conversational speech. This *transitional* genus, in turn, must start with a form of social-speaking that, through its pleasing nature, inclines a listener to become *psychologically receptive*, not *resistant*, to listening to the speaker—the chief aim of the liberal art of rhetoric and any masterful teacher, involving the disposition of *docility* possessed by any real student.

To easily understand why Adler *professionally* proceeds the way he does is simply to recall that, in writing his book, like any artist, or any psychologically healthy human being, he is being guided by commonsense organizational principles. And the commonsense organizational principles he is using in his text on communications art he is intentionally taking from Aristotle as interpreted chiefly by Saint Thomas Aquinas.

Recall, too, that the biggest intellectual mistake we human beings make is not one of bad reasoning, or asking badly-framed, or the wrong, questions. The biggest intellectual mistake all human beings make related to thinking and talking is not knowing precisely what is the chief subject about which we are thinking and talking: intellectually being on the wrong page—not realizing that to know some numerically-one thing essentially involves first placing it within a real, proximate genus, or organizational whole.

The chief reason that, as Aristotle cautioned us centuries ago, small mistakes in intellectual investigations related to first principles tend to grow into larger mistakes as the investigations proceed is because first principles are what we know best, use as commonsense or common-understanding, *intelligible unit measures* to know everything else we know and about which we form images and concepts, make judgments and reason, and *measure* truth and falsity. What we know best is what we know immediately, evidently, *by commonsense understanding*. Judging and reasoning essentially involve applying *commonsense* principles (*common-sense unit measures of intelligibility—understanding* and *truth*) to multitudes to make them comprehensible to us as essential parts existing within an organizational whole.

Commonsense principles only exist within, and as, organizational, composite, wholes. To know, understand, as well as to make intellectual mistakes, is always to do so *within or in relation to* a real genus (or, as some people often say today: *within a framework*). We human beings are incapable of forming any concept, making any judgment, much less a commonsense one, without doing so as understanding these as part of an organizational whole, or as the organizational whole considered as the harmonious effect generated by cooperation of its parts.

If you do not believe me, try forming any idea, judgment, without conceiving of it in terms of it being, or being essentially related to: 1) part of an organizational whole (genus, species, individual); 2) something conceived of analogous to a genus, species, or generic or specific part of a composite whole; or 3) a composite of genus and species (a composite whole), or something conceived of analogous to a composite of genus and species (analogous to a composite whole).

Everything about which we think we can do so only as an individual—some being with numerically-one identity (numerically-one genus, species, or individual): some one thing or being—not a no thing or non-being. *Psychologically, all human beings first form concepts through an act of negating/denying (in the form of an act of intellectual resistance to)* total or partial opposition. And we first form judgments by relationally uniting or denying concepts.

All negation, in short, is a form of total or partial opposition. To conceive of anything, we have to conceive of it as *some one being*. Our first awareness of unity, however, is of an undivided being: that which is undivided, *an ordered multitude*.

However, ordered multitudes (parts) only exist within organizational composites: composite wholes. And they do so only through an act of *relationally* uniting them through some sort of *qualitatively internal resistance to division*. Our first awareness of unity is not of mathematical unity. It is of qualitative unbreakability (resistance to breakability) of a composite whole: a real genus. As I repeatedly say, in agreement with Étienne Gilson, the only way to unify a multitude is to order it; and the only way to order it is by positionally relating parts within a composite, organizational whole. (Étienne Gilson, *Painting and Reality*, 20, n. 17)

Reasoning is a secondary, *qualitatively inferior*, way of knowing. It is only so good as the generic understanding upon which the *commonsense* principles it uses/applies essentially depend. One person can reason well, commonsensically, only to the extent that he or she correctly understands the genus within which exist the principles he or she is using to reason. To do this he or she must comprehend these principles as measures of intelligibility of something that exists from which these measures have been intellectually derived just as parts from a whole. The same is true of a multitude of persons reasoning or cooperating together *as a team or enterprise.*

An organizational whole exists in and through the harmonious unity of its parts. An organizational whole without any internal, harmonious unity is no organizational whole at all. A team that has no internal, harmonious unity is no team at all. A totally unharmonious, essentially anarchic, whole is essentially unimaginable, inconceivable, and unthinkable—makes no common sense! Even a person who verbally disagreed with me about this preceding claim could only attempt intellectually to refute me through some species of organizational sound in the form of speech.

Similarly, the principles of grammar are not the principles of engineering. As any engineer with common sense knows, principles of grammar cannot be used as the chief measures, standards, rules by which engineers measure truth in engineering and structural soundness of bridges and buildings. Measures are always homogeneous (belong to the same genus) as what is being measured. Truth, not desire, is the first measure of *doability*. We do what we can, not what we wish.

As a form of understanding, reasoning, all philosophy/science is a species of commonsense, organizational human psychology. In addition, without the existence of some form of qualitative resistance to being a total unity existing within organizational wholes, organizational wholes could not be organizational wholes; and no art or science could exist related to them. Real artists, scientists/philosophers (as well as anyone possessed of any form or intellectual or moral virtue) can only be artists, scientists, philosophers, or intellectually or morally virtuous by understanding, and being able to overcome, some degree of organizational resistance to taking direction from their subjects of respective interest. Every species of human skill, talent, virtue, essentially involves overcoming difficulties, obstacles to imposing human direction on some organizational material or subject—possessing leadership skills! For this reason, totalitarian despots can never become, or be, good leaders.

While this realization was something to some extent absent from the psyche of the youthful Mortimer Adler, this understanding of the nature of philosophy as organizational psychology that I have explained above radically distinguished Adler's later comprehension of philosophy; and enabled him to distinguish himself as a great educational leader, and from all of the other leading intellectuals of the twentieth century. This helps to explain why, like Aristotle and Aquinas before him, Adler was such a great organizational genius.

A short, but necessary, digression to consider Adler's initial introduction to philosophy so as to enable us better to comprehend how this served as a commonsense first principle for all his subsequent interest in, and under-

standing of, philosophy as an organizational, behavioral psychology and social-science enterprise.

Well known to students of Adler is that, prior to his entering Columbia College in 1920 at about age 18 on a full-tuition scholarship, he had been a high school dropout. Several years earlier (at age 15), he had started working as secretary to the editor-in-chief of the New York *Sun* newspaper, averaging a salary of "between $30-$35 a week—an enormous sum in those days." (Mortimer J. Adler, *Philosopher at Large*, 4)

While serving in this capacity, Adler had the good fortune to be able to come across and read John Stuart Mill's *Autobiography*. This led him to discover Plato's teachings. Borrowing from a neighbor a selection of several of Plato's dialogues, Adler first read the *Euthyphro*, followed soon after by reading the *Apology*, *Phaedo*, and *Crito*. "By that time," he says, "I had become so fascinated by the Socratic method of questioning that I persuaded my friends to engage in mock dialogues that would allow me to exercise my skill as their Socratic interrogator." (4 and 6)

Having fallen in love with the character of Socrates and the Socratic method of learning, Adler reports he "bought a secondhand set of the Jowett translation" of Plato's dialogues, "in five volumes and began to spend time at my desk at the *Sun* reading the dialogues of Plato instead of doing the work that earned my weekly paycheck." (6)

By this time, his discovery of Socrates had formed in Adler his "early resolution to become a philosopher." (1) This being so, and because he had realized he could not long continue reading the dialogues of Plato while drawing a check from the *Sun* for doing work for them he was not doing, Adler decided to go to college for "the only reason which," in his judgment, "justifies embarking on that venture—to study just for the sake of learning and for no utilitarian or adventitious purpose to which the learning might be put to use." (6)

While Adler had later wished he could say the time he had spent earning a living between high school and college had helped him acquire emotional maturity, docility, "depressingly ample evidence existed that I had not become emotionally mature by the time I entered college." (7) Worse is the fact that, Adler had to admit, "Emotionally immature I remained for many years thereafter—not only during the years that I was a member of the faculty of Columbia University, from 1923 to 1930, but also to a serious extent during the greater part of the twenty-two years I held a professorship at the University of Chicago": (years 1930 to 1952). (7)

When Adler entered Columbia College, and a few years later the Columbia University Graduate School, he did so wanting more than anything else in life to become a philosopher in the tradition of Socrates, and teach full time at the University at which, more than anywhere else in the world, he had one day hoped to teach: Columbia. Sadly, Adler's later admittedly obnoxious student behavior—especially toward the amiable Professor John Dewey—prevented this dream from ever becoming a reality for him.

During the time he spent in the Columbia University Graduate Psychology Department, Adler said his experience studying in both academic worlds of classical philosophy and modern psychology had convinced him that most contemporary philosophical problems, especially regarding pursuit of truth, had been caused by modern behavioristic psychologists and other contemporary social scientists attempting to understand psychological, social science, and philosophical problems without referring them to the human *mind*. While he had apparently not realized this at the time, like Socrates discovering the failure of Anaxagoras to follow his own prescription to understand and explain the behavior of everything in terms of *mind*, Adler had found most psychologists, social scientists, and even philosophers of his graduate-school days doing the same thing.

Recall that, in the *Phaedo* (97c–99e), Socrates reports the following experience he had related to the celebrated philosophical teachings of the great Anaxagoras of Clazomenae (b. ca. 500 B.C.; d. 428 B.C.):

> I once heard someone reading from a book, as he said, by Anaxagoras, and asserting that it is mind that produces order and is the cause of everything. This explana-

tion *pleased* me. Somehow it seemed right that mind should be the cause of everything, and I reflected that if this is so, mind introducing order set everything in the way that is best for it. Therefore if anyone wished to discover the reason why any given thing came or ceased or continued to be, he must find out how it was best for that thing to be or to act or be acted upon in any other way…

These reflections made me suppose, to my *delight*, that in Anaxagoras I had found an authority on causation who was after my own heart. I assumed that he would begin by informing us whether the earth is flat or round, and would then proceed to explain in detail the reason and logic on the necessity for this by stating how and why it was better that it should be so. (Jowett trans./my italics added)

Socrates maintains that he was so delighted by Anaxagoras' reputed way of explaining the nature things and their behavior in terms of a *unity* of more or less perfect parts (goods) hierarchically *ordered* to a most perfect part (final cause, or highest good) that he was prepared to give up looking for any other causal explanation for the ordering and behavior of things and to receive the same kind of instruction from Anaxagoras about other things, like the orbits and velocities of the sun and the moon. As a result, he reports he "lost no time in procuring the books (of Anaxagoras/my addition) and began to read them as quickly as" he "possibly could, so that I might know as soon as possible about the best and the less good."

Unhappily, no sooner had he started to read the works of Anaxagoras than Socrates had

> discovered that the fellow made no use of mind and assigned to it no causality for the order of the world, but adduced causes like air and aether and water and many other absurdities. It seemed to me that he was just about as inconsistent as if someone were to say, the cause of everything that Socrates does is mind—and then, in trying to account for my several actions, said first that the reason why I am lying here now is that my body is composed of bones and sinews, and that the bones are rigid and separated at the joints, but the sinews are capable of contraction and relaxation and form an envelope for the bones with the help of the flesh and the skin, the latter holding all together, and since the bones move freely in their joints the sinews by relaxing and contracting enable me somehow to bend my limbs, and that is the cause of my sitting here in a bent position. (Jowett trans)

In short, instead of identifying a universal, *providentially guiding*, cause that unequally relates and harmonizes a multitude of other causes to cooperate to become parts of one whole ordered unit of action (one ordered whole acting unit:

acting organizational whole) to make intelligible, explain, how and why Socrates was doing what he was doing, Anaxagoras was simply sequentializing, in the form of a physical description, the way different parts of a whole unit physically join together first, second, third, and so on—like parts of a machine—when they move or do not move.

Once Socrates had discovered that Anaxagoras was not actually practicing what he had preached, Socrates adopted as his own famous *Theory of Forms* (his version of the method he had initially thought Anaxagoras was preaching) and used it to launch what is often called Socrates' *Second Voyage* in philosophy. Analogously, in my opinion, while a graduate student in the Psychology Department at Columbia University, making a similar discovery, Mortimer Adler decided he had to launch himself on a second philosophical voyage similar to that of Socrates. Once he had concluded that the behavioral psychologists, philosophers, and social scientists of his time were aping the materialistic and mechanistic scientific positivism prevalent during the same period, he became increasingly aware that, in some way, he would have to reinterpret the nature of all three disciplines in relation to the human mind and order them within things and in relation to the human mind considered as composite wholes generated by some internal harmonious cooperation of parts, and not by a mechanistic external union.

Helping Adler to do this was his reading of Professor Arthur (Schauffler) Oncken Lovejoy's 1916 presidential address at the annual American Philosophical Association national conference (published in 1917 and entitled, "Some Conditions of Progress in Philosophical Inquiry"), which Adler reports, "because of its insistence that philosophy should become a cooperative enterprise instead of continuing to be, as it had been for centuries, a series of solo performances" had a lifelong impact on him personally and on his professional career as an educator and philosopher. (Adler, *Philosopher at Large*, 39) In addition, a further lifelong impact upon him from reading this paper were some implications related to the nature of *truth as a matter of fact*.

One such implication relates to a difference between rationally-debatable *matters of truth* and non-rationally debatable *matters of taste*. Reflecting upon this difference, which he mentions repeatedly in later books and articles, Adler says his main concern at the time had been the contrary opposition between: 1) those who understood "philosophical systems as work of the imagination, great intellectual poems each presenting its own *weltanschuung*": solitary metaphysical poets and sophists and 2) those who held the contrary opposite understanding of "philosophy as dealing piecemeal with problems that can be solved in much the same way that scientists solve theirs" as parts of an ongoing historical enterprise—real philosophers. (40–43)

The first case appeared to Adler to be that of *solitary matters of taste and talk*, all the species of which he would be inclined summarily to dismiss with the exclamation: *That's just rhetoric!* The second case appeared to him to have an affinity with the method used in contemporary physical science, in which, "the truth and falsity of a philosopher's statements, sentence by sentence (*as parts of a whole argument, explanation, or demonstration*/my addition), resembling a team effort, would have to be considered and recognized as such." In this case, a person would not be satisfied with attributing some kind of *solitary* truth to an emotional urge but would have to consider truth historically in its logical relation "to his world vision as a whole," that is, in relation to a logically-articulated metaphysics, common-sensically known to be essentially grounded in reality. (41)

A third implication Adler drew was that, if a philosophical proposition involves no question about truth, "no need to worry ourselves about how philosophy can be made cooperative" exists because, "the conception of philosophy as a *cooperative enterprise* . . . implies a conception of philosophy as a system of propositions, the truth of which philosophers are cooperatively attempting to demonstrate" (41/my italics). In some way, philosophy would have to involve two-way, trans-generational talk—be a trans-generational, cultural enterprise.

Adler reports that what bothered him most at the time "was the fact that if philosophy were to have no commerce with truth and philosophy in the ordinary sense of those terms" (that is, as *matters of truth rooted in commonsense experience,* or *commonsense understanding*): philosophical knowledge could not exist, "for how can there be knowledge divorced from truth?" (that is, from *evident understanding as its chief measure of intelligibility*). Even worse, "Why bother to become a philosopher or even a student of the subject?" (41)

As he said in the opening chapter of his 1965 monograph *The Conditions of Philosophy*, "the very first condition prerequisite to philosophy's being a *socially respectable enterprise* in which one may engage with some measure of intellectual self-respect is that it achieve knowledge of the same sort that science achieves and that is recognized as knowledge by the general public." (41) *To become socially respectable, philosophy must make common sense to the public at large. As matters of truth, parts of a commonsense, social-science enterprise*, just like propositions in physical science, philosophical propositions must be, and become publicly (commonsensically) recognized as, disjunctively true or false. (42)

While he appears not explicitly to have realized this at the time, in focusing attention on this disjunction, and on the radical difference between matters of truth and matters of taste, Adler had started to discuss a crucial *psychological problem* related to a proper understanding of philosophy in the classical philosophical tradition of Aristotle and Saint Thomas Aquinas as a psychological habit (a habit of a rational animal: a free, personal act involving the person as an integrated, psychological, personal whole) considered as a proximate cause and first principle of a trans-generational, cultural, social-science enterprise of executing doable deeds.

In addition, Adler was starting to become a man on a quixotic-like educational quest to transform worldwide the then-prevailing understanding of the nature of philosophy as essentially involving *solitary matters of taste* into understanding philosophy to be a *social-science defender of matters of truth* (hence: common sense) wherever it might exist.

Adler had also started to realize that, *as a matter of taste*, he had fallen in love with philosophy (which he had reduced to systematic logic and had conflated with metaphysics) as the sole measure of truth. As a graduate student, this understanding of philosophy and his "unabating passion for logic and using it to get at the truth" caused him to develop a psychological blindness, lack of tolerance for, and *angst* about the real possibility that truths might exist (including in his love of philosophy) that were not measurable by principles of logic.

Whatever could not be measured by principles of logic, he tended to banish to recesses of poetic imagination (*That's just rhetoric!*). This would include his own love of philosophy, fear of never being able to become a philosopher in the tradition of Socrates, and hope that he could someday become one. Could all these emotions have no truth in them?—be only matters of taste, sophistry/rhetoric? This possibility psychologically tortured him and made him largely unteachable by faculty members at Columbia that he thought disagreed with him.

Thinking about such psychological conflicts at the time caused him to suffer a great psychological depression after having witnessed a theatrical performance of George Bernard Shaw's *Back to Methuselah*: Then, as never before, did he as "clearly and fully appreciate the significance of Plato's banishment of poets" (among whom, beyond lyrical writers, Adler had decided he needed to include composers of all species of imaginative literature, including novels and plays, John Dewey, and apparently everyone who did not subscribe to his understanding of philosophy). (42)

Unhappily, shortly after this event, Adler agreed to read a paper entitled "God and the Psychologists" at a philosophy conference hosted by the Columbia University Philosophy Department and organized by John Randall in May 1924. As Adler reports, this paper caused him to become a *persona non grata* in the eyes of the Columbia University Philosophy Department faculty and Dean. (47–49)

In the talk, Adler had contrasted the approach to philosophy taken by a classical and God-centered metaphysician like himself to that of a godless, poet/sophist man-centered humanist, or pragmatist (someone who, at the time he had read the paper, I suspect Adler had identified in his mind with a conflation of John Dewey and a poet that, in Book Ten of his *Republic*, Plato would have banished from his ideal city!). What Adler failed to recognize, however, was that, in treating Dewey the way he was, he was pretty much behaving in the way that in Book Seven (535c–538a) of the same work, Plato describes as the behavior of a youthful *philosophical bastard*: an obnoxious young person short on metaphysical wisdom.

While reading the talk some forty years later (1965), Adler reported he could "still whole-heartedly subscribe to the opening section, which expressed" his "adverse judgments about experimental psychology and especially about J. B. Watson's brand of behaviorism, a doctrine which has become a little more sophisticated, but not much sounder, in the hands of B. F. Skinner," he was emotionally and intellectually distressed to discover "outrageous errors and caricatures of all the philosophers he had discussed." (48)

The most distressing part of the paper to Adler was its concluding section in which Adler directly criticized what he had characterized as John Dewey's "alignment of recent pragmatism with a psychological approach to the problems of human thought and conduct"; and "the prevalence of the genetic fallacy in this approach." Adler had claimed this accounted for philosophy's then-current, "deplorable state," in which "Philosophers were for the most part neither engaged in understanding the physical universe or in attacking the problems of man's social welfare." (48)

After this, Adler directly quoted the following statement from the American Philosophical Association's then-most-recent published report: "Philosophy recovers itself when it ceases to be advice for dealing with the problems of philosophers, and becomes a method, cultivated by philosophers for dealing with the problems of men." Reacting to that assertion, Adler stated, "Were philosophy to follow that prescription, it would die . . . at the end of its convalescence; and there were ample signs that the denouement was well on the way." (48–49)

Continuing his suicide mission to destroy any possibility of his ever becoming hired as a member of the Graduate Philosophy Department at Columbia University, Adler then referred to John Dewey, who was sitting a few feet away from him. He stated that, because of Dewey's concentration on "the problems of men" to a point of almost exclusively limiting philosophy's nature to "consideration of socio-political problems," such as that of social and political freedom, Dewey's understanding of philosophy was essentially reductionistic.

Apparently, in his mind, Adler was criticizing Dewey of reducing all philosophical statements to humanistic, poetic-like, matters of taste, one-way talk, just rhetoric—not matters of truth. Adler then quoted the following two sentences from Dewey's *Reconstruction in Philosophy*, "The task of future philosophy is to clarify men's ideas as to the social and moral strifes of their own day. Its aim is to become so far as it is humanly possible an organ for dealing with these conflicts." (49)

Chapter 3: Uninterrupted Speech

Quixotically reacting to this passage with youthful bravado, Adler curtly replied to it, "There is certainly nothing of the love of God in this utterance, no sense of the infinite weavings of the cosmos, wherein the human is but a pattern; no impulse to detached contemplation of the non-human as well as the human, so that the problems of humanity can be envisioned in proportions in terms befitting man's position in the total scheme of things." (49)

Adler reports as follows Dewey's reaction to Adler's disrespectful treatment of him: "John Dewey seldom raised his voice or gesticulated for emphasis. I doubt if anyone had ever before seen him explode with rage. But on this occasion, annoyed by my contempt for scientific psychology, angered by the general drift of my remarks, and probably irritated by some infelicitous phrasing of the point I was trying to make, he pounded the arms of his chair, stood up, and walked out of the room muttering that he did not intend to sit around listening to someone tell him how to think about God; he would do that in his own way." (49)

In spite of the fact that Dewey had more than ample justification never to forgive Adler (as did many others, including Sidney Hook) for his disrespectful treatment of Dewey, Adler reports: "Dewey himself bore me no grudge. I may have become a *persona non grata* with others, but not with him. He would certainly have been justified in paying no further attention to the impertinent young whippersnapper who had been so annoying—and so presumptuously smug about it, to boot. On the contrary, three years later, when my first book, *Dialectic*, was published, John Dewey 'went out of his way to write a highly complementary review of [it].' (49)

While, abstractly considered, Adler might have been correct about Dewey's having a simplistic and reductionistic understanding of freedom, with no true metaphysical and anthropological grounding, as he started to realize shortly thereafter from Dewey's gracious and amiable treatment of him, Dewey was a far more social, amiable, and benevolent human being than was Adler with a far better, *commonsensical* understanding of the nature of philosophy as a historical and cooperative enterprise—to which Adler in practice appears simply to have given lip service at the time.

Ironically, this realization appears to have been so strong that it personally and professionally transformed Adler's chief philosophical interests and pursuits more or less into educational ones analogous to those of Dewey. As, in a way, he told Sidney Hook in 1965, it appears to have *changed his spots* regarding Dewey at least to the extent that he had become "willing and able to recognize the genuine worth of Dewey's philosophical thought, . . . and to praise his revolutionary educational insights, while still criticizing the followers who had misunderstood the message of his books on education, especially his epoch-making *Democracy and Education*, published in 1916." (50)

At the time, Adler continued to think that experimental, or scientific, psychology had very little to contribute to our understanding of human nature or of the human mind; and to blame "the current state of philosophy on the substitution of psychology for a metaphysics as the ruling discipline," and the "dearth and rottenness of philosophy in" his time to humanism and psychologism influencing philosophers to abdicate "the problems of metaphysics, logic, and ethics over to the anthropologist, the psychologist, and the sociologist" (50). Unwittingly, however, when making these statements, Adler did not realize how much, in fact, *when properly understood*, anthropology, psychology, and sociology, social science, and scientific psychology (such as in the teachings of Aristotle and Saint Thomas Aquinas) actually contribute to our understanding of human nature, the human mind, metaphysics, logic, and philosophy/science considered as a whole.

Dewey's amiable acceptance of Adler's abuse *and his pragmatic common sense* transformed Adler's personal and professional disposition from solitary to social in a way that no amount of logical argument could ever have done. In addition, it transformed the chief focus of Adler's personal and professional attention from reducing philosophy to systematic logic to understanding philosophy to be a species of *scholastic humanism*: a transgenerational educational, behavioral, psychological enterprise crucially dependent upon the communications arts of listening and speaking, reading and writing, and especially the docility-generating art of persuasion (rhetoric) and the commonsense moral virtue of prudence for its success.

That's just rhetoric! Or is it?

Through his amiable behavior, a great lesson John Dewey had taught Mortimer Adler was that having truth and logic on our side is not enough *to persuade* people to listen to us. Common sense tells us that, as any good salesperson well knows, psychologically we tend to be receptive to listening to people we like and to resist listening to people we do not like. *Understanding, not argument, is what tends to persuade human beings*!

Adler's learning experience through the fallout at Columbia over his treatment of Dewey taught Adler that he was seriously lacking in the art of persuasion and that possessing this art (rhetoric) was a necessary condition for him to master if he ever wanted to succeed in getting people to like him and listen to him at all, and especially to listen to him as a philosopher. The reason for this is chiefly because, for philosophy to exist as a long-lasting, social-science, or any other kind of cultural, enterprise, its practice must have cultural supports, especially among societal leaders, in the form of a cultural psychology receptive to listening to philosophical talk and other forms of philosophical communication.

Chapter 3: Uninterrupted Speech

By attending the *Columbia University School of Hard Knocks*, Adler had started *to understand* the difference between the philosophical skill of rhetoric that inclines people to become receptive to listening to the truth and what, in the *Gorgias* (962b–966b), Plato had called its fraudulent imitator—the *knack, or routine, of flattery*: sophistry. According to Plato, through use of flattery and pleasing speech (feigned benevolence, friendship), sophistry chiefly aims to mislead ignorant people into accepting as true something that is actually false. Prior to this realization, Adler had considered every species of persuasion other than logic to be a matter of taste, not a matter of truth. He had considered the liberal art of rhetoric and sophistry to be identical and invidious, to be avoided by anyone who considered himself or herself to be a serious philosopher.

By the time he had written his masterful *How to Speak. How to Listen*, however, Adler had radically changed his psychological disposition toward rhetoric. Therein, about people who hold the above misunderstanding of the liberal art of rhetoric—including himself as a youth—Adler stated:

> Fortunately, those who harbor this view are mistaken. It would be very unfortunate, indeed, if sophistry could not be avoided, for then no honest or morally scrupulous person could, in good conscience, have anything to do with the process of persuasion. Yet most of us find ourselves inclined or obliged to try to persuade

others to act or feel in ways we think desirable and honorable. Rare is the person who can completely bypass the business of persuasion. Most of us, in our daily contacts, are involved in it most of the time.

There are some skills that can be used for good or evil purposes. They can be used scrupulously, in good conscience, or unscrupulously. The skill of the physician or surgeon can be used to cure or maim; the skill of the lawyer, to promote justice or to defeat it; the skill of the technologist, to construct or destroy. The skill of the persuader—the political orator, the commercial salesman, the advertiser, the propagandist—can be used with a high regard for truth and to achieve benign results, but it can also be as powerfully employed to deceive and injure. (27)

By this time, Adler had come to *understand* that the skill of rhetoric is not identical with, or reducible to, the knack of sophistry. Hence, he maintained that the sophist is always unscrupulous, always, by any means possible, mainly aiming at persuading others simply as a means for taking personal advantage of the ignorance of other people, especially an audience, and achieving personal success in winning an argument. In contrast, Adler had maintained that Plato had considered a philosopher to be a person who would never misuse the knowledge of logic in general, or persuasive argumentation, to win an argument. He or she would only use the knowledge to facilitate communicating truth.

According to Adler, every form of knowledge can be misused. Right and wrong moral use can exist related to all tools, which, following Aristotle, Adler had considered logic and rhetoric, by nature, essentially to be. Hence, he said that honesty and dishonesty can exist related to selling and all other attempts at persuasion, just as it can in many other species of human interactions. And while he asserted he was aware that, in some social circles, words like *sales talk, salesmanship, persuasion,* and *rhetoric* connote essentially evil human practices, he claimed, once a person understands that sophistry has no essential connection to any of these species of human activity, he "could see no reason for giving the terms up. They refer to activities in which all, or most, of us engaging can do so without recourse to reprehensible trickery, lies, or deception." (28)

Rhetoric: An ancient and honorable art.

By the time Adler had retired from teaching for several decades and had concentrated on writing commonsense philosophical books for the public at large, he no longer considered rhetoric to be identical with sophistry and to be a matter of taste. Instead, he considered it to be a matter of truth, and more than simply a form of knowledge or information. He considered it to be a species of enlightenment, saying:

> The ancient and honorable art of rhetoric is the art of persuasion. Along with grammar and logic, it has held an important place in education for almost twenty-five centuries. That place was much more important in Greek and Roman antiquity, when an educated person was expected to be something of an orator, and also in the seventeenth and eighteenth centuries, when emphasis was laid not just on substance but on style in speech and writing.
>
> These arts have all but vanished in the basic schooling of the young today. Of the three, rhetoric (*and with it the skill of docility in listening*) is the one most strikingly absent from the first twelve years of education. A few of those going on to college may take courses in public speaking, but most have not been trained in the skills of persuasion (*and listening*).
>
> Throughout its long history, the teaching of rhetoric has been concerned mainly, if not exclusively, with oratory and style. Style in the use of language, style that makes the communication of a substance either more elegant (*that is, beautiful*/my addition) or more effective is a quality common to both the written and spoken word. Whether or not elegance is always desirable, it may not always render the communication more effective as

an effort at persuasion. (25/parenthetical additions are mine)

Since Adler's interest in rhetoric in his book was mainly concerned with effective persuasion in speaking to others, in rhetoric's lengthy history what caught his attention was the way it was so closely, almost exclusively, associated with oratory that they appear to have been considered identical. "In antiquity and early modern times," Adler states, "the descriptive epithet 'oratory' was interchangeable with 'rhetorician.'" (25)

While Adler does not mention the reason for this, this conflation is easy to understand. Like philosophy, rhetoric, in the West, was first born among the ancient Greeks into a culture that was chiefly dominated by the spoken, not written, word. Its first practitioners were epic poets in the form of wandering minstrels. Poetry, rhetoric, sophistry, philosophy, science, wisdom were conflated ideas.

As Westerners started to develop the art of writing, the distinction between orator and rhetorician could start to be made. In addition, with the loss of widespread literacy in the Western Roman Empire with the decline of Rome around the year 400, rhetorical and oratorical skill also started to decrease. These did not start to become revived until the tail end of the Middle Ages, during the thirteenth century, after universities had come into existence. Prior to this, from about the years 800 to 1000, focus of educational attention in the West was on first restoring elementary reading and writing skills—the liberal art of grammar; followed (about the year 1000 to 1200) by recovering the liberal art of logic; and after that reviving the liberal art of rhetoric.

As Paul Oskar Kristeller has well documented, the distinction between rhetoric and oratory did not become revived in any major way before the start of the fourteenth-century, Italian Renaissance, through the works of Italian humanists, who were poetic and rhetorical analogues of Medieval Scholastic philosophers and theologians. According to Kristeller, these thinkers were chiefly poets and rhetoricians mainly interested in reviving the whole of classical learning—not just philosophy and theology—for the chief aim or reviving Italian, especially Roman, culture. Hence the great, well-deserved reputation of Italians like Marc Antony, Dante Alighieri, and Andrea Bocelli for their respectively elegant rhetorical styles in oratory, poetry, and music.

Spread of rhetoric and the distinction between rhetoric and oratory to other parts of Europe (such as Germany, Spain, Great Britain [to which Adler will refer in the next section of this Lesson], Poland and parts of Central and Eastern Europe) took several centuries as the influence of Italian humanism tended first to enter universities in these areas, initially through the influence of Marsilio Ficino's Platonic Academy within the School of Cambridge Platonism on the works of Benjamin Whichcote (b. 1609; d.

1683 and considered to be the founder of the School), Henry More (b. 1614; d. 1687), and others.

Regarding this revived distinction between rhetoric and oratory, Adler asks and answers:

> What's wrong with this? Simply that oratory consists of attempts to persuade others to act in one way or another. The rhetorical skill of the orator is aimed solely at a practical result, either a course of action to be adopted, a value judgment to be made, or an attitude to be taken toward another person or group of persons.
>
> A practical result, however, is not the sole use of rhetoric, not even its more frequent or most important application. We are frequently concerned with moving the mind of someone else to think as we do. That is often as important to us as moving someone else to act or feel as we wish them to (*that is, psychologically changing a person's mind, intellectual disposition, to think* [understand, reason, and appetitively agree with] *the way we do*/my addition: achieve a meeting of minds, or commonsense agreement). Our rhetorical aim then is purely intellectual, one might almost say theoretical, rather than practical. When we try to exert a rhetorical skill for this purpose, we are persuaders of a different kind than when we engage in oratory for a practical purpose. (25)

In part, I disagree with what Adler says in this paragraph immediately above. As he notes, the chief aim of the orator is never—even considered theoretically—simply or purely to change a person's mind considered simply as an intellect. This might be the chief aim at some moment to achieve a main goal of oratory or rhetoric considered according to its nature; but the chief purpose of the rhetorician or orator is always, longer term, to change a person's psychological disposition, including a person's will and emotions, which, to an orator or rhetorician, are subjects he or she seeks most to influence as a means to changing a person's mind: to like, love, and as a result, choose one action over another, and think this way, not that way. The orator and rhetorician beautify language to influence and, often change, what a person chiefly loves, as a means to changing a person's short- or long-term behavior. Like philosophy, oratory/rhetoric, is a species of behavioral, organizational psychology.

Returning to Adler, he maintains that, considered from the standpoint of its use for chiefly a practical aim, what is wrong with calling *rhetoric* by the name *oratory* is that this tends to create in the minds of contemporary listeners the reduction of rhetoric to "the political platform, the court room, or the legislative assembly." (25) From this standpoint, Adler makes a good point. "Politics is not the only arena in which human beings need rhetorical skill. They need it in business. They need it in any *enterprise* (preceding is my italics) engaged *with* others or *against* others in

Chapter 3: Uninterrupted Speech

attempting to achieve some personal result." (25–26) Such being the case, Adler makes a good point avoiding conflating the arts of rhetoric and oratory.

Another reason to do so is because the art of the orator is chiefly oral, not written. Like a singer, the orator beautifies oral speech, while the rhetorician beautifies oral and written speech. Oratory is a species of the wider genus of rhetoric. In both instances, the rhetorician acts like a sculptor, painter, even a dancer or actor. In all these areas, Adler maintains, just as in politics, analogously, we are trying to, or mainly, selling something to somebody. (26)

Since, according to Adler, "practical persuasion in all its myriad forms is salesmanship," he tells his readers, throughout the rest of his book, he will "adopt the lowly phrase 'sales talk' as the name for the kind of speaking to others that involves persuasion with an eye on some practical results to be achieved." For the species of persuasion that he considers to be chiefly intellectual or theoretical he will employ the names *teaching* and *instruction*. (26)

At the same time, Adler cautions his readers to remember:

> Instruction takes many forms. Sometimes the teacher is not simply a speaker addressing an audience that consists of silent listeners. When teachers perform that way, they teach by telling rather than by asking. Teaching by telling is lecturing, and good lectures are

just as much concerned with persuading listeners as good sales people are.

Though persuasion is involved in both instruction and selling, the one for purely theoretical or intellectual results, the other for a practical result, I think it most convenient to adapt the following terminology. I will refer to all attempts to achieve for a practical result as 'persuasive speech,' and all attempts to achieve a change of mind (without any regard to action) as 'instructive speech.' What I have called the 'sales talk' is persuasive speech. The lecture is instructive speech.

I shall discuss these two main types of uninterrupted speech before I consider special variants of each of them: in the next chapter, the sales talk; and in the one following, the lecture. (26)

When, if ever, can we use rhetoric too much or too little; and, if sometimes we can, how can commonsense wisdom help us determine this?

Unlike the cardinal moral virtues of justice and prudence, and the intellectual virtue of wisdom—which a perfectly moral person could never use in a way that is too much, too little, or badly—as Adler understands, we can over, and under, use the liberal art of rhetoric—as well as use it in the wrong place, at the wrong time, or both. Toward the start of his Chapter 3, with help from a glaring example,

Adler explains precisely how rationally to know, measure, when and where to employ the art of rhetoric.

The example Adler uses concerns a major committee meeting at which he was present during the mid-1940s at the University of Chicago. It was comprised of a group of prestigious faculty members that included two persons of contrary-opposite psychological dispositions. One was Giuseppe Antonio Borgese (a well-known poet and Professor of Italian Literature). The other was "the staid, prosaic, matter of fact Dean of the Harvard Law School," James Landis. (21)

On this occasion, Adler reports, "Professor Borgese addressed his colleagues on a subject dear to his heart. As he warmed to his subject, his voice rose, his eyes flashed and his language became more and more forceful, reaching a crescendo of poetry and passion that left all of us spellbound—all except one": Dean Landis. (21)

"In the moment of silence that ensued," Adler reports, "Dean Landis fixed Borgese with a cold stare and said in a low voice, 'That's just rhetoric!' Borgese, equally cold but with anger, and pointing a finger at Landis that might have been a pistol, replied: 'When you say that again, smile!' (21)

"What did Dean Landis mean by that remark? What could he have meant?" Adler wondered.

Certainly not that Borgese's speech was ungrammatical and illogical, leaving it no qualities of utterance at all except those which were rhetorical. Though English was not his native tongue, Professor Borgese was a master of the language. From having engaged in many arguments with him, I can vouch for his analytical prowess and the cogency of his reasoning. He had a flair for embellishing (*beautifying*) his remarks with imagery, with metaphors, with well-timed pauses and staccato outbursts that riveted attention on what he was saying and drove home the points he was trying to make.

Therein lay the rhetorical power of his address, a power that the equally well-phrased and well-reasoned remarks of the reserved Anglo-Saxon Dean of the Harvard Law School almost always lacked. Why did the Dean object to this quality in his Italian colleague's utterance? What was wrong with it? He may have restrained himself from resorting to the devices so skillfully employed by Professor Borghese, but their temperamental difference in style did not justify his dismissing the speech of Borgese as 'just rhetoric.' (22/my parenthetical addition)

Before reviewing Adler's psychological analysis of the behavior of Dean Landis and Professor Borgese related to Borgese's rhetorical presentation, I call the readers' attention to my parenthetical insertion of the term 'beautifying' in the next to last paragraph above. I did this to stress the etymological origin of the word: *to make beautiful*. In my opinion,

Adler used this word precisely because he knew that, in the first sentence of the last paragraph, he had planned to state, as he did, that use of this term had given the presentation its "rhetorical power." And, in my opinion, he did so precisely because he understood that what gives anything its power, strength, is the amount of goodness of its nature that it contains, *how qualitatively great/perfect* it individually is in being what it generically and specifically is: qualitatively maximizing the real definition of what it is, its nature or essence.

The word 'beautiful' signifies *perfection in goodness*. In saying this, I do not mean that, when referred to a finite being, composite/organizational whole, 'beautiful' signifies something being totally good in the way a religious person might say Almighty God is perfect. I mean it in the sense that anything existing within a real genus has achieved a maximum in qualitative execution of its organizational unity and/or existence, and/or activity that cannot be qualitatively surpassed. It has reached the qualitative limit of the strength of its individual, specific, and/or generic goodness— achieved the maximum of goodness/qualitative (intensive quantity) greatness in action achievable, really doable, in this or that genus of activity. For example, someone who has done something so good that nobody does, can do, it better—like the football Quarterback Tom Brady in the United States in the year 2021. This does not have to be forever. It might be the case only for one instant. For example, being the world's record-breaking weight lifter in Olympic weight-lifting competition.

Well known is that Aristotle had defined *good* as a motivating cause, some being that moves something else to become united with it: a final cause, aim, end. Once united with this end, Aristotle had maintained that a subject moved by an end stops moving, rests. Considered as such, the good is what is attractive, or attracts. In this respect, the subject that had been moved has achieved as much as it actually can achieve.

Emotionally, when human beings totally realize a human good, human desire becomes maximally satisfied. In this respect, no good can be added to it or taken away from it. It is in a state of total, or perfect, satisfaction. In short, it is in a state of perfect pleasure, or enjoyment. Such a state is fittingly called 'beautiful.'

I often define 'beauty' simply as *the shocking good*. By this I mean having a qualitative intensity or concentration of good that, like a strong concentration of liquid, is so powerful that it shocks all-knowing and appetitive human faculties: such as intellect, will, imagination, passions/emotions, and one or more external sense.

By doing this, if what is beautiful is something visible, it arrests human attention in such a way that we instantaneously do what in English we call 'a double take.' We have to look back at what we just saw and cannot take our eyes off it because it is something we call 'drop-dead beautiful' or 'gorgeous.' If it is audible, we cannot stop listening to it. Related to any and all our senses, we often say 'it knocks our socks off,' causes us to 'jump with joy.' And, sometimes, for example, when watching an athletic competition, musical, or theatrical performance, we *do* jump with joy because the joy is so intense/strong that it causes us to jump.

I think Adler well understood that Aristotle and Saint Thomas had considered any and every virtue, skill, talent, art to be a psychologically beautifying quality such as I have just described: a beautifying quality of the human soul. When a psychologically healthy human being familiar with the nature of some virtue, skill, talent, art, science recognizes the existence of this nature as a cause of action, he or she naturally inclines psychologically to react in the way I have just described above.

Psychologically healthy, adult human beings evidently understand the reality of good and evil. For them, this needs, can have, no rational demonstration. Were this not the case, if nothing could be really good, better, or best/and bad, worse, and worst, human beings could not reasonably hope or fear anything, because nothing could actually improve or harm us. By nature, experience of the emotions of hope and fear as being related to real goods and evils would be psychologically disordered, unhealthy, a sign of being out of touch with reality, lacking in common sense—which is the way utopian socialist ideologues tend to conceive of these passions.

Such being the case, equally evident to such healthy human beings is the reality of real, generic, specific, and individual perfections. A chief reason for this is because, if a person denies the reality of such perfections and their contrary opposites, he or she cannot rationally affirm the reality of real good and real evil; or of better and best in any genus or species of individual activity.

Among commonsensically educated human beings (and, at times, even, some human beings with little common sense), and, especially among great rhetoricians, recognition of the reality of good, evil, perfection and imperfection is considered to be psychologically healthy: a sign of being higher educated. And they take advantage of this knowledge to change the minds of their better educated listeners as suits the occasion and is the chief aim of the rhetorician.

Turning now to Adler's analysis of the reactions of Dean Landis and Professor Borgese to the Professor's rhetorical presentation, as benignly as possible to communicate the psychological cause that had triggered Dean Landis's criticism of Borgese, Adler interpreted his meaning *not* to signify that Borgese's "oration was *just* rhetoric, but rather that it was *more* rhetorical than the occasion required" (22). Note that neither Adler nor the Dean had denied that Borgese's act was rhetorical. They had recognized professionally who he was, what he was doing, how he was doing it, with what he was doing it, and related to whom he was doing it. Their objection was mainly to how, where, when, and why he was

Chapter 3: Uninterrupted Speech   109

doing it as, in some way, being specifically out of place, *qualitatively too much for their occasion*: a serious flaw for a rhetorician of Professor Borgese's skill and reputation.

This is a crucial point to note for several reasons, but especially because, whether he realized it or not, Adler was referring his and the Dean's criticism of Borgese to what are often identified as the eight (although some disagreement exists among some classical scholars as to their actual number) circumstances of a moral act given by Aristotle and as interpreted by Saint Thomas Aquinas: 1) who is: 2) doing what; 3) to what or whom; 4) with what; 5) where; 6) when; 7) why, and 8) how (see *Summa theologiae*, 1–2, q. 18, esp. arts. 3, 10, and 11). While Scholastic theologians and philosophers almost universally think about and apply these actions solely to the nature of an act as morally virtuous or vicious, as is evident from the fact that both the manner in which Adler had described the way the Dean had chosen to critique it, and the manner in which Borgese had reacted to the way the Dean had critiqued it, all three had recognized who, professionally, Borgese was—to what professional genus he belonged: a rhetorician, and a reputedly highly skilled one at that—at least, abstractly considered.

All knew professionally and abstractly what Borgese was doing, chiefly why he was doing it, with what he was doing it, and how he was doing it. Their disagreement lay in concretely how, where, and when he was doing it: the way he was doing it. This point is crucial to understand because the circumstances of an act are not limited to determining a generic human act as specifically and/or individually morally virtuous or vicious. They also apply to specification of any act considered according to its nature, as well as to its moral good or evil. As Aristotle said, for a person to be a murderer, thief, or the like, he or she must kill the way a murderer kills and, to be a thief, must take the property of another the way a thief takes it, and so on. Making the appropriate changes, the same is true related to any human action.

Recall the example I gave in Lesson 1 about a person who attempted to ignore using principles of mathematics, especially geometry, to building a bridge, but instead chose to limit the principles to those of grammar. He or she would not be, and could not reasonably be called, *an engineer.* Abstractly considered, the circumstances of an act play no role in specification of a nature. For example, logically considered, Socrates is a human being no matter where, when, or with what he acts. Concretely considered, however, human beings are not specified to be engineers by applying principles of grammar to bridge-building materials. Concretely considered, to be specified an engineer a human being must rightly apply mathematical principles to bridge-building materials: must do what real engineers commonsensically do and do them the commonsensically way real engineers do them.

In the current instance, Adler appears to be applying the term "occasion" according to its non-moral reference. And

Chapter 3: Uninterrupted Speech

he appears to be critiquing Professor Borgese and Dean Landis for ignoring some essential circumstances of measuring both their performances as, *or as not,* rhetorical masterpieces. Borgese appears to have been angered by the Dean's reaction to his performance precisely because he had taken it to be a criticism of his failure to understand the nature of his art *qua* art, rhetoric *abstractly considered* as rhetoric. Apparently, Borgese had taken the Dean's criticism to reflect some defect in Borgese's oratorical skill as a knowledge, which it appears partly to have been. In addition, as described by Adler, the way Borgese had angrily reacted to the Dean also appears to have displayed to a *concrete* lack of moral prudence.

Adler had criticized psychologically-cultural Italian, Borgese for apparently *concretely* mistaking himself for Marc Antony, thinking he was present in the Roman Forum, giving Julius Caesar's Funeral Oration. And he had critiqued Anglo-Saxon Dean Landis for *concretely* mistakenly thinking Professor Borgese was a first-year law student at Columbia Law School and displaying lack of moral prudence for treating him as such. In short, both appeared to Adler to be on psychologically the wrong page about what was the real genus of human action in which they were involved and were acting somewhat imprudently, lacking in common sense.

Hence, Adler said:

Borgese was not on a platform addressing a large audience of strangers, whom he was trying to persuade. He was sitting around a table with colleagues who were engaged with him in an undertaking the underlying presuppositions of which they all shared. The issue under consideration called for the examination of a wide assortment of facts and the weighing of many reasons pro and con.

That, in the view of Dean Landis, could only be done well by sticking, closely and cooly, to the pertinent matters, eschewing all irrelevant digressions that I added more heat (*emotion*) than light (*understanding or reason*) to the discussion. Hence his curt rebuff to Borgese that in effect said: 'Cut the unnecessary rhetoric out!' (23/my parenthetical addition)

At this point, Adler pondered the term *unnecessary* that he had put into the mouth of Dean Landis to express what the Dean was precisely thinking. What could the Dean have meant by thinking Borgese's rhetoric was unnecessary? Was it unnecessary because was *too much* for the occasion (where/place and when/time) it was being employed? Or "because it is never needed at all?" (23)

Adler immediately denied this second possibility could not possibly have been Dean Landis's meaning because, "To think so amounts to thinking that speaking grammatically and logically always suffices for the purpose of hand." But, according to Adler, anyone with common sense knows speaking grammatically and logically does not always suffice "for the purpose of hand." To claim it does, he maintained (in a fashion radically different from the way he would have done as a Columbia University graduate student), "One might just as well say that speaking to others never requires any consideration of how to get them to listen to what you have to say or how to make what you have to say affect their minds and hearts in ways that you wish to achieve." (23) In short, we might as just as well say that talking to them never requires we consider how to get them to listen to us and to change their minds about what they think or feel.

While such an attitude might suffice for writing "a private memorandum to file away for future reference," the more emotionally mature, prudent, wiser and commonsensical Adler claimed that, using language skillfully to change people's intellectual and appetitive dispositions (their minds and hearts) demands a qualitatively different talent than grammar or logic—rhetoric. Hence, Adler stated, "Rare as the need for rhetoric may be when we are speaking only to ourselves, we are unlikely to be able to do without it when we are speaking to others. The reason is clear. We almost always have to try to persuade them not only to listen to what we have to say, but also to agree with us and to think or act accordingly." (24) Precisely how to do this is the topic Adler considers in his second division of Part 2, to which I will now turn my attention.

—CHAPTER FOUR—

Lesson 4—Analysis of "The 'Sales Talk' and Other Forms of Persuasive Speech"

Adler explains his use of 'The Sales Talk' as part of this Chapter's title.

Mortimer Adler begins his Chapter 4—"The 'Sales Talk' and Other Forms of Persuasive Speech"—by saying, "The title of this chapter may arouse the reader's misgivings. What does a philosopher know about how to make a sales talk? This is hardly a subject which falls within his ken." (30)

To calm his reader's psychological concerns, Adler said he would start his Chapter by doing what the philosopher, and master of persuasion, Aristotle had "recommended as the first step to be taken by anyone trying to persuade anyone else about anything, especially in the sphere of the practical." He would apply the oratorical principles of persuasion (*ethos*, *pathos*, and *logos*) that Aristotle had first identified centuries ago in his lengthy book entitled *Rhetoric*. In fact, Adler reports this is precisely what he had done many years before when—as Director of San Francisco's Institute of Philo-sophical Research, which he had established—he had received an invitation to give a talk at a luncheon meeting of the associated Advertising Clubs of California.

Since the invitation had included a request that he give them a title of the talk, accepting the invitation and thinking he should speak on a topic "sufficiently shocking to them," Adler suggested he speak about "Aristotle on salesmanship." To his knowledge, "no one had ever before connected the name of Aristotle with salesmanship—or with advertising, which is an adjunct of selling. Hence, he had thought that the title would be provocative enough to attract their attention, which it did. (30)

Going into the details of the talk, Adler states he started it by explaining its title by asking the following, common-sense, rhetorical and leading question: "Advertising is a form of selling, is it not?" (30) Once they universally nodded agreement, he followed with a second commonsense, rhetorical and leading question, "Is not every form of selling an effort at persuasion, in this case an effort to persuade potential customers to buy the product advertised? Again, they nodded in agreement." (31)

Having secured their commonsense agreement on these two points, Adler told them Aristotle is the master of the art of persuasion, about which, centuries ago, he had written a lengthy treatise entitled *Rhetoric*. To present his message for the occasion in summary form, he told them that Aristotle had identified "three main tactics" (by which he meant *principles*) to be used by anyone who wanted to "succeed in the business of persuasion"; and he immediately added that no better names existed for these three main tools of persuasion than the words the Greeks used for them: *ethos, pathos*, and *logos*, which he then proceeded to explain.

In his Chapter, Adler then reports that the advertising experts present for his presentation were so impressed by it and Aristotle's *know-how* related their advertising business that, as he learned afterwards, "the book-stores of San Francisco were besieged that afternoon by members of the audience trying unsuccessfully to buy copies of Aristotle's *Rhetoric.*" (30)

The meaning of the Greek words *ethos, pathos*, and *logos*.

Having given this general introduction to his Chapter, Adler starts to go into its specific details by explaining the meaning of Aristotle's three essential principles of rhetoric, out of which all its activities naturally grow. According to Adler, "The Greek word *ethos* signifies a person's character. Establishing one's character is the preliminary step in any attempt at persuasion. The persuader must try to portray himself as having a character that is fitting for the purpose at hand." (30)

In this situation, Adler's choice of the word *character*—which he does not limit to moral character—captures its wider scope of reference in relation to the practical, not liberal (speculative), art of rhetoric. Etymologically, most readers of Adler's text can recognize that the Greek term for *ethics* is derived from the Greek word *ethos*; but, depending upon whether the Greek letter 'e' is accented as short or long, the meaning switches from its moral sense to a more general sense captured by the Latin term *mores*, referring to custom, or expected behavior.

The term *character* generically considered (which is the way Adler is applying it) captures more than a person's moral disposition, whether a person is morally virtuous or vicious. More generally, it signifies a person's psychological *virtus*, skill-set, considered as a whole: volitionally, emotionally, and intellectually. To do this, a good rhetorician or salesman must start out by persuading a listener that what he or she "has to say is worth listening to." To do this, in turn, Adler says a speaker must present himself or herself as being the type of person who knows what he or she "is talking about and can be trusted for" his or her "honesty and goodwill." A speaker "must appear attractive and likable to them as well as trustworthy." (30)

To achieve this goal with his audience of advertising specialists, Adler related to them two stories about himself. (31)

The first was about a conversation he had had with one of *Encyclopaedia Britannica*'s bankers when the Company was expending lots of money on producing *The Great Books of the Western* World, of which Adler was editor. "The bankers," he said, had come "to that meeting highly skeptical

Chapter 4: Analysis of "The 'Sales Talk'" 119

of the saleability of the product on which the company was spending so much money, and especially skeptical about the strange thing called the *Syntopicon* that threatened to consume more than one million dollars—a lot of money in those days—before it was completed. What good would the *Syntopicon* do anybody that might arouse their desire to purchase a set with the *Syntopicon* attached to it? 'I, for example, I am interested in buying and selling,' the banker said; 'and if I went to the *Syntopicon's* inventory of 102 great ideas, would I find one on salesmanship?' (31)

According to Adler, because the word *salesmanship* does not appear among the names of the 102 Great Ideas, the list of 1,800 subordinate terms that provide an alphabetical index referring to aspects of the 102 great ideas (later changed to 103/my addition), for an instant, that question had stumped him. Becoming immediately un-stumped, Adler replied to this banker by asking him one common sensical, rhetorical question, (commonsensical and rhetorical because Adler already knew, how, as a professional businessman, he would likely reply): whether he agreed "that to sell anybody anything one must know how to persuade them to buy what one wanted to sell?"

After this person immediately agreed, Adler reports he "clinched the matter by telling him that one of the 102 great ideas is rhetoric, which is concerned with persuasion, and that, if he consulted the *Syntopicon*'s chapter on that idea, he would find many extremely helpful passages in that chapter, even though none of the great authors cited there ever used the word 'salesmanship.' That was all I had to do to put an end to the banker's qualms about the money being spent on the production of the *Syntopicon*. I had sold him on it." (31)

After finishing that story, Adler proceeded to tell his audience of advertising sales experts the story about how he "had to sell five hundred sets of *Great Books of the Western World* in order to raise enough money to defray the printing and binding costs for the edition." (32) He reports:

> I did this almost single-handed, first by writing a letter that Bob Hutchins (who was then president of the university of Chicago) and I sent out over our signatures to 1,000 persons who might feel honored to become patrons of a special first edition of the set by purchasing it in advance of publication at the cost of $500—again a lot of money in the nineteenth fifties.
>
> That one letter brought in 250 purchase orders accompanied by checks. The 25 percent rate of return on a single appeal struck my audience of advertising men as an unparalleled success in the business of direct-mail advertising. I followed that initial success by selling the remaining 250 sets to individual patrons, either on the phone or by visiting them in their offices.
>
> On one such occasion, I sold the head of a chain of over eighty department stores forty-five sets—one to be given away by each of the forty-five stores in its home-

town to the local library or college as a public relations gesture. This particular sale took less than thirty minutes to make. The chief executive clearly indicated that he had little time to give me on a late Friday afternoon where he was about to leave town for the weekend. So I cut my sales talk to the bone in order to avoid impatience on his part, thereby gaining his goodwill.

By the time I had finished the second story, the advertising experts in my San Francisco audience were sufficiently impressed by my own personal involvement in the business of persuasion and selling to be all ears when I then went on to explain how Aristotle had summed up the essence of salesmanship in his analysis of the three main factors in persuasion. I had succeeded in establishing my own *ethos* with them before I started to explain the role that *ethos, pathos,* and *logos* play in persuasion.

And that is what I hope I have just done with you by telling you these two stories about my own personal experience as an advertiser and a salesman. (32–33)

Adler's analysis of the nature of *ethos*.

According to Adler, unless a speaker has previously established his or her character as a credible speaker and made himself or herself personally (and he should have added, 'professionally') *attractive* to his or her listeners, he or she is not likely to sustain their attention, much less to sell them on buying or doing what he or she wants them to buy or do. Of the three aforementioned rhetorical principles, following Aristotle, Adler maintains that *ethos* should always come first.

Only after they are persuaded that a person is morally and intellectually trustworthy (not just honest) will listeners be inclined to listen further and more intensely. Being honest is not enough if what a person needs to sell a listener about is his or her courage or prudence or knowledge about the courageous or prudent act to choose at this or that time in this or that situation. *If and only if* a person can first establish professional moral and intellectual competence about a subject in general can he or she persuade a knowledgeable listener to pay further attention to what he or she has to say about something else. (33)

Adler maintains that many ways exist to do this. For instance, by telling stories directly about yourself. He adds that such stories become especially effective if they provoke laughter, especially so if the laughter results from a self-deprecating tale. A second way to do this is indirectly—"by underestimating your credentials to speak about the matter at hand, thus allowing the listeners to dismiss your under estimation as undue modesty. You can also do it by suggesting your association with others whom you praise for certain qualities that you hope your listeners will also attribute to you." (33)

Adler then refers to the famous, classic illustrations of *ethos* and persuasion in the form of attempts to move Roman citizens to take different courses of political action made by Brutus and Marc Antony in William Shakespeare's *Julius Caesar*. (33–34)

Since little likelihood exists that anyone reading this text is unfamiliar with Brutus' and Marc Antony's orations, I will not give full, direct citation of them here. Regarding that of Brutus, I will mention two points Adler makes: 1) Brutus starts his talk by encouraging his audience to listen to him because he is an honorable man; and 2) if any dear friend of Caesar in the audience were to wonder why Brutus rose up against him, he did so not because he did not love Caesar; he did so because he loved Rome more than he loved Caesar.

About Brutus' short speech, Adler initially remarks that it "mainly illustrates the role of *ethos*." After that, Adler states, "Brutus, satisfied that he has exculpated himself and his fellow conspirators, does not try to arouse the citizens to any course of action. He asks them only to allow him to depart alone." (34)

Clear from Brutus' presentation is that Brutus knew the Romans were angry at him for participating in Caesar's assassination. As Adler indicates, Brutus conceived his sole aim to be to quell this anger, prevent them from killing, or in some other way, hurting him. Hence, Adler says, "Satisfied that he has persuaded them that the assassination was justified, Brutus yields his place to Marc Antony. Before

Antony can speak, the populace, completely won—or sold—by Brutus, shower him with acclaim and proclaim the public honors they wish to bestow upon him in dead Caesar's place. Brutus quiets them and implores them to listen to Antony, to whom he has granted permission to speak." (35)

Thus introduced, Antony addresses them, beginning with the famously stirring words, "Friends, Romans, countrymen, lend me your ears; I come to bury Caesar, not to praise him. The evil that men do lives after them; the good is oft interred with their bones; so let it be with Caesar." (35)

Commonsense political wisdom about Ancient Rome indicates that, unbeknown to Brutus, Antony had no intention of following Brutus with some glowing oration letting Brutus off the hook for participating in Caesar's killing. All along, Antony had planned to use Brutus' oratorical skill to hurt, not help, Brutus. Only someone lacking in ordinary commonsense political wisdom—a political fool or ignoramus—could believe Brutus had thought he would be softening up an already angry crowd for the chief aim of enabling an enemy of his to be able to enrage them against him. As Adler remarks, in contrast to Brutus, Antony "has a further (by which Adler means *contrary opposite*) purpose in mind. He wishes to avenge Caesar's death by arousing the multitude to take drastic action against the conspirators, especially Brutus and Cassius. (Honorable men indeed!) To do this, he resorts to *pathos* and *logos*, the other two factors in persuasion." (36)

The natures of *pathos* and *logos*.

Pathos:

According to Adler:

> Whereas *ethos* consists in the establishment of the speakers credibility and credentials, his respectable an admirable character, *pathos* consists in arousing the passions of the listeners, getting their emotions running in the direction of the action to be taken.
>
> *Pathos* is the motivating factor. It makes its appearance fairly early in Antony's speech, commingled even in the opening passage with the development of the speaker's *ethos*. Antony reminds them of all the things that Caesar did for Rome from which they benefitted, and as he recounts these benefactions, he repeatedly asks them whether they can believe that Caesar displayed self-seeking ambition rather than dedication to the public good.
>
> Antony thus succeeds in changing the mood that Brutus had established. One citizen cries out: 'Caesar has had great wrong'; another exclaims: 'he would not take the crown; therefore, 'tis certain he was not ambitious'; and still another expresses the admiration for Antony that Antony's use of *ethos* sought to produce, saying: 'There's not a nobler man in Rome than Antony.'

Satisfied now that he has established his own good character and also that he has their emotions running in the right direction, Antony proceeds to reinforce the passions aroused by adducing reasons for the action that he has sought to motivate. (36–37)

Logos:

Of the three chief Aristotelian rhetorical principles, Adler claims that use of *logos* comes last during the defense that Brutus and Antony made. The chief reason he gives for this is:

> Just as you cannot bring motivating passions into play, feelings in favor of the end result you are seeking to produce, until your first aroused favorable feelings toward your own person, so there is little point in resorting to reasons and arguments until you have first established an emotional mood that is receptive of them.
>
> Reasons and arguments may be used to reinforce the drive of the passions, but reasons and arguments will have no force at all unless your listeners are already disposed emotionally to move in the direction that your reasons and arguments try to justify.
>
> How does Antony in the concluding portion of his address commingle *pathos* and *logos* so effectively that he succeeds in moving the citizens of Rome to take arms

against Brutus, Cassius, and their associates? First of all, in the course of other remarks he slowly gets around to mentioning Caesar's will and intimating that, when the citizens learn of its provisions, they will find themselves Caesar's beneficiaries.

The citizens beseech Antony to reveal the contents of Caesar's will to them. But before he tells them that the will provides a gift of seventy-five drachmas to every citizen, he launches into a peroration that raises their passions to a fever pitch. (37–38)

Then, Antony tells them he remembers the first time Caesar had put on his mantle in a battle camp on the summer evening the day he had defeated the Nervii. Physically, Antony points to, and tells them to look at, different places where the assassins, supposed friends, had driven their blood-stained daggers into him and pulled them out. He especially calls attention to the cut made by the person he calls "Caesar's angel": *beloved Brutus*, about whom he says "how dearly Caesar loved him! This was the most unkindest cut of all" because, when Caesar saw that Brutus was the person stabbing him, the traitorous nature of the evil deed caused Caesar's "mighty heart" to "burst." He could not look at Brutus. All Caesar could do was muffle up his face in his mantle and fall. And, according to Antony, when mighty Caesar fell, all the citizens of Rome fell, "whilst bloody treason flourished over us." (39)

Adler maintains:

> This speech has the calculated effect. The citizens cry out for revenge against the assassins and their cohorts, calling them traitors and villains. They are no longer honorable men. But Antony, to be sure that he has won the day and sold the populace of Rome the action he wishes to be taken, takes one more step to consolidate his gains. As the opening lines of his speech indicate, this action plays once more on the *ethos* of Brutus as compared with the *ethos* of Anthony, epitomizes the reasons—the *logos*—for the action to be taken, and confirms the feelings—the *pathos*—he has already aroused. (39)

While pretending he has no intention of stirring up the crowd to mutiny, that he is no great orator like the honorable Brutus, Antony uses his exceptional oratorical skills to do the contrary opposite. As a result, just after he concludes his speech, the citizens shout: "We'll mutiny!"

> We'll burn the house of Brutus and we'll go after the other conspirators. Then, and only then, does Antony clinch the matter by revealing how every citizen of Rome benefits from Caesar's will. That does it. The citizens cry out 'go fetch fire. . . . Put down forms, windows, anything.' Satisfied that he has now done the job, Antony

retires, saying to himself: 'Now let it work. Mischief, thou art afoot, take thou what course thou wilt!' (40)

How to be effective in use of *ethos*, *pathos*, and *logos*.

Two essential, commonsense rhetorical principles crucial to use to be an effective speaker, and how rightly to use them

According to Adler, to be effective in using *pathos* (moving the human emotions) chiefly to cause a desired effect of favorable emotional impulses toward the speaker, persuasive speakers must recognize *commonsense human desires* they can take for granted exist in, and passionately tend to move, all psychologically healthy human beings—such as, the desire for human freedom, justice, peace, pleasure, wealth, honor, good reputation, social position, preferential treatment. Taking for granted and identifying the existence of commonsensically known, human wants and needs that generally exist among all human beings and passionately motivate all psychologically healthy human beings enables speakers and writers rightly to use them by skillfully calling them to the attention of listeners in this or that situation for the chief goals the speakers aim to realize.

Rightly to use them, however, demands the speaker focus on, and have the knowhow effectively to use, *logos*: be able rationally to explain to listeners why this or that choice and/or way of behaving is a better way of securing what they chiefly want than is some other one that a competitor might suggest.

Why effective use of ethos, logos, and pathos, *essentially demands that a persuader understand that he or she is chiefly a commonsense, behavioral, organizational psychologist.*

While Adler does not explicitly mention this point, essential to recognize is that, unlike a speculative logician, as any business person or salesman immediately understands (knows by immediate, commonsense induction), the focus of a smart rhetorician's attention is, and needs always to be, chiefly on human action—really doable human deeds in this or that situation. For this reason, even before considering a choice, professional business people, sales persons: 1) constantly tend to think about whether or not this or that individual action is a really doable deed for this or that person or organization at this time, in this or that situation; 2) know that trying to solve such a problem and approach it like a speculative logician is deadly.

As professional business people instinctively tend to recognize, needed, instead, is concrete, *commonsense logic, practical means-ends logic,* in the form of prudent decision-making of appropriate means to choose to secure this or that goal in this or that situation. For this reason, deadly to a business is to have as head of its organization's HR (Human Resources) department, or some other crucial, decision-making, organizational division, pretty much anyone who thinks like a speculative logician, or anyone who has received an academic degree in psychology or sociology from any contemporary college or university. While some exceptions exist to this general rule, doing so tends to make no common sense.

Another point Adler fails to mention is that, like any good sales person, *a rhetorician is chiefly a commonsense, organizational, behavioral psychologist*—something Adler was not while at Columbia University; but which he later became after immersing himself in the uncommon commonsense wisdom of Aristotle and Aquinas. Whether he explicitly knew it or not, a chief point Adler was trying to make to his readers in this part of his text was that this is the case with all good persuaders.

For this reason, great sales people will often think of themselves as psychologists, and also as people who have common sense, and good instincts about human behavior and how to use commonsense logic. This is true whether this salesperson happens to be, as Adler notes, someone advising a politician in an election campaign or legislative debate about opposing policies—such as peacekeeping policies, protecting human rights, or securing welfare benefits. Persuaders with common sense, he says, "do not have to create a desire for peace, liberty, or welfare." Their common sense tells them that desire already exists. "They need only argue that the candidate or their policy serves that purpose better." (41)

Those persuaders, who actually have common sense, also know that they "cannot always count on desires that are generally prevalent in their audiences and ready to be brought into play. Sometimes they must instill the very desire that they seek to satisfy with their product, their policy, or the candidate." (41)

According to Adler, such listeners are individuals who have an actual desire that exists in what he calls a "dormant" condition, one that needs to be awakened, which a commonsense persuader knows how to create in this or that situation, at this or that time.

> Sometimes people have needs or wants that are dormant, needs or wants of which they are not fully aware. These, persuaders must try to awaken and vitalize. Sometimes they must try to create a desire that is novel—generally inoperative until they have aroused it and made it a driving force. This is what must be done with a new product on the market. So, too, this is what a candidate for public office must do if his or her claim to it is based on a novel appeal. (41–42)

In this situation, Adler notes:

Chapter 4: Analysis of "The 'Sales Talk'"

The element of *ethos* may either precede or be combined with the employment of *pathos* in the sales talk. The role of the PR experts or the Madison Avenue consultant is to make the company that is trying to sell a product look good as well as to make the product itself more desirable than what the competition has to offer. When such experts in persuasion work for a political candidate, they work in the same way. They try to paint a glowing picture of the candidate's character in addition to activating the motives for subscribing to the policies for which he or she stands. (42)

After *ethos* and *pathos* have been well established, three essential commonsense principles that need to be commonsensically applied in the individual situation to be effective in commonsense use of *logos*.

KISS (Keep It Simple, Stupid!)

According to Adler, once a persuader has been able to cause *ethos* and *pathos* to become operative within a listener, '*logos* remains the winning trump in the persuader's hand.' (42) Adler then: 1) lists the things to be avoided and to be well done and 2) explains the reasons why they need to be avoided and how they are to be effectively achieved.

While he does not label in the following way the first principle a persuader needs to apply, it is the well-known, commonsense principle in the arsenal of any good salesperson: *Keep it simple, Stupid!* (*KISS!*). Expressed in more formal academic form, Adler says,

> the persuader should avoid lengthy, involved, and intricate arguments. The test to be preferred is not to produce the conviction that can result from a mathematical demonstration of scientific reasoning. Effective persuasion aims at much less than that—only a preference for one product, one candidate, or one policy over another. Here the argument to be employed should be much skimpier, much more elliptical, much more condensed. (42)

The three classical, commonsense rhetorical principles any good salesperson applies to a sales talk when applying the general rhetorical principle of KISS!: 1) Enthymeme; 2) Immediate induction/arguing from example; and 3) Rhetorical questions.

Immediately to capture and arrest the attention of listeners, like any good orator, Adler recognizes that good sales people skillfully use a form of *commonsense logical argumentation* that omits many steps in strict syllogistic reasoning: "The classical name for such reasoning is the Greek word *enthymeme*, which signifies a process of reasoning with many premises omitted. The unmentioned premises must, of course, be generalizations that the persuader can safely assume will be generally shared"—that are commonsensically understood. (42–43)

In other words, the salesperson or debater must know the listener possesses a commonsense understanding of some steps in reasoning that makes mentioning them altogether unnecessary, or makes no common sense in this or that situation, in this or that time or place. Common sense enables a debater or salesperson immediately to understand, *take for granted*, that, in the here and now, mentioning some premises in an argument wastes valuable time, could annoy a listener, and defies common sense. For example, Adler states:

> In an argument before a judicial tribunal, counsel for the prosecution or defense can take for granted certain generalizations of which the court takes judicial notice because, being generally acknowledged as true, they do not have to be explicitly asserted.
>
> With such generalizations (*commonsense understandings*/my addition) taken for granted, the persuader can go immediately from a particular instance, one that falls under the assumed and mentioned generalization, to (*jump to/induce*/my addition) the conclusion that the applicable generalization entails. This is arguing from example. If I wish to persuade my listeners that a particular product of policy should be bought or adopted, I

can do so effectively by showing how it exemplifies a generally accepted truth. (43)

For instance, he adds, most of the time we do not need explicitly to state that everything that strengthens someone's health is something good. All we need do is describe how this or that product does that, and as completely as possible. A main point Adler is making when talking about use of economy in a sales talk is that two other principles—in addition to reasoning by use the *enthymeme*—unite to form the complete nature of the well-known sales prescription, *Keep it simple, Stupid!* (which appears to be a specific application to sales talk of the teaching principle often called *Ockham's Razor*).

The third *KISS!* principle is, whenever reasonably possible, use rhetorical questions. According to Adler, "Rhetorical questions are those so worded that one and only one answer can be generally expected from the audience you are addressing. In this sense they are like the unmentioned premises in abbreviated reasoning, which can go unmentioned because they can be taken for granted as generally acknowledged" (43–44); and, *to any good salesperson, these are simply commonsense questions!*

For this reason, in his situation, as Adler notes, Brutus asks his fellow citizens of Rome: "Who is here is so base that would be a bondsman?" Then he immediately adds: "If any, speak, for him have I offended." And: "Who is here so vile

Chapter 4: Analysis of "The 'Sales Talk'"

that will not love his country? Let him so speak, for him have I offended." To Brutus these are commonsense, rhetorical questions that he dares to ask because he knows, as Adler says, "full well that no one will answer his rhetorical questions in the wrong way." (44)

"So, too," Adler remarks, "Marc Antony, after describing how Caesar's conquests filled Rome's coffers, asks: "Does this in Caesar seem ambitious?" And after reminding the populace that Caesar thrice refused the crown that was offered him, Antony asks: "Was this ambitious?" Both are rhetorical questions to which one and only one answer can be expected." (44) For this reason, in his situation, any orator with commonsense would ask them, or others like them, and do as did Antony.

How and why every form of speaking chiefly for a practical goal is a sales talk.

Next, Adler explains more precisely how the three essential rhetorical principles of *ethos*, *logos*, and *pathos* (any kind of speaking with a practical goal/sales talk) work to give rhetoric its effectiveness.

While we normally restrict use of the term *sales talk* to evident instances of selling in advertising and marketing commercial goods and services, because we consciously speak with a practical goal in political venues, legislatures, and court rooms; at public ceremonies honoring someone or commemorating a special event; and related to private kinds of speech that might involve a Chairman of the Board speaking to other Board members, the proponent of some policy at a business meeting, or even by one member of a family with other members, Adler analogously and more widely extends use of this term. "All these," he says, "no less than winning customers for a product, involve selling." (44–45)

Adler notes that classic expositions of *practical* rhetoric (not the *speculative* liberal art of rhetoric, but rhetoric—mainly oratory applied in a contingent situation) from Aristotle, Cicero, and Quintilian to the present, make no mention of terms like *selling* and *salesmanship*. Classical, practical application of rhetorical species of speaking tend to be divided under three headings: 1) *deliberative* (chiefly referring to political oratory in legislatures); 2) *forensic* (mainly referring to the way lawyers address members of a jury), and 3) *epidictic* (which refers to acts of praising or dispraising someone or something, be that some person, policy, or something else). Despite absence of contemporary use of the above-mentioned contemporary terms for these ways of speaking, Adler maintains that, considered "as forms of persuasion," all species of the genus of classical oratory are specific forms of selling, species of salesmanship. (45)

Widely used, less eloquent, but highly effective forms of practical persuasion and speech that Adler omits mentioning, but that are crucial to understand.

Often, being persuasive, even as a speaker, requires, no extensive vocabulary. Sometimes, it involves use of no vocabulary at all. Exceptional actors know this fact well. So did Professor Borgese. A simple glance, raising an eyebrow, smiling or frowning, an intense stare, ruffling a piece of paper, nodding one's head one way or another, pointing a finger, remaining totally silent, entering, or standing next to someone in a courtroom are some ways often used by human beings to persuade a person, or persons, one way or another.

My father was an exceptionally persuasive, but not exceptionally articulate, person. In part, this was due to the fact that he had an incredibly amiable nature, tended to love everybody, speak and think ill of no one—and he was an organizational genius, one of the two leading community organizers within my neighborhood of Bay Ridge and Dyker Heights, in Brooklyn. For 10 years, among the five local community organizations he ran, he was Grand Knight of the Archbishop John Hughes Council, Knights of Columbus.

At the time he was elected Grand Knight, this Council was one of the most politically influential in New York State and the United States. And, while its name suggests that its membership was chiefly Irish-American—and that was the case when it was first founded decades before—by the time my Irish/Scottish father ran for Grand Knight, its membership had become chiefly Italian-American. Included among these was a close personal friend of my father—with whom he had worked on many church projects—the other leading community organizer and great business entrepreneur in our area: well known to Italian-Americans in the United States and internationally as "The Olive Oil King."

In and of itself, that accomplishment of getting elected Grand Knight of that Council is glaring evidence of my father's persuasive nature. I often tell people that my father's becoming elected Grand Knight of the Archbishop John Hughes Council Knights of Columbus at that time in my neighborhood was more difficult than Donald Trump's becoming elected President of the United States in 2016. Like Trump, immediately after he had announced his candidacy, my father had experienced some resistance to it—an insurrection among some Italian-American Council members. Nonetheless, that insurrection was short-lived. With all due respect, apparently using appropriate, economical forms of *KISS!*, and *talking nicely* with the *all due respect* species of rhetorical speech the situation demanded, some other Italian-American member(s) of the Council quickly put the insurrection peacefully to rest.

Needless to say is that, as a youth, I was surrounded by highly persuasive, organizational geniuses. By themselves, several of these people heavily influenced the politics of New

York City, State, the entire United States, and other countries. Despite the fact that, like my father, my ethnic background is mainly Irish and Scottish, in grammar school and high school my brothers and I became close personal friends with some of the sons of these Italian organizational geniuses. I learned much from these people about the nature of organizations, how they are formed, how they excel in operational unity, last, and decline. In addition, they taught me much about leadership, common sense as a species of shrewdness, and the crucial importance of knowing how to talk to other people, and how always to do so *respectfully*, *nicely*, and *persuasively*.

One such individual was my high school Latin teacher, saintly Brother Meric (Jerome Meric Pessagno), who, aside from teaching Latin, was a brilliant linguist, orator, and coach of the high school debating team. So successful was he as a debate coach that, while I was in attendance at the school, his debaters won four successive national Catholic High School debating championships in Washington, D.C.

While he was a religious Brother, as a youth Meric had been surrounded by great wealth and privilege. For example, a relative of his (my recollection is that it was his uncle) had owned and operated the *Circle Line Boat Tours* around Manhattan. In addition, in appearance, he looked, spoke, and carried himself like the actor Claude Rains. While his standard mode of dress at the school was the typical black religious habit and white collar, when he left the high school he always covered this habit with a full-length black cape.

The story I am about to tell of simple, *one-way* oratorical excellence (which, for the situation, appeared to be *two-way* conversation) was reported to me personally by him several decades after he had left teaching at the high school. It does not relate to his oratorical skills, but to his common sense and to the masterful, commonsense rhetorical skills of one of our local Italian-American community organizers.

Since Meric was exceptionally proud of his debaters and wanted to reward the debating team members for all the great work they had done during their first three years, he desired to take the team *in style* to Washington, D.C., for its last debating performance. To do this, he planned to have them all driven to our national Capitol in a stretch limousine and housed while there in a penthouse suite at one of D.C.'s leading hotels.

To do that, common sense told him he needed money—which he estimated to come to a minimum of $2,000. To get the money, he decided to write to the presidents of the eight local banks in and near Bay Ridge, Brooklyn, at the time. In the letter, he explained the reason for his requiring the money, and the fact that he thought their contributing to honoring the students in this way would be great local public relations on their part for which they would be publicly praised by the school and eventually richly rewarded.

To his amazement, after waiting over two weeks, he had received not one reply from any of the bank presidents. Undeterred by this minor wrinkle in his plan, since the high school had many persuasive and influential personages whose sons were in attendance at the time, Meric spoke to one of them he had as a student in class—the son of Tony Anastasia (affectionately, *with all due respect*, a resourceful *self-provider* in our neighborhood referred to simply as *Tough Tony*). Tony was the brother of another great, local community organizer and self-provider—Albert Anastasia, who had met with an unfortunate death in a barber's chair in Manhattan a few years earlier.

Knowing that his father was head of the International Longshoreman's Association (ILA) at the Brooklyn waterfront, and that his union collected dues from its membership, Meric asked Tony's son whether he would be willing to set up an appointment for him to talk to his father. Tony's son was happy to accommodate.

This being the case, several days later Brother Meric went to the Brooklyn waterfront early one morning to meet with Tony Anastasia in his office. After spending a few minutes in his waiting room, Meric said he was invited in and sat down across from the union boss. Before relating to me the rest of the story, Meric told me that the immediate sensation he had of meeting Tony was that of being in the presence of brute animal power. He said the only experience he had ever had that approximated this was an interview he had conducted with Jimmy Hoffa.

Understanding his situation and respectfully relaying the tale of the letters he had written to the bank presidents and the way that not even one had had the courtesy to reply to him, Meric told me Tony was totally dumbfounded by his report. For several minutes—which had seemed much longer to Meric—he said Tony was so shocked by this act of disrespect and lack of common sense that all he could do was shake his head back-and-forth to the left and right, while quietly muttering, *sotto voce*, "This is terrible, Bruddah. This is terrible."

After repeating this phrase three or four times, with all due respect, Meric inquired of Tony what precisely he had meant when he said, "This is terrible."

Immediately, Tony responded to him like a no-nonsense, commonsense man on a commonsense mission who had immediately figured out precisely what was the problem and how immediately to resolve it. In answer to his question, he told Meric: "Obviously, what happened here, Bruddah, is that the bank presidents never got your letter. I'll tell you what I'll do. I will have my secretary phone each of these bank presidents right now while you are here, and I'll see whether we can straighten this problem out today."

And that is what Tony immediately did. A few minutes later, the first bank president phoned him, and Tony reported the problem to him. He said, "I have a Bruddah

Chapter 4: Analysis of "The 'Sales Talk'" 145

Meric from X high school in Bay Ridge in my office. He tells me something terrible has happened. A couple of weeks ago, he wrote you a letter asking you to donate $4000 to his debating society as a gesture of good public relations for which eventually you would be richly rewarded. . . ."

As he was speaking, Meric tried politely to interrupt and correct what Tony was saying by holding up *two* fingers to indicate that the monetary figure was $2000, not $4000. Tony's body-language response was to shake his head back-and-forth, left to right while holding up *four* fingers. He then continued, saying: "Obvious to me is that you never got the letter. I would like for us to resolve this problem now. So, would you please have someone from your office deliver $4000 in cash to Bruddah Meric by 4:00 P. M. today at X high school?"

Regarding the result of the meeting, Meric told me that, after leaving Tony's office and returning to his high school, at around 4:00 P.M. on the dot, the school's doorbell started to ring. Thanks to the persuasive speech of Tony Anastasia, he received $32,000 (no small sum of money in those days) in cash in brown paper bags!

While Tony's sales talk might have lacked some linguistic eloquence, it masterfully and succinctly contained and applied with highest *KISS!* intensity and economy in the form of commonsense exposition and reasoning, concretely and precisely comprehending the nature of his audience and the way to speak to them, the three principles of *ethos*, *pathos,* and *logos*—traits of a masterful commonsense rhetorician and salesman that not even the linguistic skill of a Professor Borgese or the rational rigor of Mortimer Adler could have surpassed.

—CHAPTER FIVE—

Lesson 5—Understanding Lectures and Other Forms of Instructive Speech

Mortimer Adler explains the difference among a sales talk, lecture, and other forms of instructive speech.

Mortimer Adler devotes his Chapter 5 ("Lectures and Other Forms of Instructive Speech") to formal, rhetorical presentations given to silent listeners. These include all species of professional and non-professional written and spoken, or memorized, addresses before large, medium, and small audiences. (46–47) Regarding the difference between sales talks from lectures and other forms of instructive speech, he states, "both kinds of presentations consist in telling, and telling is always teaching, though there are other forms of teaching than by telling. When I tell you what I know, think, or understand and do so with the intention of instructing your mind, I am engaged in teaching you. Herein lies the essential difference between the sales talk, on the one hand, and the lecture and other forms of instructive speech, on the other." (47)

Many species of talk exist. Adler gives baby talk and small talk as two examples. In this chapter, he is concerned with the species of persuasive and instructional speech. And he claims what causes them to be essentially different is that "the aim" of persuasive speaking is to affect the actions and feelings of the listeners while the other aims at influencing their minds: "Both involve persuasion, but for a different purpose." (47)

Strictly speaking, because it is not precise enough, what Adler says in the paragraph immediately above is only partially true. Precisely speaking, the *chief aim* (not the aim) of both forms of speaking is to affect the whole person in relation to a specific and individual psychological disposition or character. Whenever we choose to act on anyone or anything, we do so for *a chief aim*, or *goal*; and one or more secondary ones, including, in some way, our own betterment, happiness.

Whenever we engage in persuasive speaking, we always affect the minds of others, and our own, because the only way we can change their actions, emotions, and wills, is by changing their minds, or, better, their intellects. And, to do that, we have to think about the means we are going to choose to do so. If we have changed their minds, we have changed their mental actions, and our own. To do this, in some way, we have to affect their passions and wills, and our own passions and will.

Chapter 5: Understanding Lectures

Knowing, understanding, emoting, willing, are actions. Whenever we change any of them, we change human behavior, personal psychology, not simply the human mind. *The entire analysis of rhetoric that Adler gives in his book is an exercise in uncommon commonsense, behavioral organizational psychology!*

The chief point Adler appears to want to make above is that the chief aim of all speech could be speculative, practical, or productive. In the first case, the only action, or doing, it chiefly seeks to change, *produce*, in some way is specific acts of knowing simply for the sake of knowing—for example, understanding or understanding better. It does not chiefly seek to effect an action in the sense that it mainly aims to add/produce something beyond knowledge or understanding. However, whenever we aim to do this, we do so with some understanding that, by changing this other person's behavior, we will *produce* some impact on improving, not improving, or, in no way, affecting ourselves (other than ourselves remaining the same).

Adler, in fact, appears to recognize the point I have just made when, in the first sentence of his next paragraph, he states, "It may be thought that lecturing as a form of teaching should aim to convince the mind rather than merely to persuade it. But conviction carries with it a degree of certitude that is seldom if ever attainable outside the sphere of mathematics and the exact sciences." (48) And I would deny that it is ever totally sought or achieved even there. In either case, however, it has an impact on the human will and emotions of the listener and lecturer. The mind cannot be freely and totally convinced or persuaded if the will and emotions refuse to allow this to happen.

Whatever the case, Adler's chief point related to mathematics and what he calls "the exact sciences"—an odd word choice, since it suggests that some human knowledge can be scientific, yet not be exact—appears to be that, since it aims only at convincing the "the minds of the listeners of its the truth of certain propositions," it "need only have the order, clarity and cogency that sound logic confers upon it. No rhetorical considerations enter." Since conviction, certainty, removes doubt, and doubt is caused by fear of being wrong or certainty of some other conclusion being right—which can only be changed by introducing doubt into a person's intellect, even in logic, mathematics, and whatever he means by "exact sciences," strictly speaking, Adler cannot be correct. The chief point he appears to want to make is that, in such knowing activities, due to the reduced possibility of contingency related to their subject matter, less need exists for rhetoric in written or oral form.

Again, whatever the case, Adler explains that his chief interest in considering rhetoric related to lectures and other forms of persuasive speech is mainly with the kinds of speaking that chiefly aim to cause a more modest effect— *mental persuasion only* "beyond reasonable doubt, or simply by a preponderance of evidence or reasons in favor of one view rather than another"—"not beyond a shadow of a doubt." (48)

In such an instance, he maintains we need more than cogent and coherent logic. We have to pay attention to rhetorical differences that exist between written and spoken presentations of identical subjects. Just as Adler had referred the term *sales talk* to many species of *practical* persuasion, so he applies the word *lecture* to refer to all species of non-practical (such as theoretical, simply observational) persuasion by means of lecture—persuasive activities that chiefly aim at "a change of mind rather than a change of feeling or of impulse to act in one way rather than another." (48)

As already mentioned, from such forms of persuasion he has already excluded the kind of learning generally employed in acquiring knowledge "in mathematics or the exact science." To these, he adds all knowing chiefly obtained through rote memorization, such as learning grammar, spelling, punctuation, and mathematical formulas. (48–49)

These exclusions having been made, Adler is left mainly with: 1) largely continuous, fifty-minute college and university lectures typical of contemporary American colleges and universities; and 2) a formal, uninterrupted, presentation made in a private or public lecture hall to an audience of any size. (49) Beyond these, however, he recognizes television, and other sorts of lectures, not restricted to some kind of lecture hall. Contemporary online lectures via the internet are good examples.

He adds that these two species of instructive speech are not its only forms. Beyond these, he includes mainly instructive church sermons, business presentations, and military staff meetings that aim chiefly to increase knowledge or improve understanding—*not* oratorical ones that chiefly aim to "change the will or conduct of the listeners rather than trying to improve their understanding." (49–50)

Related to instructive church speech, he refers to a church sermon from a pulpit commenting on and explicating a biblical passage. Regarding instructive business speech he mentions, a conference of business executives addressed by a company's chief executive or employee, military staff meetings, dinner-table or drawing-room conversations "for the purpose of imparting knowledge of the business at hand, for the purpose of analyzing a business problem to be solved so it is better understood, or for the purpose of stimulating thought about the operation of the business." Regarding all the preceding, he restricts his attention and that of his readers to "the kind of teaching by telling that consists in uninterrupted speech, with the listeners remaining silent until the oral presentation is completed." (50)

Adler says he does so because: 1) in Part 3 of his monograph, he wants to focus his attention on what an audience of silent listeners to an uninterrupted instructive speech have to do to make their listening intellectually

Chapter 5: Understanding Lectures 153

effective. And, 2), in Part 4, he wants to concentrate on two-way instructive talk—both the kind of verbal exchange that happens in two-way instructive conversations involving all kinds speakers and in teaching by means of discussion and the kind in which listeners are engaged in cross-questioning and answering (like that which happens between listeners and an instructive speaker of any kind once the speaking stops and the speaker speaking invites questions from listeners, including sales talks). (50)

Clearly, in both Parts, from the way he explicitly talks throughout this book about what he is doing and why he is doing it, Adler is consciously proceeding as an uncommon commonsense, organizational behavioral psychologist; and he is considering rhetorical persuasion and instructive lecturing as different species of the same real genus.

Why lecturing is more difficult to do well than is writing.

Adler claims that, analogous to the way in which listening is a more difficult activity to do well than is reading, for the same reason, lecturing to a live audience is more difficult to do than is writing an article or a book. Unlike writing and reading, which a writer has time to edit in draft form before providing a final draft for publication for a public readership, "the silent listener must catch on the fly what is being said. That imposes on the audience of a lecture the obligation to be persistently attentive. What is lost by flagging attention, or by turning the speaker off while one's mind turns to other things, is irretrievably lost." (51)

The uninterrupted speaker suffers from an analogous difficulty. With no break, he or she has to keep an audience's constant attention. Such being the case, while Adler does not put his case precisely the way I am doing, the speaker must proceed like an organizational behavioral psychologist (which is precisely what Adler does in his book). "In the limited time allowed for a lecture or a speech, the speaker must so arrange the parts of the speech that listeners are able to follow easily what is being said and preserve it in their minds as they are moved from one point to another by the continuous flow of the speech." (52) This being the case, according to Adler, and commonsense experience, instructive speech involving silently listening on the part of the listeners tends to be most effective when two-way talk follows it in the form of—"conversation or discussion, by questions and answers, by some kind of forum in which speaker and listener can engage in an active interchange." (52)

If, for some reason, a lengthy speech has to be presented to silent listeners without giving them a break and follow-up discussion, Adler recommends a speaker do what any experienced public lecturer with common sense tends to do: before starting the lecture, provide hand-out copies of notes (today, also, use an overhead projector with slides) that contains, in written form with images, the substance of remarks. No need exists to tell silent listeners why this is needed. Anyone who has had to suffer through a boring lecture or sermon, as well as giving one, knows the commonsense answer only too painfully. (53)

Why use of the oratorical principle of *ethos* is also essentially demanded of mathematicians and in the 'exact' sciences.

Turning to lectures that chiefly aim to inculcate knowledge related to mathematics and what Adler calls "exact sciences," he states the aim of the logical reasoning essentially related to the subject necessarily controls the order of presentation. Having said this, he understates the reality of the situation by maintaining that "the only rhetorical skill required to give such lectures effectively is making sure that the problem to be solved is understood before the solution is offered, and then being as clear as possible about the steps to be taken in reaching the solution. Here, too, the steps should be ordered so that one leads to another in a manner most cogent." (54)

Because that claim was not precisely true, Adler immediately had to qualify it by adding:

> Of course, there is more to effective instruction even in the sphere of mathematics and exact sciences. If laboratory demonstrations are involved, a certain amount of showmanship in setting them up and carrying

them off contributes to the effect that is sought. Above all, intellectual excitement on the part of the teacher (even though what is being dealt with is old hat to the teller) serves to produce like excitement on the part of the listener. Without it, the telling, however logical and clear, remains a dull recitation that turns the audience off rather than on. (54–55)

To any psychologically healthy adult, the reason for what Adler has just said is commonsensically clear. In fact, previously in this work, Adler has already told us why. We human beings like to listen to people we like, to someone amiable, friendly. In addition, by nature, pleasure tends to attract, and pain repel, all of us. All healthy, adult human beings, even children, tend not to be interested in listening to what psychologically they consider to be boring—painful to which to listen. As a commonsense, organizational, behavioral psychologist, a good lecturer (especially one like a Professor Borgese!) has to know his or her audience and what tends to interest and not interest them. In addition, he or she has to know how to present this information to them in a way they find attractive, beautiful.

In short, beautification of a subject discussed—an essential quality of the skill of rhetoric—is the first step any good instructor takes in causing *docilitas* within an audience. All teaching worthy of the name essentially contains it. As Adler had painfully started to learn early on at Columbia

University during the 1920s—but which, even as late as 1983 when he copyrighted his *How to Speak. How to Listen* apparently had not fully sunk into his thick skull—logical coherency and cogency of a presentation is never enough for fully effective, attractive, teaching. A good teacher must also be theoretically, practically, and productively prudent!

Hence, he continues to backtrack and qualify his initial claim about what is essentially needed for a good lecture in mathematics or the "exact sciences," saying that, once a lecturer ensures the content of a presentation is good, he or she:

> must have some of the gifts of a good actor. Each time the curtain goes up, no matter how many times it has gone up before for the lecture, it should always seem like a new performance for the audience. The sense of novelty should be heightened by the sense that the speaker is discovering for the first time the truths he is expounding. The skill of lecturers in dramatizing the moments of discovery will draw listeners into the activity of discovering the truths to be learned. Without such activity on their part, there can be a little genuine learning. What results will be a little more than a stuffing into a memory of matters soon to be forgotten. (55)

Adler adds that what he has just said applies to every form of instructive speech, and even more so when an instructor is not "imparting information" related to mathematics and the exact science—when he or she has to speak about issues that essentially involves persuading "the minds of listeners to adopt a certain view that has not been theirs before or to change from a view they have held to a view that is offered to replace it." (55)

Again, Adler's psychological inclination to reduce radical changes of psychological dispositions that involve intellect, will, passions, imagination, and other human faculties psychologically inclines to obfuscate and oversimplify the complexity of the issue about which he is talking. More precisely put, Adler is actually talking about a lecturer changing a person's entire, prior psychological attitude—intellectual, emotional, volitional, and imaginative disposition—*character and characteristic reaction* toward someone or something (like taking the psychological attitude a person has toward Donald Trump and replacing it with the same attitude toward Joe Biden). Hence, he says, "In all such efforts, the speaker must take into account the character of the audience being addressed." (55)

By "character" Adler means the entire, or at least *prevailing*, psychological disposition (*ethos*, *pathos*, and *logos*) of the audience. He is saying that, in approaching any audience as a lecturer, a speaker, any instructor, even any artist, must approach them as a commonsense organizational behavioral psychologist attempting to change their group, or *generic*, character. Hence, he immediately adds, "A

Chapter 5: Understanding Lectures

lecture on a given subject with a given end result in view should not be given to any audience at random. I have often been invited to talk on a particular topic to an audience for whom, in my judgment, it would be inappropriate to speak on the subject chosen. One must have a certain degree of confidence that the subject selected is one that holds some initial interest for the audience to be addressed and that the general background will enable one to enlarge that interest." (55–56)

For the same reason, when lecturing in Staten Island, New York, in ethics courses, through use of a glaring example related to the moral virtue of *prudence*, I would often admonish students, if they were ever invited to an Italian wake and they wanted to be well received, never to sing "Danny Boy" or "When Irish Eyes are Smiling"!

For this reason, too, almost every semester of my college and university academic career, I have had to fight with academic deans—whose chief aim in admitting students into a course tends, somewhat understandably, to be "to put asses into classes"—and essentially, in part, to be organizationally dysfunctional academically: to behave in a way the contrary opposite of what should be the chief aim of education—academic excellence and the best interest of their students.

Chiefly to maximize economic profit, academic deans often admit academically unqualified students into this or that class—even long after start of classes. To make matters worse, they often do this simply because this or that student prefers this or that timeslot for a course, irrespective of the nature of the class and his or her qualifications to take it. In such a situation, a student tends to start a course in which he or she is, by nature, academically unqualified to succeed with an added handicap of having to play *catchup* related to previously assigned, not completed, work!

In the face of such realities, I caution new college and university teachers that their crucial, commonsense first step in starting off a new course is to start like any good sales person—*by beginning to qualify students* to become commonsense members of a commonsense team of teachers, who incline to like and teach one another—and to make sure to tell students they are doing this and precisely why they are doing so. In this process, a classroom teacher has to function much like a commonsense athletic coach, finding out as quickly as possible the qualification of potential team members, and indicating as respectfully and gently as possible to those not qualified that, in their own best interests, they should seriously consider dropping out of this course, going somewhere else, and doing something for which they are actually better qualified from which they can, in some way, at this moment improve themselves. *Needless to say, behaving in this way has not endeared me to many a dean*!

As my brilliant, commonsense colleague Frank Slade, at St. Francis College in Brooklyn—where I had taught part-time for many years—had taught me, most students do not

Chapter 5: Understanding Lectures

learn much, if anything, from classroom instructors in class. They learn chiefly from other students, and in the *rathskeller*, or something like it, outside and after class—and they do so chiefly by talking to each other about something that had gone on in class and had interested them.

Crucial to note is that good teachers, lecturers, actually have to like, befriend, their students or audiences; and the best classes or audiences are ones in which the students like each other like members the same team; and, throughout the course—share a commonsense understanding of precisely what they are doing and why they are doing it.

Only after guaranteeing that he or she has a commonsense understanding of an audience considered as a real genus—organizational whole composed of psychological dispositions ranging from least to most receptive—about which a speaker must make prudent estimation about how personally to approach (sometimes, even on the spot) can any teacher start to think about how to talk to them in a way that will make them docile to listening to what he or she has to say. (56)

Such being the case, Adler *prudently* states:

> To persuade listeners to change their minds by adopting views contrary to ones they have persistently and, perhaps, obstinately held, it is necessary to undermine their prejudices in a manner that is as firm as it is gentle.

> Long-standing prejudices are barriers to persuasion. They must be removed before positive persuasion can begin. Removing them opens the mind that renders it receptive to views of a contrary tenor. (56)

Again, removing such prejudices does more that "open the mind" in such a way that it makes it "receptive to views of a contrary tenor." It changes a person's entire psychological makeup: especially the intellect, will, passions, and imagination—often, a person's entire life, character, and personality. I know this well from over fifty-two years of teaching experience on the college and university level; and in high schools, elementary schools, correctional facilities, and online programs going from elementary grades through university; plus over forty years of lecturing nationally and internationally at some of the West's leading academic and cultural institutions.

Given the magnitude of such influences teachers have on other human beings, every teacher worthy of the name must (as I mentioned previously in this chapter, and Adler now explicitly has to admit) think about himself or herself in relation to the task at hand being or not being "a doable deed" for him or her. Hence, Adler states:

> Thinking about the state of mind of the audience you are going to address and its relation to the subject about what you are going to speak is still not enough. You must

also think about their state of mind in relation to your own person. Your listeners may harbor prejudices or suspicions about you that constitute obstacles to be overcome before positive persuasion can begin. Portraying your *ethos* in a favorable light plays a role in lecturing that is important to a degree only slightly less important than what is required by an effective sales talk.

If you cannot rely upon the fact that some favorable impression of your character and competence has been conveyed to your audience in advance of your speaking to them, you must do whatever is necessary to establish your authority to speak on the subject chosen. (56–57)

Why an effective lecturer must, beyond *ethos*, display *pathos*—and how to do this.

Having established the proper, commonsense *ethos* of a professional teacher (someone who actually knows what he or she is doing and why he or she is doing it), Adler adds that, *like a good salesman*, a good lecturer must *close the sale* on creating listener docility by calling upon "*pathos* in a way that qualitatively intensifies to a maximum his or her persuasive effort." (58)

In a lecture that chiefly aims at practical persuasion, he states a speaker should attempt to effect emotional responses favorable to choosing an action he or she wants them to make. This involves more than arousing this or that emotion. It involves doing that and then steadily moving them passionately more intensely in the direction of the action he or she wants them to execute.

In doing this, Adler notes that a lecturer must keep in mind that controlling passion, *pathos*, works differently in instructive speeches that have as a chief goal simply conveying information or theoretical understanding, not practical outcomes—including productive ones, even though Adler does not explicitly mention this.

In this situation, as Adler does explicitly state, the best lecturers must speak with passion—physically display as deeply as possible personal attachment to the views he or she is advocating. Personal indifference on the part of a speaker in such an instance, he states, "is deadly." Unless the views a speaker advocates and encourages his or her audience passionately to adopt are convincingly presented to his or her audience as ones the speaker possesses with the completeness of his or her being, Adler contends he or she can hardly expect to generate passionate, or even some, interest in them in others. (58)

Even related to teaching, logic, mathematics, and "the exact sciences," Adler maintains that a good lecturer needs to display passion in what he or she has to say and how he or she says it. (58-59) Backtracking on what he had previously and initially said related to teaching these subjects to be effective, he states, more is needed than being cogent, coherent, and clear. The teaching must be persuasive. The

Chapter 5: Understanding Lectures

thinking in which a public lecturer is engaging must always have *personal gravitas—physically display a synthesis of emotional passion and intellectual power*. Hence, Adler adds, "the minds of your audience must be moved as well as instructed. And their emotions, stirred by your own, are needed to do the moving." (59)

But, once again, at this point Adler does not go far enough. The bodies, the whole of their beings, as well as the minds of the audience members must be moved to *jump with joy*! And, from what he immediately adds, this is what he had intended to say:

> The more abstract your argument becomes, the more remote from everyday experience it tends to be, the more it may appear 'academic' to your audience, the more it is necessary for you to overcome the difficulties your audience is likely to have in listening to and following what you have to say. How? Strangely enough, by being more rather than less overtly physical in the manner of your presentation.
>
> By this I mean the amount of physical energy you put into your voice, in the stance of your body and in the gestures that employee motions of your head, your body, and your arms. Somehow the manifest concreteness of your bodily movement in what you have to say in the physical energy expended in saying it compensates for

the abstract us and the remoteness from life of the ideas you are expressing. (59)

Just as, in Ernest Hemingway's masterpiece, *Old Man and the Sea*, when he goes out fishing every day, the passionate fisherman Santiago repeatedly asks, "What would Joe DiMaggio do?," Adler is saying the truly passionate (but, not necessarily totally prudent) orator in the situation he is describing would ask, "What would Professor Borgese do?"—or, better, a Professor Borgese who had not forgotten to take into account the psychological dispositions of his audience. Beyond reference to this glaring, commonsense example, no need exists to present any others to readers, listeners, possessed of any commonsense rhetorical wisdom.

Returning to a crucial point Adler is attempting to convey in this part of his text, he maintains:

> Most human beings, even those who have had sufficient schooling, find it difficult to rise above their imaginations or to think without appealing to vivid images and concrete examples. But abstractions—and often abstractions of a fairly high-level—are indispensable to thinking about any important subject, certainly any subject that involves fundamental ideas.
>
> Thinking about such subjects can seldom be done well entirely in concrete terms; what is worse, such thought is often distorted or confused by appeals to the

imagination or to concrete examples that tend to obscure rather than clarify the ideas involved. It is, therefore, necessary to lift the minds of your listeners to levels of abstraction that exceed the reaches of their imaginations. (60)

While elevating the intellect of your audience, never insult them by talking down to them and never undermine their confidence by talking too high over their heads.

In making the above claim, Adler is evidently following Galileo Galilei's sage observation in his work the *Assayer* that a necessary condition for extending the breadth, width, and depth of the human intellect is first *to stretch the human imagination*. In doing this, Adler gives his own sage advice to his readers based upon his more than fifty years of giving formal lectures in many different venues: "Never talk down to your audience about any subject. If you do so, they will quite rightly turn you off. Why should they make much effort to listen to you if you are telling them things they already know or fully understand? (61)

Instead, he recommends:

Always risk talking over their heads! By the emotional fervor of your speech, by its physical energy and your manifest bodily involvement with materials that are obviously abstract, you should be able to get them to stretch their minds and reach up for insights they did not have before.

It will not hurt if some of the things you say may be beyond the reach. It is much better for them to have the sense that they have succeeded in getting some enlightenment by their effort to reach up (even if they also have the sense that some things to be understood have escaped them) than it is for them to sit there feeling insulted by the patronizing manner in which you have talked down to them. (61)

In giving this advice, Adler is simply analogously extending the same advice he had been giving to decades to readers regarding how to attack understanding the intellectual content of a *great book*, which he often compared to physically exercising with heavy weights.

The truly great books, I have repeatedly said, are the few books that are over everybody's head all of the time. That is why they are endlessly readable as instruments from which you can go on learning more and more on each rereading. What you come to understand each time is a step upward in the development of your mind; so also is your realization of what remains to be understood by further effort on your part.

So far as enlargement of your understanding is concerned, any book that does this for you is, ipso facto, a great book *for you*, though it may not be one for others.

What is true of books to be read is true of lectures to be listened to. The only lectures that are intellectually profitable for anyone to listen to are those that increase one's knowledge and enlarge one's understanding. (61–62)

While making the above recommendations, Adler tempers them with an admonition to lecturers to make sure the talks they give contain enough easily intelligible material for the audience at hand to which to refer to help make intelligible to them the materials that are over their heads. While lecturers pitch what they have to say over the heads of his or her audience, Adler prudently, commonsensically, cautions them accurately to measure the intellectual ability of their audience so that what a lecturer tells his or her audience does not so far exceed their intellectual ability "that there is nothing for them to hold on to in their effort to reach up." (62)

With these admonitions made, Adler adds a final one regarding *logos*. Just as *ethos*, *pathos*, and *logos* are essential principles that comprise the nature of any good sales talk, so, too, are they essential principles in a good instructive lecture—but with one difference: "Whereas the arguments involved in selling, or in any other form of practical persuasion, should always be as abbreviated and as elliptical as possible, often to the point of being barely detectable, the logical content of a good lecture or an instructive speech should consist in arguments of extended length and fully explicit about the steps to be taken. The *logos* should be spelled out in detail." (62)

My opinion about the chief reason Adler gives this recommendation is that he had considered the chief aim of such instructive lectures to be *to convey commonsense understanding* of the nature of a subject that is essentially difficult to comprehend. Given the complicated nature of the subject to be understood, repetition is crucial, so long as it is done in a variety of ways. And, as Adler notes, "If an argument is elaborate and extended, as it often must be, it should be followed by a compact summary—boiled down to a statement of its message in a few brief and striking sentences." For example, "*Here it is in a nutshell.*" (63)

One crucial, final caution implied in what Adler has already said, and that he will subsequently mention, is that, in pitching difficult, and, especially, abstract material over the heads of an audience, a lecturer should always do so by using vocabulary the audience can easily understand; and in a way they can easily understand it. Avoid technical jargon! And, if you have to use it, give an alternative, more simplified, term to refer to it—especially one that is easily imaginable to the audience so that the listeners can refer to

Chapter 5: Understanding Lectures   171

it to make intelligible to themselves the concept that the technical jargon attempts to articulate.

Two final and essential principles that apply to intelligently organizing and giving an instructive lecture.

Taxis and *lexis* are two other classical Greek terms that rhetoricians use to refer to essential principles that apply to a lecture which is both instructive and persuasive. *Taxis* signifies a lecture's essential organization as a composite whole comprised of three parts: 1) introduction (proem), 2) main part of the speech, and 3) conclusion (peroration).

Unlike the organization of most sales talks, in which the order of rhetorical principles is first to establish a speaker's *ethos* (moral character and professional competence), quickly followed by *pathos* in the middle, and *logos* left for the conclusion, Adler correctly notes that organization of an instructive speech is more complicated. Generally, its introductory part should consist of a brief outline, division of the parts of which it consists, and mention of the order they will be presented in relation to the whole. Hence, Adler recommends instructional lecturers start their lectures to their listeners by setting "forth the three or four main sections that constitute the structure of the speech—so that the audience is advised in advance of what they can expect to hear. (63) Giving them such expectations enables them to listen more carefully and to follow closely what they are listening to. (63–64) Their having from the outset a kind of map or chart of the journey to be taken through the speech makes it possible for them to detect, from time to time, what stage has been reached in the forward, ongoing flow of the speech"—*helps them understand precisely what they are doing and precisely why they are doing it!* (64)

Adler maintains, further, that the introduction to an instructive lecture should achieve one main goal: using language and expressing it in a way that guarantees a speaker will capture the listeners' attention. Stumbling over words at the start of an instructive speech is deadly. As Adler says, at the very start of a lecture, "the speaker must not stumble in the least. In those opening moments, what the speaker has to say should be said loud and clear, in simple forceful sentences, and without any hesitation or backtracking. Not only will such speaking get the attention desired, it will also set the tone and pace for the rest of the speech." (64)

Once this has been successfully accomplished, Adler asserts that the lecturer then needs to deliver the main part of the speech in the order in which he or she had initially told the audience he or she would do so. This simply involves maintaining *commonsense ethos* (audience trust) by following the plan the speaker had outlined for the listeners in the introduction and reminding them of precisely where the speaker is at different parts of the talk, as he or she enters and exits from one part to another. Proceeding in this way helps prevent audience members from getting lost about precisely what a speaker is talking, and precisely when he or she is so doing in relation to the other parts of the talk. Execution of the plan in this way enables an audience to follow it in a way similar to that they do when following a play according to *Acts* and *Scenes*.

In addition, Adler adds the helpful comment that, if the main body of the speech consists of several main parts, a good idea is to: 1) "conclude each part with a summary of what has been said," and 2) "include a transition to what is coming next. Repetition may be necessary to help the listeners discern where they have been, where are they now are, and what they are about to move on to." (64)

While, in writing, repetition is sometimes avoided because in some articles and books readers can easily return to an earlier page to refresh their memories about what an author has said, in an instructional lecture, this is not the case. Prudently executed, commonsensically timely and well-placed repetitions is crucial "precisely because the listener cannot turn back to something said earlier and hear it all over again. The speech is continually moving forward, and the speaker must repeat something said earlier if the listener needs to have it in mind in order to understand the point being made later." (64)

Regarding a lecture's conclusion, Adler rightly recommends it be brief in length, much like the culmination of an orchestral performance:

It should manage to provide a summation of the whole in the shortest possible scope and with maximum clarity. The closing sentences, like the opening ones, should be carefully constructed and eloquently delivered. They should be spoken slowly and in a tone of voice that conveys to the listeners the assurance that what has been said fulfills the promise made at the beginning concerning what was to be said. It should also carry some emotional manifestation of the speaker's sense of the importance to the listeners of what they have heard. (65)

—CHAPTER SIX—

Lesson 6—Commonsense Rules for Composing and Delivering a Speech

Achieving the 'Churchill effect' when delivering an impromptu speech.

Mortimer Adler begins his Chapter 6 (entitled "Preparing and Delivering a Speech") by making the following hyperbolic claim: "The only speech for which no preparation is possible is the one you may be unexpectedly called upon to deliver by the toastmaster at a dinner party."(68) Anyone who has ever been called upon unexpectedly to give a talk is well aware that what Adler has just said is false.

Just why Adler would make such an exaggerated assertion, I do not know. Especially odd about it is that he could have made the simple, commonsense point he sought to achieve by saying, "The only speech for which no preparation is possible is the one you may be unexpectedly called upon to deliver." The truth of even this case is questionable, since other situations exist in which a person knows he or she is expected to deliver a talk, but is still unable to make adequate preparation. For example, a person has agreed to give a lecture at a specific time, date, and location and then get seriously ill or involved in some sort of accident that he or she did not expect to happen.

Whatever the case, Adler's point is simple enough. Sometimes we are unexpectedly invited to give a lecture that has to appear to be extemporaneous, or off the cuff, to this or that group; and knowing how to do this is a worthwhile skill. He gives examples of different people who had this talent, including Winston Churchill, who, according to Adler, was so skilled that he could write out a speech beforehand and cunningly deliver it in such a way that it appeared as if it were totally impromptu.

Developing precisely this ability is the chief goal of the recommendations Adler reports he is going to make in his Chapter 6. While he states the suggestions, he is going to present will not "turn anyone who follows them into a Churchill," he thinks they will "enable anyone to achieve a modicum of Churchill effect in delivering a speech." (69)

According to Adler, a crucial difference a lecturer must always keep in mind is that when a writer composes a speech chiefly for a listening audience he or she can and should write it so as to be able to anticipate before giving the talk the way it is non-verbally delivered will accomplish their desired effect. As he has often repeated up to this point in his text, a great deal of difference exists in writing work for a face-to-face oral presentation in front of a specific group, in a specific place and time, and one simply to be read by an invisible audience.

Preparing a talk for face-to-face listening is radically different in many respects from doing so for an audience that, in a sense, is *invisible*. One is that the nature of time causes the oral presentation continuously to move forward without interruption in a way not required of a written presentation.

The listener to a face-to-face presentation cannot rewind the speaker like he or she can turn back a page in a book. Even though the interest of a face-to-face audience and one invisible to a writer might be identical, strictly speaking, the audience for an oral speech and a speech written only to be read can never be exactly the same. And to be maximally effective, a writer must take this reality into consideration. As Adler says, "the written word to be read is unaccompanied by bodily gestures, facial expressions, modulation to voice, differential pauses, and all the other subtle paraphernalia of eloquent oral delivery." (70)

An author composing only for readers has to achieve whatever effects he or she seeks to realize solely by word choice, and shaping, placing, and positioning (organizing) words within a printed page. The orator, in contrast, in advance, and sometimes on the spot, must physically express (organize) words that will be spoken so that they will realize their maximum qualitative effect through the speaker's nonverbal delivery.

According to Adler, and in reality, the ability to do this with maximum effectiveness is a rare skill possessed by a handful of geniuses. For the rest of us, the benefits of organizing notes in advance appears to be a matter of common sense. (70)

And in doing this, a speaker needs to take into consideration commonsense time constraints that a writer of a book or journal article does not have. While both tend to be constrained relative to the length of what they will be presenting (sometimes, for example, by a book publisher or journal editor in the case of these forms of writing), a speaker is generally given time limits for an oral presentation before this or that group. And knowing the word count for such a talk in advance is a skill all of its own, which essentially involves knowing the audience before whom a person will be speaking.

Never presume you can ignore time limitations for an invited presentation.

To fit all the parts of into speech together in proper proportion to each other within the given time, crucial for a lecturer is carefully to organize a talk by having its plan of presentation well typed out and easily visible at a podium or table. (72–73) If a speaker decides to use notes to help give a presentation, Adler recommends a choice between two possible forms to employ: 1) a skeletal outline of topical

Chapter 6: Commonsense Rules

phrases, not full sentences or paragraphs; or 2) the talk composed as if it were a final draft ready for publication. (73)

He rightly observes that a speech delivered by scholars at annual conferences generally takes the form of a completely composed speech to which most listeners do not tend to pay attention because "it is almost impossible to listen to and seldom, if ever, it deserves the monumental effort required to do so with sustained attention." (73)

At the opposite extreme, Adler says, is the second form of written preparation—a brief skeletal outline in the form of topical phrasing. About this, he comments that, in general, the briefer, more skeletal and topical it is, the better. (74)

Nevertheless, he does not always recommend using it because he has found it only works well for subjects in which the speaker is so fully in command of the matter to such an extent that he or she can easily present it in an orderly way. To work well, the speaker has to know the subject inside out—so well that his or her mind "is saturated with all the words, phrases, and sentences needed for a clear, orderly, and cogent utterance of his or her thought about it." If such is not the case, he states, "then he or she had better have something more on the lectern than a brief topical outline in skeletal form." (74)

This does not mean, however, that the speaker must use the deadly-dull, scholarly lecture presentation, which Adler encourages us to avoid. Instead, he recommends the one

Winston Churchill had used during World War II, which appeared to be entirely impromptu, but, in actuality, was partly impromptu and partly written. (74–75)

This middle ground approach—which, *from practical experience teaching speed-reading courses*, I had decided to use prior to reading Adler's recommendation that speakers employ it—involves writing out single or multiple, short sentences in outline/resume form using wide margins, together with resume-style tab-spacing, divisions, and subdivisions. Doing this enables a speaker quickly to see and comprehend in an instant multiple sentences and raise his or head as if not reading from a paper or notes at all. (75) As Adler rightly observes about this method, using it enables a speaker to have "complete control" over what he or she is saying; and it tends to guarantee that he or she will say it, without rushing, within precisely the right time allowed for the talk. (75–76)

Since Adler's description of this method did not suffice to make it intelligible to a reader, I substituted my own way of describing it for his. However, he prudently presented an example of it as "Appendix 1," calling it his "middle ground between the brief topical outline and skeletal form in the fully written essay." (76 and 201–203) Readers of this present chapter of mine would do well to take a look at Adler's text and imitate it in their own presentations.

Adler's early stages of preparation to write a speech in middle-ground form.

Having described and given an example of his method of composing a speech that is a combination of brief topical outline in skeletal form of fully written essay, next Adler specifies four steps he follows to prepare his lecture:

1) He refreshes his memory of his earlier thinking about a subject that he finds in essays he has already written and published. (77)

I do the same thing, except that I cut and paste entire articles and chapter presentations I have previously written into the work I am presently composing. As I work, I will also do the same thing with works in the public domain from classical authors like Plato, Aristotle, and Saint Thomas Aquinas that I download to my computer. As I do this, I will make notes to myself of citation information for later footnote and bibliographical use. In this way, I will have all this information readily at hand later on and will not have to waste time trying to find precisely what I need precisely when I need it. This enables me to compose enormous amounts of exceptionally difficult material in much shorter periods of time—for example, a 200- to 300-page book within a few months, as I have done with this monograph. This is a feat I could never accomplish if I were not employing this method.

If I am not able to download an internet copy of a work in the public domain that I need, I will find a paper copy. Then I will dictate the passage or passages I want directly to quote or paraphrase into the body of an email message to my iPhone. From my iPhone I will forward the message to my computer email account. After doing this, I will cut and paste that material into the article or chapter I am writing into a computer file from which I will produce final copy.

I will also do this with original narratives that, for one reason or another, I have decided to compose. For simple health benefits, instead of sitting at a desk typing for hours, I will lie down, or sit in a reclining chair, and dictate material to myself for later cutting and posting. Frequently, I will do this at night, if I am awakened in the middle of sleep by some thought I do not want to forget. Instead of jotting it down on a piece of paper, I will simply use the dictation feature in my iPhone to capture the idea, sometimes while continuing to lie down. I will also do this in many other venues—when sitting in an automobile as a passenger waiting in a parking lot for someone to return from shopping, or even while another person is driving, if he or she does not care; even resting in an airport waiting for a flight, and so on.

2) Next, Adler says he takes a large yellow pad and starts to put down some random notes related to whatever comes into his mind, in whatever sequence, almost like that a free association. (77)

I do something radically different. I always start with a generic definition of my subject matter. Since I always consider my subject matter to be an organizational whole that proximately causes action, I always think about: 1) what is the organizational whole about which I am thinking (of creating or dismantling an organizational whole); and 2) what essential parts need to exist and harmonize together to cause such an organizational whole to come into being and cause the kind of actions it does in the way it does.

This gives me the genus and species of a real organization. Since, as Aristotle and Aquinas maintain, the whole of a science is contained in its first principles which are contained in its real definition, *I start to write by thinking about the implications contained in the definition I have just given. In this way, an outline of the whole of any work I am composing naturally flows out of the implications of the definitions I have first induced.*

I never write an article or a book from an outline I have arbitrarily composed. *I write an outline from a definition I have induced.* I allow the article or book naturally to flow out of the implications I see/induce starting to grow out of the definition into an outline. The definition of the subject matter is the proximate cause of the outline, and the outline is the proximate cause of the article or the book. Again, working in this way, saves me enormous time trying to guess how to start writing something for publication or lecture.

3) After Adler finishes his step two, he says he examines his notes and decides which "points are related to each other and how they form a major unit of the speech." (77–78) What he is describing is almost exactly the same process I have described immediately above to be the one I use. By "points" Adler means "principles," parts of a real definition of a subject. First, using free-flow association to induce what is able to fit together, actually be harmoniously related, he identifies his *generic* defining principles. Then, like the organizational psychologist he always tries to be, he tests what he can harmoniously and *specifically* relate into a composite whole so as to define precisely what he considers himself to be doing and precisely how he considers himself to be doing it.

My extensive reading of Adler, together with that of thinkers classical thinkers like Plato, Aristotle, Aquinas, and their commentators—all of whom proceeded to analyze their subject matter as organizational psychologists—is precisely what, after decades of personally behaving in this way—caused me to realize I was, and am, chiefly an organizational behavioral psychologist, not a systematic logician.

4) After going through this procedure, Adler remarks that he writes out his speech in full in the outline form he has described. Then, he revises it once or twice before delivering it. After delivering it, he often revises it again before doing

Chapter 6: Commonsense Rules

something else with it—perhaps giving it as a talk somewhere else, or publishing it as a journal article or growing it into a book.

Regarding this last step, he remarks that he is always amazed about what he is able to learn from giving a speech that he is unable to discover prior to this experience. The same thing happens to me. I often recognize some point I had made that I had not fully understood before presenting it to an audience and getting the reaction of listeners.

As Adler notes:

> The reaction you get from your audience tells you something about how to improve your speech. Certain discomfort you experience in the actual delivery of the speech calls your attention to things you must change in order to make the speech more comfortable to deliver.
>
> Audience reaction is an essential ingredient in this whole business of speaking. What do you see on the faces or in the eyes of your listeners tells you almost instantaneously whether you were getting across, and what other effects are occurring. Such feedback is indispensable to effective speaking. (78)

Again, Adler is spot on related to the observations he makes immediately above. The audience serves as an analogous kind of *generic*, publishing, copy editor and movie critic from whom a speaker derives crucial information about the *specific* strength and weaknesses of a performance. For this reason, Adler's says, "it is always wise to insist upon the kind of lighting that enables you to see your listeners clearly." (78) The audience helps a speaker specifically and individually define himself or herself as effective or not effective, good or bad, and so on at this moment and location. In so doing, the listeners to a speech are as crucial a means every lecturer needs for precise self-understanding as qualitative principles measuring his or her professional, performance excellence as are a theatrical audience for actors, actresses, dancers, musicians; or sports fans are for professional athletes. In effect, audience reaction is a chief qualitative measuring principle of professional excellence that any and every speaker has!

Moving on to other crucial observations and recommendations Adler makes regarding public lectures is that a speaker go beforehand to the site where his or her lecture will be given and check it out—much like any good golfer will check out the golfing range before playing on it. Quite often a podium is not in the right place or totally nonexistent; a microphone is not working, or not there; an overhead projector that a speaker has expected to be in place is missing. As Aristotle admonishes, small mistakes in the beginning of an investigation tend to grow in multitude and magnitude as an activity proceeds. The same is true regarding a lecture. (78–79)

Two other steps that I use when composing a speech or writing an article or book chapter, which Adler does not mention, are stylistic habits I have adopted from observing Aquinas's Aristotelian commentaries and extensive work I have had as a newspaper editor, speed-reading teacher, a book copyeditor, and book-series executive editor from which, I synthesized my method of outlining lectures: 1) In growing my outline, following Aquinas, I do so in a numbered, syllogistic form—especially when referring to material from another author in a paraphrased way. 2) In doing this—adopting a method I learned from my colleague and friend Richard Hull—I always get rid of every form of passive voice, change this to active voice. In addition, I get rid of every unnecessary word and phrase—always, as much as possible, expressing what someone else has said in a more economical fashion. And, beyond this, I avoid every species of ambiguity. I avoid use of indefinite reference (such as: he/she/it is/was/had been/will be; and they are/were/had been/will be) and use of pronouns. Instead, whenever possible I use proper names. And I encourage all my students to do the same when they write or speak.

One of the most brilliant people I ever met, Herbert I. London (R.I.P.—for many years a close personal friend and colleague and former Dean of the Gallatin Division at NYU, President of the Hudson Institute, and Founder and President of the London Center for Policy Research) used to write and speak this way. Regarding his way of talking, I often say about him: "Herb always talked in final draft." And, having an incredible memory, he always used to do so with no notes!

Like Adler learned from his procedure presenting talks to audiences, I am amazed what I learn by writing in the way I do. As I go through it as a mechanical procedure, most of the time I do not understand much, if anything, about what an author is saying. *Some readers of my works might say I never get beyond this stage!* Whatever the case, at this point, I am just cutting and re-ordering material. At this moment, I do not try to read my final product for understanding anything at all. After I finish this gutting process, I start to read for understanding. Only after I *gut* what someone has written—like a general contractor demolishing an old house to get down to its frame—do I think about adding essential elements and doing the final trim, beautifying a work with rhetorical flair. When, later, I do this, I am often absolutely amazed what an author is actually saying in contrast to the way I find that he or she has often been misinterpreted, including by me!

Some final admonitions about public speaking that Adler gives.

Adler concludes his Chapter Six with several final cautions. The first is absolutely to refuse to talk about the subject selected for a special occasion before the talk is to be given. Doing so tends to spoil the rhetorical value of a presentation.

The second is that what he has said about speaking face to face equally applies to television presentations. Today, they would, also, apply to internet lectures. On television, a teleprompter can replace notes and outlines. Notes and outlines can be strategically placed next to a computer for internet video or audio presentations.

In both cases, as Adler correctly states, a lecturer has the advantage of looking directly into a camera. "By looking directly into the camera," Adler says, "he or she will be looking directly into the eyes of each person watching the television screen. When someone looks you directly in the eye, that tends to hold your attention. It is impolite to turn your eyes away." This is not possible in other venues, like an auditorium or a lecture hall, no matter how well-lit they might be. (80)

As Adler notes, however, a great disadvantage of delivering lectures via the internet or television is that you cannot see your audience and get immediate feedback from them. In this sense, this form of one-way presentation becomes less intellectually rewarding and more dangerous—especially because how well or badly the talk was received cannot be well determined until after exiting a television site or computer room and receiving later reports from critics. (80–81)

—CHAPTER SEVEN—

Lesson 7—Silent Listening as a Commonsense Liberal Art Activity

Mortimer Adler begins Part 3 of his text, dealing with "Silent Listening" with his Chapter 7 entitled, "With the Mind's Ear." (85) Again, I think the title of this Chapter represents an oversimplification of a much more complicated activity. Better would have been for Adler to have called it, "With Human Ears," or, "With Ears of a Whole Person."

I say this because when human beings listen actively, attentively, to something, we do this with our entire person: intellect, will, memory, imagination, emotions, and external sense faculties, and so on—not just with these and one or two ears; or one or both together with an individual mind. For example, when we listen attentively for the sound of an enemy, and hear something that resembles it, this can simultaneously cause hair to rise on a person's arms, his or her breathing dramatically to change, and his or her legs to freeze up or get set to run. And when we listen to enjoyable music, we experience the listening in and with our legs, even in our entire body, as well as in our ears and mind. To make an analogy, as the great Thomistic scholar Anton C. Pegis used to say, "the knowledge of a pianist is in his or her fingers."

Hence, I disagree with Adler when he states, "Listening, like reading, is primarily an activity of the mind, not of the ear or the eye." (85) It is mainly an activity of the whole person, hylomorphic unit.

I can attest to this fact from decades of on-campus, college and university teaching during which *I observed many students pained by the sound of words being read from a book, and even by the sight of a book*! The entire body of a student would become contorted, and he or she could not sit still for any extended period of time following a passage being read from a book in class.

Nevertheless, when this holistic act is not involved in reading, I agree with Adler that this whole activity "should be called hearing, not listening; seeing, not reading." In addition, I would say any noise coming out of the mouth of a person should be called *sounding out*, not *reading*.

And I agree with him when he says, "the most prevalent mistake that people make about both listening and reading is to regard them as passively receiving rather than as actively participating." (86)

As he correctly notes, reading and listening as forms of human communication through use of words are comparable to the skills of actively and athletically catching something pitched. If we do not use all our psychological and physical faculties—not just individual eyes, ears, and minds—as cooperative partners in a single act of commonsense understanding, we do not comprehend or engage in the activity essential to reading and listening as forms of human communication. "The result is," as Adler states, "failure of communication, a total loss, a waste of time." (87)

Adler's exposition of the rules students need habitually to apply to develop the liberal arts virtue of commonsense listening, and why these rules are inadequate and misleading.

Within this chapter, Adler tells his readers he is going to consider "the effort and skill required for active and effective listening." (87) By this he means he will reflect upon the extent of effort and skill an active reader needs to exert to follow what someone is saying "so as to understand it to a degree that approximates the understanding a speaker seeks to achieve"—which is what Adler has previously called in his monograph "a meeting of minds," and I would call a *mutual commonsense understanding*. (87) And the means he will to use to do this is to provide positive rules that listeners can follow which, through habitual application, will enable them to develop effective listening skills, or what we might more precisely call the *liberal arts virtue of commonsense listening*.

Adler answers the question, "What are these rules?" by asserting they "are essentially the same as the rules for effective reading." (91) I agree with Adler that the reason this is so should surprise no one; but I do so for a slightly different reason than he gives (which he states is because both "require the mind to do"). The chief reason the two processes are alike is that they require a person to develop the liberal arts virtue of commonsense listening—not simply use, or skillful use, of the mind in cooperation with eyes and ears. (91)

In the skills of both effective reading and effective listening, Adler maintains:

> The mind of the receiver—the reader or listener—must somehow penetrate through the words used to the thought that lies behind them. The impediments that language places in the way of understanding must be overcome. The vocabulary of the speaker or writer is seldom if ever identical with the vocabulary of the listener or reader. The latter must always make the effort to get at the meaning that can be expressed in different sets of words. The listener must come to terms with the speaker, just as the reader must come to terms with the writer. This, in effect, means discovering what the idea is regardless of how it is expressed in words. (91)

Until it arrives at the last sentence—which is inadequate and misleading—I entirely agree with the claims made in the above paragraph. Listeners and readers must come to terms—with speakers and writers by doing more than discovering what is the idea both express; and they cannot disregard how the idea is expressed because how an idea is expressed involves more than different vocabulary: how the vocabulary is judgmentally being used to express the idea. For example, is the idea being expressed theoretically, practically, or productively? Rhetorically? Ideologically? For the chief aim of conveying understanding—or in some other way?

Active readers must chiefly discover: 1) what the ideas themselves chiefly express/signify—*real definitions*; 2) what the real definitions mainly express/signify—real organizational wholes and organizational actions they naturally incline to generate; 3) and the way these ideas are chiefly being expressed—mainly how and for what chief goal.

The first experience we human beings have of ideas as children and throughout human life—especially as great ideas—is not as abstract essences in an abstract mind. It is as concrete principles that cause existence, unity, and action in some really existing, organizational whole! And, in relationship to art, philosophy/science, we always experience these in relationship to individual and personal commonsense, psychological wonder about how this or that organizational whole is internally united, organized, with these or those parts—how these or those parts are essentially related/harmonized to cause some organizational whole to behave the way it is doing in this or that situation.

Not surprisingly, the method Adler advocates to use in active listening is analogous to the one that, for decades, he had encouraged readers to use when reading a great book. "In most discourses," he rightly notes that, "whether spoken or written, the number of truly important propositions being advanced is relatively small. The listener, like the reader, must detect these and highlight them in his mind, separating them from all the contextual remarks that are interstitial, or merely elaborative and amplifying." (92)

Explicitly knowing this or not, Adler tells his readers, in order to engage in active listening, any and every reader must analyze the subject matter to which they are listening like commonsense, organizational behavioral psychologists would do. Hence, he explicated his first rule for active listening as follows: "Like a written document, however long or short, the speech being listened to is a whole that has parts. If it is worth listening to, its structure (the way the parts are organized to form the whole) and its sequence (the way one part leads to, or connects with, essentially relates to, another) will be perspicuous and coherent. Therefore, the listener, like the reader, must make the effort to observe the relation and sequence (that is, the order) of the parts as constituting the whole." (92/my parenthetical additions immediately above)

That is, he or she must apprehend the order of the parts in their essential relationship to the whole. To do this, however, he or she must *understand* the chief aim that exists within the organization of a speech. Consequently, Adler states, "Like the writer, the speaker proceeds with some overarching and regulative purpose or intention (chief aim) that controls the substance and style (organization) of what is being presented. The sooner the listener, like the reader, perceives the focus of this controlling purpose or intention, the better he or she is able to discriminate between what is a major and what is a minor significance in a discourse that is to be understood." (92/my parenthetical additions immediately above)

Adler continues that, involved in intellectually grasping a speech's identity as an organizational whole essentially involves exercising three essential operations as an active and effective listener employed by an active and effective reader: 1) "understanding what the speaker is trying to say"; 2) "perceiving how he or she is managing to say it"; and 3) "noting the reasons given or the arguments advanced for the conclusions that the speaker seeks to have adopted." (92)

While these aforementioned activities are necessary conditions for active and effective listening and reading, Adler rightly states "they are never enough." (92) At the same time, what he says about why they are not enough, is not enough—is as inadequate as it was when he first mentioned it decades before in his bestselling *How to Read a*

Book: "With regard to anything that one understands, either by reading or listening, it is always necessary to make up one's mind about where one stands—either agreeing or disagreeing." (93)

Adler's 3 rules for adequately reading a book (especially a great one) or listening to a speech (especially a great one) and precisely why they are essentially inadequate.

Before going into detail about precisely what causes Adler's three rules adequately for reading a book or listening to a speech to be essentially incomplete, inadequate, some need exists for me to cite exactly what Adler says are these rules and precisely why he proposed them in *How to Read a Book*:

> First, there were rules for analyzing the book's structure as a whole and the orderly arrangement of its parts. One should be able to say what the whole book is about and how each of its parts successively contributed to the significance of the whole.
> Second, there were rules for interpreting the contents of the book: by discussing the principal terms of the authors conceptual vocabulary, by identifying the authors main propositions and contentions, by recognizing the arguments the author employed in supporting or defending these propositions, and by noting the

problems the author through the book solved, as well as the problems the book left unsolved, whether the author knows it or not.

Third, there were rules for criticizing the book by indicating matters about which the author appeared to be uninformed or misinformed, by noting what appeared to be the author's errors in reasoning from the promises or assumptions that seem valid, and by observing the respects in which the author's analysis or argument appeared to be incomplete. (93–94)

While the rules Adler states above are incredibly thorough, and he should be rightly praised for having identified them—especially in relationship to reading and making somewhat intelligible to a listener or reader a great book or speech—because they omit the three following most-crucial elements all authors and lecturers use as chief means for skillfully organizing books and speeches (especially great and beautiful ones), Adler's rules are glaringly inadequate:

1) The definitions that the ideas authors and lecturers use chiefly express.

2) The way authors and lecturers essentially relate these definitions to each other—usually in the form of necessarily connected arguments—throughout a book or speech as

essential parts out of which proximately to grow the book or speech into a perfect and beautiful organizational whole.

And 3), precisely whether and why—given an author's or lecturer's chief aim, goal, or purpose—he or she behaved in a professionally reasonable or unreasonable way skillfully to execute his or her final product.

Omitting explanation of essential definitions and arguments an author or lecturer uses to compose a book or speech and the way he or she positions and places these throughout his or her work is like: 1) a drama critic omitting from an evaluation of a play position and placement of actors and their actions in relation to the organization of the play as a whole; 2) a fine arts critic omitting from evaluating the worth of a great painting the skillful organization of different parts of paint and figure, intensity of color and light, in it in relationship to each other; or 3) a sports broadcaster trying to explain why this or that game was or was not excellent by omitting to identify plays made in different parts of the game at different times utilizing this or that athletic equipment. Such omissions would be glaring, would make no common sense.

For analogous reasons, Adler's omission in his following 4 questions of the crucial import of definitions and the way the authors and speakers organize them to compose books and speeches, especially great ones, is glaring. It makes no common sense—especially in light of Adler's sage observation that the essence of being a good reader or listener is to be a demanding reader or listener and the questions he maintains a demanding reader or listener to a speech should ask as he or she is reading or listening (95–96):

1) "*What is the whole speech about*? What, in essence, is the speaker trying to say and how does he go about seeing it?"

2) "*What are the main or pivotal ideas, conclusions, and arguments*? What are the special terms used to express these ideas I had to state the speaker's conclusions and arguments."

3) "*Are the speaker's conclusions sound or mistaken*? Are they well-supported by his arguments, or is that support inadequate in some respect? Was the speakers thinking carried far enough or were matters that were relevant to his controlling purpose not touched on?"

4) "*What of it*? What consequences follow from the conclusions to speak of wishes to have adopted? What are their importance or significance for me?"

If we consider the glaring omission Adler has made related to: 1) identifying the crucial importance that understanding the nature of definitions authors and speakers use to compose their books and speeches and 2) how they utilize, order, these definitions throughout a book or speech to make it an intelligible whole to an audience, evident is that Adler has woefully failed to include in his rules an essential element needed for any and every demanding reader completely to fulfill his or her nature considered as such.

Nevertheless, toward the end of his Chapter 7, added to the much other sound points Adler makes therein, he adds one more that a demanding listener should take to heart and practice as part of his or her arsenal to become as effective as possible in his or her nature. Because the nature of active and effective listening cannot be done in exactly the same way as active and effective reading is done (for example, an active listener cannot generally write questions in a book or article as a speaker is speaking–unless a lecturer has handed out a copy of the speech or parts of a book beforehand), "both while the speech is going on and after it is over, when one reviews ones notes and reflects on them," skillful note-taking becomes crucial for developing and maintaining the habit of skillful listening. (96–97)

—CHAPTER EIGHT—

Lesson 8—How to Apply the Commonsense Liberal Art of Listening to Taking Lecture Notes

A brief, but necessary, clarification.

Mortimer J. Adler spent the major part of his life writing books and lecturing with the chief aim of making reading and listening more pleasurable and profitable for other people. At the start of Chapter 8 from his monograph *How to Speak. How to Listen*, he mentions his 1940 best seller, *How to Read a Book*, and his 1941 article, "How to Mark a Book," as his two most successful attempts, among volumes of others, to achieve this end. I call attention to this fact at the start of this lesson because, despite the fact that, in my last Lesson, I was critical of some of Adler's teachings, that criticism was aimed solely at omissions Adler had made in his text, which I thought commonsense dictated he should have included at this or that precise point.

Were Adler with us today, I am convinced he would agree with me about my critique. In no way was I maintaining Adler was not aware of the truth of what I was saying. I was doing the contrary opposite. Precisely because I had recognized that the principles I was articulating are implicitly contained within his own teachings, I know—at least implicitly—he had to be aware of these commonsense truths I wanted to emphasize to my readers. As someone who considers himself to be a student of Adler, I have no doubt he would have wanted me to do this, just as, related to my work, I would want my students to do in the future.

I have no doubt that, were a person to research Adler's voluminous works, he or she would find him, at some time in his life, in other contexts, making precisely the same points I made in Lesson 7 of this book. The only reason I have been able to call attention to these points is precisely because of the great fortune I have had to be able to take pleasure in and profit from reading many of Adler's great works, as well as that of several other students of Plato, Aristotle, and Saint Thomas Aquinas.

Commonsense liberal-arts virtue of note taking during a lecture.

That clarification having been made, I now turn my attention to some statements Adler makes in Chapter 8 of *How to Speak. How to Listen* about what I *call the commonsense liberal-arts virtue of note taking*. Just like the other commonsense liberal arts of communication—such as reading well and speaking well chiefly for the aim of

Chapter 8: How to Apply the Commonsense Liberal Art 205

understanding how to do these—a commonsense, liberal arts, virtue-tradition of note taking exists with Western culture. It came into existence over the centuries as a result of the hard work and extensive reading and listening experience of different scholars. Having immersed himself in this tradition, at the start of Chapter 8, Adler's lengthy experience with it enabled him easily to explain the necessity for anyone who seriously wants to read or listen "with a questioning mind" to know how artistically to take notes. (99)

Beginning with note taking essentially related to actively and effectively reading a great book, Adler authoritatively states: "*How to Read a Book* has insisted upon the necessity of actively using one's mind while reading, always by reading with a questioning mind. That can be done without pen, pencil, or pad. But the best way to make sure that you are incessantly active while reading is by making notes, page by page, as you read—not in bed or in an arm chair, but at a table or desk." (99)

While I agree with Adler that reading with a questioning mind is an excellent way to engage in and maintain incessantly active reading, as Adler well understood, doing so is best when this questioning mind is also a *wondering mind* actively conversing with an author. Adler's focus of attention on the rules involved in proper note taking, however, caused him to omit at this point in his text giving an explanation of precisely what he meant by "reading with a questioning mind." For all a reader might know, Adler could mean reading with a skeptical, or doubting, mind.

While that might likely have been the attitude Adler would have recommended as an annoying undergraduate at Columbia College or graduate student at Columbia University, in contrast, as an experienced, adult educator, Adler actually meant *reading with an enquiring mind*—looking at active reading as engaging in pleasant conversation with a friend; and wondering why this friend would be making this or that point at this or that time within a conversation. To talk *with* the author of a text, the best way to do so is to write in the text at the precise point where a reader has a question to ask or a comment to make. *For an experienced reader, who is reading chiefly for understanding, doing this just makes common sense.*

According to Adler, doing so while listening to an instructive lecture is also desirable and productive. He considers taking notes while listening so as intellectually to record what a speaker is saying to be the first step in what I have called *the commonsense liberal-arts virtue of listening*, regarding which he adds:

> That record enables you to go onto the second step, which I regard as equally important to the activity of listening. What you have noted during the course of listening, together with what your memory retains of what was said, provides you with food for thought.

The thinking you then do should lead you to make a second set of notes, much more orderly, much more comprehensive, and much more critical. These concluding notes constitute the completion of the task of active listening. You have used your mind as well as possible in response to what, in the speech you heard, you thought it was worthy of attention and comment. (100)

As someone does this, Adler cautions against talking to oneself, in the sense of thinking about arguing with a speaker, instead of actively listening to what he or she is saying. Doing so, he states, "is counterproductive." (100) He especially cautions listeners *not to* "make the mistake of trying to combine your record of what you are hearing with your own reactions to it. Listeners who are more concerned to express themselves than to pay close attention to what someone else is trying to express (which is precisely the mistake Adler repeatedly made decades before as a student at Columbia University!/my addition)—are very poor listeners—they really wish they were making the speech rather than listening to it." (101)

Adler's four rules for making running notes while listening to an instructive speech.

In providing his four rules for note taking related to an instructive speech, Adler cautions his readers that such speeches differ in quality from those that are exceptionally well ordered and organized to those that are exceptionally badly ordered and poorly organized. (102–103)

Rule 1:

At the start of what purports to be an instructional speech, a well-ordered—and I would say *commonsense—*speaker will summarize for an audience precisely what he or she is going to do and precisely how he or she is going to do it—from introduction, through the middle, to the conclusion. Such being the case, Adler remarks that a seasoned—and I would say *commonsense—*note taker will start making notes from the beginning of the talk.

In the case of a disorderly, rambling, speaker, one with no commonsense speaking ability, a note taker is more or less on his or her own as to being able precisely to know what to record and not record. This being the case, given our contemporary situation, I recommend that, in addition physically to taking notes, audience members use their cell phone option to record a talk. Doing so enables members of an audience more easily to take subsequent notes related both to well, and badly, ordered and organized lectures. Listeners who fail to do this will have to pay special attention, as Adler's cautions, not to allow the wandering musings of a poorly organized speaker to cause a listener to become lazy and inactive, bored and nodding off. In such a situation, prudence/common sense dictates listeners do the contrary opposite—listen with even greater intensity.

Rule 2:

Regarding both types of lectures (commonsensical or non-commonsensical), and whichever way notes are recorded, Adler rightly advises listeners to pay special attention to conceptual vocabulary, the main ideas about which a speaker says he or she will be talking, and the way he or she will be talking about them. Beyond this, while Adler makes no mention of it, to make as intelligible as possible to a listener precisely what a speaker is saying and precisely why he or she is saying it, crucial is for listeners to pay special attention to the definitions a speaker gives about the main ideas and technical jargon he or she is using to express them.

As I have previously mentioned and emphasized, every instructive lecture consists in logically (or illogically) ordering definitions in relationship to a chief organizational aim, end, goal, or purpose. In listening to both well, and badly, ordered and organized lectures, audience members must actively focus attention precisely on understanding (hearing) what is the chief end, aim, goal, or purpose a speaker gives for a specific presentation, the chief means he or she states will be used to achieve it, and how these will be so used. Failure actively to do these things will cause a listener to become intellectually lost related to the nature of the entire lecture or to this or that part of it.

Rule 3:

In well or badly arguing for or against some claim he or she is making, a speaker will, or will not, make evident to listeners some assumptions (commonsense principles), he or she is taking for granted to be true, and the way in which the ideas he or she is using need to be defined. In his third rule, Adler cautions readers to be especially attentive to such assumptions, but he fails to tell us to be equally careful about precisely understanding the way speakers *are defining* the chief terms they are using. Generally, these are precisely the most crucial assumptions listeners intellectually have to grasp in an instructive, and especially a rhetorical, speech—as should be evident to any reader who recalls the speeches given by Brutus and Marc Antony after the death of Julius Caesar. For this precise reason, *commonsense listeners must pay special attention to hearing and understanding these definitions when a speaker mentions them.*

Rule 4:

Beyond paying special attention to claims a speaker makes and the assumptions he or she is making throughout a speech, and especially at the beginning of it, Adler states that every instructional lecture will contain reasons in the form of arguments intellectually to justify the claims he or she is making. No matter how easy or difficult is apprehending and following these arguments, Adler rightly maintains that a listener "must make the effort to jot down in some shorthand fashion a record of how the speaker tried to carry you from his starting points to his conclusions." (105)

To this sage advice, I need to add that, when focusing attention on how the speaker tried to do this, *a commonsense listener must pay special attention to looking for the definitions the speaker is using.* The reason for this is because these are the chief means any and every speaker essentially must use logically to carry an audience from his or her introduction to his or her conclusion. And this means that the listener must pay special attention to the words, technical jargon, a speaker is using at this or that point in an argument.

At times, speakers will introduce these definitions through use of an example; and they will tell you precisely that they are doing this by using the terms "for example," or "for instance." *Examples and instances are always signs of ideas* (ideas expressed in the form of physical images), and ideas always express definitions. In his famous dialogues

Plato generally orders arguments by introducing these arguments into the characters who first introduce definitions. *New characters introduce new ideas containing new definitions that introduce new arguments.*

Note that I have just used reference to Plato's method of lecturing through dialogue method as an example (species) of how to locate definitions within ideas, contained within arguments, introduced by new characters that lead listeners from introductions to conclusions in Plato's dialogues considered as instructional speeches. In so doing, I have defined one of Plato's chief instructional techniques! To readers who have understood what I have just said, in one short paragraph I have hopefully made intelligible to them how actively and effectively to read Plato in a way that achieves what Adler would say arrives at a meeting of minds: the way Plato had sought to be understood by those who had read his dialogues during his own time and had likely also listened to Socrates speak in the Agora in Athens—the most intellectually enjoyable and profitable way of all to understand mostly all of Plato's dialogues! Beyond this, I have revealed an essential element that Adler necessarily has to include maximally to achieve and make intelligible to himself and others precisely what he means when he talks about completely achieving *a meeting of minds*!

In addition, analogously transferred to dramatic and comedic works considered as species of instructional and/or persuasive lectures (such as the plays of William

Shakespeare), the same method and results achieved in effecting a meeting of minds with Plato relative to understanding the intelligible content of most of his dialogues proportionately apply to understanding the nature of characters and character development from Act 1, Scene 1 through the concluding Act and Scene in his plays. Again, in telling readers this, in one somewhat lengthy sentence, hopefully, I have made intelligible to them how to achieve a maximum meeting of minds with that of Shakespeare actively and effectively to read and more enjoyably and profitably understand mostly all his plays!

Adler's two rules for composing a retrospective summary after listening to an instructional speech.

Given the difficulties taking notes during a face-to-face instructive lecture, after such listening to this species of lecture, Adler provides the following two rules for active readers to apply to achieve what more or less approximates what he calls *a meeting of the minds* between the listener and the speaker.

Rule 1:

Extract from running notes and memory of the speech a summary of it and write it down, including in it as much detail as you can, in as unbiased a representation as you can, of what the speaker actually said.

Rule 2:

Include in this summary "the speaker's initial premises or assumptions, the words he used in some special sense that were his crucial terms, the conclusions at which he aimed, and the ways in which he tried to support those conclusions." (106) In addition to this, I would add to include the ideas the speaker said (or you reasonably suspected) he or she sought to express by these terms, especially technical terms/jargon; and follow these with the crucial definitions he or she gave for these.

I would also refer to these words and definitions according to their order of appearance in his or her speech (if possible, indicating for yourself the page numbers according to their order of appearance). Doing this will facilitate your ability to follow the order of the speakers arguments as parts of a whole from the introduction, through the middle, to the conclusion. They will also create a historical record—bookmark of sorts—to which you can return in the future if you ever wish to re-read a book to brush up on your understanding of its contents.

Once a listener does this, he or she is in a reasonable position rationally to react to the talk as a whole as an unbiased listener. According to Adler, expressing reactions to a speech in this way "is as much a part of actively listening to a speech as it is a part of actively reading a book." (106)

If a listener has understood a speech in this way and totally agrees with its conclusion, in my opinion, he or she will have achieved what Adler would call a complete or total meeting of the minds, a listener and speaker will: 1) have the exact same understanding—a mutual, commonsense understanding—of what the speaker understood himself or herself chiefly to be saying (sought to say); and 2) completely agree with it. In such a situation Adler states a listener's reaction to the speaker's presentation will be "to say 'Amen.'" (107)

If this does not happen, if a listener partly understood and partly did not understand what a speaker was saying, or attempted to say, Adler maintains the first task of the listener is to write down questions expressing what he or she thinks a speaker did or did not do that might have caused this failure in understanding on the listener's part. Specifically, what did the listener think were weaknesses in the speaker's talk? In the form of the following questions, Adler gives examples of these questions expressing actions taken or not taken by the speaker:

> Why did the speaker say this or that? Why did he think that the reasons or evidence he advanced were adequate to support his conclusions. Why did he fail to comment on objections that might be raised to what he said? What did he mean by this or that word which he

used in a special sense without explicitly calling attention to the sense in which he used it? (107)

After doing this, regarding the issues concerning which a listener thought he or she had had a good enough understanding of what the speaker was saying to agree or disagree with it, the listener should write down with what he or she agreed or disagreed; and, sometimes, why (if some profitable purpose is served by so doing).

If, after listening to a speech, a listener cannot determine whether or not he or she totally or partially agrees with a speaker, and cannot explain to himself or herself precisely why, Adler maintains that the reasonable move to make is to suspend final judgment before completely making up on one's mind.

Whether or not a listener agrees, disagrees, or suspends judgment about the contents of a speech, the last thing a serious listener should do is to ask the following question about the speech, "So what?" Or, as Adler puts the question, "What of it?" That is, what personal consequences, if any, follow from the fact that you agree, disagree, or have suspended judgment about agreeing or disagreeing with a speaker's conclusions and the way he or she might have, or might not have rationally justified them? (108)

According to Adler, asking this final question involves a listener thinking about the personal significance of the speech considered as a whole. Why bother following the cumbersome rules and recommendations Adler has given related to note taking unless a listener is convinced "that the character and substance of the speech is rich and important enough to deserve all the effort called for"? (108) The rational answer to such a question appears evidently to be that *doing so makes no common sense.*

For this reason, after asking this question, Adler immediately adds that the way a person answers this question must be determined *by the precept of prudence— which is what most of us, most of the time, understand to be identical with practical and productive common sense*: "The precept of prudence in following the recommendations suggested is simply to make whatever adaptation or use of them the substance, style, and importance of the speech deserves, making the maximum effort for the best of speeches, less for those that are less worthy, and not at all for those that were not worth listening to in the first place." (108)

And, Adler adds, this is just as true for other forms of uninterrupted speech as it is for instructive speech. In both species, both the speaker and listener can often benefit from post-speech question and answer sessions because these provide an opportunity to get answers to questions that listeners have to what a speaker has said to which they might want to hear a speaker reply; and a speaker might want to give one. (108)

According to Adler, once again, the chief aim of human communication "is the meeting of the minds in such a way that they share a common understanding, whether or not they agree or disagree." (112) Such being the case, whether such speech be chiefly persuasive or instructive, wherever and whenever possible, he maintains the one-way species of talk essentially characteristic of uninterrupted speech and silent listening should always "be followed by two-way talk, the kind of interchange between speakers and listen to us that his conversation or discussion." (112) This is the only way, as much as possible, to guarantee that speaking and listening can achieve a maximum commonsense meeting of understandings and maximum benefit for both parties involved.

—CHAPTER NINE—

Lesson 9—How to Use Question and Answer Forums to Learn to Excel at All Forms of Social Talk

Passing beyond solitary to social speech.

Chapter 9 of Mortimer Adler's monograph, *How to Speak. How to Listen*, starts Part 4 of his text. In so doing, it abandons his talk about human communication in terms of one-way speech and mainly silent listening. To prepare his readers for this transition from a less, to a more, social form of talking, in his previous chapter he had started to have us begin focusing attention on the crucial importance of speakers getting audience feedback so as completely and precisely as possible to determine the extent and depths to which they have been able to achieve a meeting of the minds with their audience.

A chief reason Adler did this is because he was convinced that, in its most perfect, adult and professional form, human communication is always social, not solitary: two-way, not one-way, talk. By nature, one-way human communication starts out as a species of maternalistic and paternalistic talk engaged in by adults when talking to children. From an educational standpoint, it is a preparatory stage in reading, listening, and speaking through which all human beings naturally have to pass before reaching the adulthood of social communication.

Without a question and answer format, Adler maintains that neither instructive nor persuasive speech can be as effective as they should be. A question and answer session needs to follow them. (116) To support this claim, he refers to the centrality two-way talk has historically played in the political life of the West: 1) beginning with the discussions that had occurred daily in the Athenian Agora and the Roman Forum; 2) moving on to parliamentary government with its long history in British political life; 3) mentioning the American tradition of Presidential candidates touring the United States via train "speaking at one whistle stop after another to track-side gatherings and responding to questions or other challenges" (116); followed later on by television debates in which direct confrontation between candidates is conducted face to face with the American people and their answer are called into question by, and required to face objections from, moderators; 4) and concluding by referring to the famous London Hyde Park Corner, Sunday afternoon soapbox speeches; the long tradition in the United States of public lectures that are advertised and include a question-answer period—examples of which are the Chautauqua lecture series that started toward the end of the nineteenth century (and remained in existence beyond that); and the Ford Hall forum in Boston and the Cooper Union Forum in New York City, the last being the place where Adler states his own experience as a lecturer had begun during the 1920s. (116–117)

According to Adler, these well-conducted, well-regulated forums "improved the listening and tested the metal of the listeners" and, at the same time, "taught the speakers much that they could not have learned in any other way." (118) Personally, he learned so much from these experiences that he deeply regretted the occasions where he had lectured and these lectures had not been followed by audience discussions. He reports, "I have learned nothing just from hearing myself speak, totally deprived there any sense about whether what I have said has been adequately heard and understood. I might just as well have been speaking in an empty hall." (118)

In contrast, he states, when a lecture is followed by a forum, he learns much about what he has said:

> I learn which of my terms need greater clarification. I learn what assumptions need to be more fully explicated. I learn what points need further elucidation and why it is necessary to change the order in which certain points are made. I learn where one argument needs amplification and another can be improved by stating it more succinctly....

> I also learn from objections raised and difficulties posed where my own thinking has been mistaken or inadequate. Objections I cannot satisfactorily meet call for serious emendations of the lecture I have given. Questions that I cannot satisfactorily answer call for additions that must be made—points added, clarifications advanced. (118)

Each time this happens Adler notices his increased learning experiences contribute to the quality of his subsequent lectures, making them more intelligible to himself and to his listeners. This proved to be so valuable to him throughout his professional career that, in 1986 (when he wrote his *How to Speak. How to Listen*), he stated, "in the last 40 years, most of the books I have written have been expansions of lectures that have undergone the testing, the learning, and the detailed improvements in both substance and style that resulted from speaking to listeners who talk back." (119) In fact, he reports this is the way he wrote his bestselling *How to Read a Book*; and he adds, it was precisely for this reason that:

> It was much better than the earlier books I had written as if I were talking only to myself in the silence of my study. I had given a lecture on the art of reading to many and diverse audiences a full year before I sat down to write it out. The lecture had undergone many revisions,

both emendations and expansions. My file of lecture notes and other notes, made as a result of facing audiences, was what produced the book. Its success in reaching a wide audience of readers persuaded me to adopt the same procedure for the writing of subsequent books.

I would almost dare to say that speaking and listening, when properly conjoined in a lecture-forum, is the best way to write a book. (119)

While what Adler reports about the nature of a forum and its benefits qualitatively to improving the acts of lecturing, listening, writing, and publishing are of tremendous educational worth, most odd, again, are several things that, given his educational background, he omitted from his analysis of a forum and the many benefits he derived from it. For example, he had greatly benefited from learning about the education the Ancient Greeks and Medieval Italians had received from daily discussions that had occurred in the Ancient Athenian Agora and the Roman Forum. He came to understand that, from similar discussions, the educated class of the Middle Ages had become so skilled in listening, speaking, reading, and writing during that time that their educational abilities in these areas had surpassed those of the educated class of his own day. Nonetheless, he makes no mention of these facts in relation to the nature of a forum and its benefits.

Furthermore, he made this omission despite the fact that Socrates was the most famous person associated with the Ancient Athenian Agora, and that what made him so famous was his commonsense philosophy—which provided the educational principles that had generated Plato's Academy, Aristotle's Lyceum, and, centuries later, gave birth, during the Christian Middle Ages (especially at the University of Paris with its different nations of students and faculty), to the uniquely-Western *International Teaching and Research University*! Perhaps even more remarkable is that Adler also omitted mentioning that, etymologically, the term 'forum' is evidently Latin in origin and is most closely associated throughout Western history and the contemporary world with the Italian analogue of the Athenian Agora—the Roman Forum and the famous oratorical speeches of Brutus and Marc Antony that Adler had gone out of his way to mention toward the start of his monograph.

Equally amazing is his failure to mention the great Medieval teaching methods of the classroom and university-wide public disputation (*disputatio*), which were Medieval analogs of the Socratic method of teaching—which had so strongly influenced Adler as a youth. These lay at the foundation of Saint Thomas Aquinas's masterful *Summa theologiae*, which Adler had discovered during the late 1920s, that had exercised enormous influence on his understanding of how to do philosophy dialectically after the fashion of a science. Both had exercised such a powerful influence upon Adler's own education that his Center for Philosophical Research and idea of developing his Great Books of the Western World essentially grew out of the commonsense philosophical principles of these Medieval *Scholastic* sources! Their principles even essentially generated the famous Columbia University/Columbia College Great Books Honors Program that John Erskine had established there and of which Adler had so much desired as a youth to become a part.

While Adler does mention in his monograph the important role the Medieval lecture (*lectio*) had played in making students at the Medieval university great readers, writers, speakers, and listeners, he totally neglects the powerful nature that the Medieval *disputatio* had played in perfecting the method of learning as a cultural, philosophical, social-science, team enterprise. This omission is most odd since he had considered it to be better than any other in representing the forum technique of learning through which is perfected what Adler repeatedly calls *a meeting of the minds*.

Especially puzzling about this omission is that, shortly after he had graduated from Columbia University in 1928, he had decided to make philosophy considered as a social-science team enterprise an essential part of his professional career. A chief mission in his life had become to help philosophy become respectable as a social-science enterprise concerned with matters of truth—not opinions or matters of taste. The teachings of Saint Thomas Aquinas he had revived his conviction that achieving these goals were really doable—not pipe dreams. In his intellectual autobiography, *Philosopher at Large*, he reports that, during the early 1930s, his exposure to the writings and lectures of Jacques Maritain had left him psychologically reinvigorated to pursue this mission as a personal and professional calling.

Immediately prior to his coming into contact with Maritain's work and personally getting to know Maritain in Chicago, Adler says the different notions of philosophy with which he had become acquainted had left him "very uncomfortable about my choice of philosophy as a career. In one way or another they downgraded philosophy to a second-rate enterprise (that is, *they had not elevated it to the status of a social science*: a transgenerational, cultural, team, higher educational enterprise), making it much less respectable than science as a pursuit of truth, either turning it into a handmaiden of science, or relegating it to the role commentator on other primary disciplines, or even worse, conceding that it was more like personal opinion or a work of the imagination than like certifiable and testable knowledge." (Adler, *Philosopher at Large*, 298/my parenthetical addition)

Of the many "intellectual debts" Adler states he owed Maritain, the greatest was "for a conception of philosophy, especially in relation to the empirical sciences, that gave it dignity and made it respectable as an undertaking to which

Chapter 9: How to Use Q/A Forums 227

one might devote one's life": that is, which made it *a social science enterprise that could become a life-long vocation.* (298) Considered as such, Adler did not have to be a one-way, paternalistic talker for the rest of his life!

Regarding the idea to which Maritain had acted as a midwife to give birth in his soul, Adler reported it became a life-changing moment for him. Not only had he had achieved a meeting of minds with Maritain. The idea Maritain had given him had dramatically and forever changed his mind and his life—"it became for me a vivid and controlling insight (commonsense understanding—a kind of *Eureka*! Moment) after I heard him expound it in one of the first lectures he gave at the University of Chicago. My efforts to assimilate and develop all its implications have taken many years, during which I produced successively more detailed, and I hope sounder and more mature, statements of the view that philosophy, like science, is a body of knowledge (that is, an organizational whole consisting of transgenerational truths in the form of inherited propositions/my addition), not a set of opinions, knowledge of the world (in the form of uncommon commonsense, social science understandings in which we live, of the nature of things, man and of society). As such it does not compete or conflict with science." (298/my parenthetical additions)

Around the same time Maritain had had this life-changing influence on him, Adler reports he gave a lecture—entitled "The Misapplication of Psychology"—at a meeting of the Men's Forum of a Detroit synagogue. Therein, he states, he critiqued "current trends in so-called scientific psychology, such as behaviorism and psychoanalysis in the light of the philosophical psychology to be found in Aristotle and Aquinas." (306) In other words, he had argued that the philosophical psychology of Aristotle and Aquinas represented a better example of true scientific psychology, or psychology as a species of social science!

Paradoxically, and some might say, *providentially*, present at this lecture was a Jesuit priest and Philosophy Professor—a faculty member from the Jesuit University of Detroit. According to Adler, after the lecture, the priest invited him to repeat his lecture before his students at the University. He explained to Adler a motive for his so doing was that his students "had never heard such things said . . . by anyone not wearing a Roman collar," and that "hearing them from" Adler "might help to *persuade* (my italics) his students that commitment to these propositions could be something other than strict adherence to a party line." (306)

This invitation, in turn, eventually led to Adler getting his foot in the door to being asked to talk at other Catholic philosophical gatherings. In my opinion, the most remarkable of these was Adler being invited to present "the Annual Association Address at the meeting of the American Catholic Philosophical Association in 1934." (306)

For this occasion, Adler chose as his topic "The New Scholastic Philosophy and the Secular University." In his talk, Adler states, he decided "to question the meaning of the word *scholastic* as applied to philosophy." In so doing, he asserted:

> If philosophy consists of such wisdom (that is, uncommon commonsense wisdom) as can be distilled by the reflective operation of the intellect (that is, by a psychological habit) to find the materials of common experience (that is, to discover the proximate first causes and principles of commonsense wisdom), and if scholastic philosophy is philosophy in this sense (that is, if scholastic philosophy is a psychological habit of uncommon commonsense wisdom wondering about and discovering the proximate principles and causes of commonsense wisdom), then the word *scholastic* signifies only that philosophy is not the work of a single man, but the work of a school (that is, philosophy is essentially a transgenerational historical and cultural, social-science enterprise) of men preserving and adding to traditional human wisdom (that is, standing on the shoulders of prior educational giants—wise men). It is only in modern times that philosophy is not *scholastic* in the sense, because each thinker insists upon the novelty of his system and hence necessarily disguise the tradition. (306/my parenthetical and italicized additions)

Adler reports that, if what he was saying was true, he questioned "the advisability of referring to a "new" scholasticism. Granting that philosophy should address itself to contemporary problems and that, to this extent it is necessary to rethink the nature of Aristotelianism and Thomism," he proceeded to ask his audience, "would it not be better . . . to refer to such efforts as a *revival* of philosophy rather than a "new" scholasticism?" (307/my italics added)

To his commonsense rhetorical question, Adler immediately replied, "this revived philosophy is no more essentially Catholic than it is Greek. It can be called Greek if we wish to refer to the accident of its origin; it can be called Catholic if we wish to refer to the accident of its adoption by the Church. But as perennial wisdom, the only proper qualification of philosophy is as *human*." (307)

Such being the case, no wonder should exist why Medieval teachers of rhetoric and poetry would consider themselves to be *scholastic* philosophers. Any professor at a Medieval university would consider himself to be a schoolman, scholastic, someone contributing as a higher-educational team member to a cultural enterprise transmitting uncommon commonsense *human wisdom*—philosophy/science—from one historical generation to the next. Considered as such, each would think of himself as an educator, philosopher, scientist/social scientist, teacher, historian, and humanist.

Consequently, no wonder should equally exist why, when students of the Medieval scholastic poets and rhetoricians moved to Italy during the fourteenth century to obtain jobs at universities and help revive Italian literacy—and through it—Italian culture, their students would eventually refer to them as *humanists*. And they would consider themselves to be historians and philosophers.

The first of the ancient Christian thinkers to be called a *scholastic* was Anicius Manlius Severinus Boethius (d. 524). The honorific title he is often given is that of "last of the Ancients and first of the scholastics," meaning that Ancient philosophy had ended with him and Christian philosophy had begun with the start, with him, of scholasticism—in the sense of forming a team of *liberal arts* scholars to preserve classical learning. Actually, scholasticism had started with the Ancient Greeks, as part of ancient Greek humanistic learning—philosophy as a cultural enterprise. Strictly speaking, Boethius was not the first of the scholastics.

Another title given to Boethius is that of a *humanist*—a name often given to liberal arts educators considered as such. Certainly, Boethius was not the first of liberal arts educators; and reduction of the whole of liberal arts today to humanities is simply a continuation of the identification of the whole of higher education with scholasticism—being a scholastic enterprise—a species of educating that requires a culture that has professional schools chiefly devoted to transmitting wisdom from one historical generation to the next.

Of course, what Adler was saying about every species of philosophy (uncommon commonsense *human* wisdom) simply being philosophy (commonsense *human* wisdom reflecting on itself) is true; but I suspect that, at the time, commonsense understanding of philosophy as the philosophy of common sense was probably lost on many, if not most, members of his audience—who I surmise, even by the 1930s, had largely reduced all species of philosophy to species of systematic logic, just as Adler had been inclined to do when he was an undergraduate at Columbia University.

This modern and contemporary lack of understanding of the nature of philosophy as a transgenerational educational—that is, *scholastic*—psychological habit (a team-effort, school practice) *of wondering* that had become institutionalized within an educational tradition, or institution of higher education was a caricature and gross mischaracterization inherited from the misnamed Western *Enlightenment*, which tended to know nothing about classical philosophy as the Ancient Greeks and Medievals had actually practiced it. This ignorance was so deep and widespread that it was even common during the first half of the twentieth century among students of Plato, Aristotle, and Aquinas—and it still continues to this day among some members of these same groups.

Chapter 9: How to Use Q/A Forums

The first scholarly attempt to challenge this caricature of classical philosophical wisdom in extensive historical depth and detail was that given by Adler's contemporary and friend, Étienne Gilson when, toward the middle of the twentieth century he published a brief account of the nature of scholasticism—*scholasticism* as a team philosophical enterprise—common to the Medieval university in his magisterial *History of Christian Philosophy in the Middle Ages*, to which I now turn my attention.

The teaching methods of the Medieval University.

According to Étienne Gilson—the twentieth-century's leading historian of Medieval thought—the main method out of which all the other teaching methods in the Medieval university grew as from a proximate first principle, or cause, was the question (*quaestio*: from the Latin for inquiry, investigation). He states, "The 'question' (*aporia*) is the typical expression of this method." (*History of Christian Philosophy in the Middle Ages*/248) He maintains the roots of this method are found in Aristotle's dialectics; and, as mostly anyone familiar with Ancient Greek philosophy knows, it is the practice most commonly associated with the teaching method of Socrates of driving opponents into an intellectual dead end, state of puzzlement, where they are actually confronted by discovering that they really do not know what they claim to know. Gilson calls this, "The living cell of school teaching"—the philosophical/scientific learning method of the Schoolmen: the scholastic method of learning as a cultural enterprise and transgenerational historical/cultural team effort that, more than anything else, essentially defined the nature of the Medieval university. (248)

Centuries later, the term *scholastic philosophy* would become pejoratively and ignorantly referred to as representing a universal, essentially intellectually backward, *philosophy* common to the whole of the Middle, or Dark, Ages. Instead, it was simply the educational nature of the classical Greek, cultural, team-method of social-science philosophizing (Greek philosophy considered as a team effort philosophically and historically standing on the shoulders of intellectual giants) inherited by Plato and Aristotle from Socrates and analogously transposed and passed on to Medieval masters like Aquinas as the Medieval university cultural team enterprise: *Scholastic philosophy*.

Hence, contrary to this erroneous caricature, Gilson states, "All the main products of this school teaching are either isolated disputed questions or aggregates of disputed questions ordered according to some organic plan" (organizational whole). And he adds that, while variations of this method "were always possible, . . . the 'question' remained, up to the end of the middle ages, the favorite mode of exposition of personal thought for the masters of the university." (248/my parenthetical addition)

As Gilson indicates, the favorite form of this instructional method among university teachers was called the "disputed question." It was the commonsense philosophical/scientific method of learning to which university students were introduced after they had mastered liberal arts psychological habits of listening and reading well through the practice of the instructive lecture (*lectio*), regarding which Adler's had spoken so glowingly in his Chapter 1, entitled "The Untaught Skills." (6–7) And it was taught in this way and order precisely because the common sense wisdom of the Medieval educators caused them evidently to recognize that hoping to achieve a shared understanding in the form of *a meeting of minds* (to use Adler's technical vocabulary) between two people who have never learned how verbally to communicate in a way in which one speaker would eventually come to understand exactly what is in the mind of the other speaker *makes no common sense*, is at the best an impossible dream. Before becoming a master at communicating, commonsensical Medieval educators had recognized a person must first become an apprentice (bachelor).

As described by Gilson, the disputed question (*quaestio disputata*) "was a formal exercise" in which teachers (masters) would choose a thesis against which either the master or his students could raise objections. After this happened, using suitable arguments, "a younger teacher (*baccalarius*)" would defend the thesis and answer the question as someone responding to it (*respondens*):

> The master had always a right to intervene in the discussion and the final conclusion was his. On the next day, the master could take up again the subject matter of the preceding dispute. He would then restate the thesis, make a choice of arguments against it, announce his own decision, justify himself as if he were the *respondens* and finally refute the objections. If he wrote it himself, it became a *Questio Disputata*; if one of the listeners wrote it for him, it became a 'reportation' (*reportatio*/my addition) of a *Disputed Question* (247/my parenthetical addition). Since the master was free to determine the number of these disputes, he could decide to hold enough of them, within a year or even more, so as to discuss completely the different aspects of one and the same question. Hence the remarkable series of disputed questions found, for instance, in the works of Saint Thomas Aquinas (*Quaestiones disputatae de veritate*, etc.), or of Matthew of Aquasparta (*Quaestiones disputatae de fide, humana cognitione*, etc.). (247)

Apart from these disputes, held in the class of a certain master at his own convenience and for his students, there were public disputations. Each master was free to hold them or not, and they were such an ordeal that not all masters cared to do so. These public disputes had to take place about the second week of Advent and the third or fourth weeks of Lent. Anybody could submit a question on any subject; hence the name of *'Quodlibetic Questions'* (*Quaestiones de quodlibet*, or *quodlibetales* [also sometimes referred to as "*Quodlibetal Questions*"/my addition]). (247–248/ my addition in brackets)

Naturally, the master could turn down certain questions as unsuitable for discussion. The dispute then followed the usual routine, with this difference however, that any number of masters could intervene in the discussion. In some cases, their number was large. Over and above these lectures and disputes, there were academic sermons preached by masters before the University; in some of these sermons, general questions pertaining to theology, sometimes even to philosophy, could be debated at length and the history of philosophy or of theology has often to learn from them. (248)

Given the highly sophisticated nature of such discussion forums with which Adler was well familiar, and the influence of the scholastic method of teaching and learning had on his entire professional career and life, I am shocked that he made no mention of them in his monograph—that, instead, he had included less rigorous methods for achieving the total meeting of minds he so forcefully sought his readers to master.

Adler's recommendations about how, to be effective, a speaker should conduct a forum.

In answer to the question of how, no matter what the circumstances, he would recommend conducting a forum, Adler offers the following format, which takes into consideration the points of view of both the speaker and the listeners.

In this plan of execution, he states that the speaker should open the discussion by asking the participants to distinguish between two types of questions: 1) those "that seek for a further or better understanding of what has been said"; and 2) those "that challenge the speaker." (122)

Trying to answer questions or objections caused by misunderstandings, commonsensically dictates to Adler that, educationally considered, the first types of questions to which he refers above should be asked first, and in the following form: "Do I understand you to say that . . ." Better, I think, would be to put this question something like this, "Would I be understanding you correctly if I were to maintain you are saying . . .?"

If, after being asked this type of question, a listener is still having difficulty understanding what a speaker is saying, according to Adler, the speaker can try to help the listener by attempting to rephrase the listener's question in a way such as follows, "Let me see if I understand the question you are asking, . . . and let me do so by restating you the question as follows."

If a listener still has problems understanding what the speaker is saying, perhaps in the form of restating the listener's question, the speaker can volunteer to become the questioner, and ask himself or herself the question he or she thinks the listener is attempting to ask. If that does not work, I would recommend that the speaker simply ask someone else in the audience whether or not he or she might be able to explain what I, as the speaker, was saying. I have used this device in the past more than once; and, generally, I have found it to be pretty effective. Often, listeners understand what I am saying better than I understand it myself.

After handling all the preceding types of questions, Adler recommends a speaker conclude the forum by posing and answering questions he or she considers to be good questions to ask, which had not been asked, and he or she would like to answer so as to elucidate what he or she had been talking about.

In relation to persuasive, instead of instructive, speeches Adler states that use of this device is especially helpful in overcoming audience resistance to a selling point a speaker is trying to make that remains hidden from his or her awareness. Using it enables the speaker to flush out these psychological obstacles, identify precisely what they are, and answer them.

Adler's recommendations about how an active and effective listener should participate in a forum.

From the standpoint of active participants in a forum, Adler recommends that he or she should use the running notes he or she had been taking as the basis for asking the speaker questions.

Related to instructive speeches, he advises the listeners have two chief goals in mind: 1) to ensure that they have fully understood what they have heard and 2) "to challenge the speaker in a manner that the listeners can decide whether to agree or disagree with what a speaker has said about this or that point." (125)

Regarding persuasive speeches, Adler maintains that listeners need to feel psychologically secure in the conviction that a speaker has adequately covered all relevant issues and has answered all relevant questions. To ensure this is the case listeners have to call to the attention of speakers all such issues and ask them all such questions they think the speakers, for one reason or another, have neglected to address and not adequately answered, or not answered at all. (125)

—CHAPTER TEN—

Lesson 10—How to Use Some Commonsense Principles of Two-Way Talk to Excel at Both Playful and Serious Conversations

The 4 species of two-way talk.

Mortimer Adler starts his Chapter 10 dealing with "The Variety of Conversations" by maintaining that four species of two-way talk exist, of which forums that follow persuasive or instructive lectures are just one. (128) He divides this genus (two-way, or social, conversations) into two extreme, contrary, opposites of "playful as opposed to serious."

Since, today, we often refer to playful conversations (such as ones we might have at a dinner party) as *social*, in this chapter Adler appears to reduce *social* to playful—even though, according to the technical vocabulary he had previously established—since it is only one species of two-way, or social, talk—strictly speaking, he should not have done this!

Because doing this is bound to get some readers confused, lost, Adler's having done so made no common sense. According to his previously-established vocabulary, all species of conversation about which he talks in this chapter are social. Nonetheless, with respect to this chapter, and this chapter only, when Adler refers to a conversation as being *social*, he might be referring to the term 'social' simply as meaning *playful*. So as not to get confused, lost, in reading this, readers need to make special note of this point!

Apart from playful, two-way conversations, which are more free-flow and off-the-cuff (tending to have no other aim than securing mutual enjoyment of the parties involved), Adler divides the genus of previously-referred-to *social*, or *two-way*, conversations (*in this chapter*, considered as *non-social*) into the second, third, and fourth species of *serious* talk: 2) Personal, private, and serious—or heart-to-heart. 3) Impersonally theoretical, serious, informative, and/or enlightening, if they chiefly aim to effect a change of mind to enable persons involved to obtain knowledge or understanding they did not previously have. 4) Impersonally practical and persuasive, if they chiefly aim to effect a change of emotional state "or the practical purpose of selling merchandise, of winning political support, of getting a business plan of policy adopted," and the like. (128–129) Unlike the first species, these other are *formal* in the sense that they are *formally-controlled* and *purposeful* to effect an emotional change in one or both parties involved in the conversation.

Personal and playful conversations.

According to Adler, personal and playful conversations tend to be most effective when they happen in relatively small numbers, "the best is often just between two persons, but the group can be slightly larger." (130) Based upon his personal experience, he claims that when a group expands beyond five or six people, it is inclined to subdivide into "two quite separate conversations. (130–131)

"By playful conversation," Adler states, he means "all forms of talk that have no set purpose, no objective to achieve, no controlling direction. In addition, like play itself which is that form of human activity in which we engage purely for the pleasure inherent in the activity in itself, conversation that is playful in intent rather than seriously motivated in conversation that is enjoyable for its own sake, and not pursuit for any ulterior purpose." (127)

He goes on to describe this species of conversation as "easy, informal talk that takes place in pleasing companionship with one's friends and associates. It may be informative, but it need not be, nor need it be enlightening, though it may also be that. It simply gives pleasure and, by doing so, it brings persons together in friendship or helps make them better acquainted with one another." (127)

To this, he adds, it "can never be planned in advance. It just happens if the circumstances fortuitously favor occurring. To set an advance what is to be discussed is to plan something akin to a business meeting." In contrast, playful conversation "should be permitted to wander. There is no goal to reach, nothing to decide." (127) Related to such a conversation, setting a formal goal or predetermined decision would make no common sense.

Personal, or serious, heart-to-heart, talk.

According to Adler, in marked contrast to the informal nature of personal and playful conversation, personal, serious, heart-to-heart, talk usually: 1) "involves two persons or at most only a few"; 2) happens under private, not public, circumstances; 3) never involves the kind of conversation the involved parties would want to have recorded like that of a public meeting; 4) does not have a prepared agenda; and 5) might occur spontaneously or, in some way, be preplanned. (129–130) "However it happens," Adler states, "it is always a signally significant event in their lives, affecting them and no one else" (at least not in any pre-planned way/my addition). (130)

In such species of talk, Adler asserts that, due to friendship or love—which tend to put the participants on a respectively equal footing, and usually facilitate their ignoring any sort of inequality that, otherwise, might exist between them—the people involved confront each other as, in some way, specific equals relative to the issue involved. (130)

To this Adler adds that, because it is chiefly concerned with emotional issues of major importance to the people concerned, "it is deeply serious, probably more serious than any other kind of talk, for it aims to remove emotional misunderstandings or to alleviate, if not eliminate, emotional tensions." (128)

This radically distinguishes personal, heart-to-heart, talk from all species of impersonal conversation, whether instructive or persuasive. (130) In every form of impersonal conversation, Adler maintains, the participants need not confront each other as equals talking to each other conversationally as equal, species-members of the same genus. And whether or not they do makes a dramatic difference related to the ultimate effectiveness of the conversation! (130)

Impersonal conversations considered in general and specifically.

According to Adler, a persuasive, or instructive, impersonal conversation may involve two or more people of long- or short-time acquaintance. In the first situation, the speakers will have some familiarity with each other's vocabularies, intellectual commitments, assumptions, prejudices, and so on. This makes impersonal conversation easier between or among them. Not so if they come together for the first time as complete strangers. In this situation, Adler observes commonsensically, "they face obstacles to be effective communication that must be surmounted and are often difficult to overcome." (130) And, while he does not say so, this is chiefly because they tend to lack any individual, commonsense understanding of each other and the way they tend to define their words.

According to him, such meetings may be informal or formal; totally or partially pre-arranged or spontaneous. The subjects to be discussed might be some pre-assigned reading material, plan, policy proposal, problem requiring solution, issue needed to be resolved, disagreement, or difference, which has to be overcome.

He maintains that, related to these conversations, differences, or disagreements, of opinion concerning actual matters of fact are worth discussing only if the conversation aims to consider "what consequences flow from one set of facts rather than another, the opposing sets a facts being treated hypothetically for the sake of discussion." (131-132)

Given such a situation, he states: "Discussion can advance and understanding of the practical or theoretical significance of supposing one set of facts to obtain rather than another; but it cannot ever decide which is the actual state of affairs with regard to matters of fact. Inquiry, investigation, or research, even if it amounts to no more than going to a reference book to look up the facts in question, is the only way to settle the matter." (132)

If these impersonal conversations chiefly aim at achieving a theoretical goal, Adler recommends the chief subject of discussion should be relevant issues and ideas, not well-formulated and relevant problems, policies, plans. (132)

In contrast, and finally, if they chiefly aim at a practical goal of one person trying to get another, or others, to do something he or she wants (or, I would add, mutual agreement about a course of action), Adler advises the participants in the conversation ask themselves the following questions: 1) Will only two people be involved in the conversation, or does it involve more? 2) If it involves more, will one act as a moderator, or will it be free flow? 3) Where and when will it happen? 4) Will it have any time limits? 5) If so, what will they be? 6) What sort of surroundings will be involved? 7) What kind of discussions will the surroundings facilitate or impede? 8) If the precise goal of the discussion is known beforehand, precisely what is it and how much time will be allotted to reach it?

Commonsensically, in *Old Man and the Sea*, Santiago would try to answer the above questions by asking and answering, "What would Joe DiMaggio do in answer to these questions?"

—CHAPTER ELEVEN—

Lesson 11—Some Commonsense Rules Applicable to Making Every Kind of Conversation Pleasurable and Profitable.

A general summary of topics Adler considers in his Chapter 11.

Toward the end of Chapter 10 of his monograph, Adler summarizes the topics he will consider in Chapter 11. He states he will examine rules and recommendations that, in general, can exercise a beneficial effect on conversations. In addition, he will suggest rules and recommendations for impersonal, theoretical and practical, social conversations. However, because they are extremely idiosyncratic, differ so widely depending upon the different, emotional dispositions and circumstances of the persons involved and the times in which they happen, he will not suggest rules or make recommendations for conducting personal, heart-to-heart discussions. (134)

Rules universally applicable to every species of conversation in relation to four chief causes of resistance to any and every form of instructive or persuasive speech: language, emotions, lack of self-knowledge, and having enough available time.

Some linguistic problems we all face in instructive and persuasive speech and how to overcome them in general, and, especially, today.

Adler begins his examination of rules universally applicable to every species of conversation by first considering them in relation to causes of resistance to instructive or persuasive speech that universally exist in them all, starting with language.

Language is the chief instrument human beings use to communicate with each another. Given the universal necessity to use it, its obscure and cloudy nature, replete, as Adler rightly notes, with "ambiguities and pitfalls of misunderstanding," makes necessity of its wide use unfortunate." (136) He adds, "It is almost impossible for any of us to use important words that will be understood by those with whom we talk, particularly words of crucial significance for us, in exactly the same sense in which we use them. (136) Even when we make a special effort to call attention to the meaning we attach to an important word, our cautionary remark often goes unheard, and the response our questions or statements elicit from the person with whom we are conversing reveals that he or she either has not heard or has not paid attention." (137)

He maintains that: 1) universal schooling in the liberal arts of grammar, rhetoric, and logic and 2) a common tradition of learning that would provide "a background of common reading" and "an understanding of a relatively small number of ideas" (both forms of *scholastic/humanistic learning* for which, we should recall, Adler had fought long and hard during his own lifetime) would help to transcend the road blocks linguistic imperfection places in our contemporary way of communicating. (137)

As Adler observes, and has already stated in his monograph, our Ancient and Medieval Western ancestors, and even some of our Enlightenment forebears, did not have to suffer from this linguistic communications collapse. Up to the start of the twentieth century, they had been lucky enough largely to escape the narrow, positivistic-scientism and its absurd and false reduction of the whole of truth and science—*and, with these, all common sense*—to mathematical physics, and acquire a classical liberal arts education in the *trivium*. In contrast, for the most part, contemporary students in the West and globally are deprived of a common, scholastic literary tradition such as the one which had endowed our ancestors "with a common vocabulary, not only of words but also of ideas." (138–139) This common vocabulary of words and ideas had "made them members of the same intellectual community"—real intellectual genus—"sharing a common background of ideas, references and illusions (plus common sense and a commonsense intellectual tradition!) that made communication between them easier and better." (139/my parenthetical additions)

In contrast to our predecessors, loss of this rich intellectual tradition makes communication between us harder and worse; and it helps explain the contemporary collapse of Western civilization, and almost universal loss of common sense in the West and globally. Worldwide today, as evinced, especially, in national and international politics and higher education, we are all suffering from "what Ortega y Gasset has called 'the barbarism of specialization'—the antithesis of the culture of civilization." (138) As Adler had well understood, the only cure for this civilizational disorder is a return to: 1) a classical liberal arts education and 2) the uncommon, commonsense philosophical wisdom—especially metaphysical, moral, and rhetorical teachings—of Aristotle as best interpreted by Saint Thomas Aquinas.

Some commonsense emotional issues that impact negatively and positively on human communication.

While Adler maintains that emotions are appropriate and necessary means of communication to be used in heart-to-heart discussions and talks that aim to be persuasive in some practical way and are controlled relative to the main goal at hand, he claims that "emotions are entirely out of place in impersonal conversations that have as their goal the achievement of better understanding and the attainment of agreement about resolution of purely intellectual issues. (138) The intrusion of emotions into such conversations spoils them, turns them into emotional conflicts when they should be purely intellectual confrontations. (138) As a result, they become battles between conflicting prejudices instead of into changes that strive for a meeting of minds about ideas or about genuinely disputable opinions, where the dispute can be settled by the adduction of evidence in the marshaling of reasons." (138–139)

I strongly disagree. Human beings are not robots, dispassionate machines, disembodied minds, or *Star Trek's* 'Mr. Spock.' Unhappily, at times, Adler appears to reduce us, and himself, to one, or all, of these.

We always intellectualize with our emotions and emote with our intellects. No intellectual activity is totally dispassionate. For the simple reason that intellectual activity is always somewhat healthy or unhealthy, and we always experience health as pleasant and lack of health as unpleasant, we always apprehend intellectual activity somewhat emotionally.

In addition, as Adler indicated quite clearly in his discussion of persuasive speech, no human being is receptive—even in a serious, somewhat 'impersonal,' way—to talking to someone he or she dislikes: finds unpleasant, unfriendly. Intrusion of the emotions of pleasure and friendliness into every form of conversation, even impersonal, serious, ones never turns them into emotional confrontations. It does the contrary opposite—is a necessary condition for making them profitable and effective. Whether serious or light, no species of human conversation is ever totally *impersonal.*

Why self-knowledge, self-understanding, is a commonsense, necessary condition for all profitable and effective human communication.

In contrast to the egregious error he makes regarding emotions entering into conversations, Adler is more or less spot on in relationship to self-understanding being a crucial condition that "facilitates intelligent conversation and, when absent, impedes and frustrates it." (139) In fact, he does not go far enough and stressing its crucial import. Lack of self-understanding does more than impede and frustrate intelligent conversation. It makes such conversation totally impossible!

Because not understanding that, when we talk about some subject, we actually become a member of the same genus or organizational whole about which we are talking, not understanding this change in personal relationship when transitioning the way we talk from one genus to another makes every form of conversation completely impossible.

Chapter 11: Some Commonsense Rules

For example, when a businessperson talks to his or her wife or husband during dinner at home and to employees at work in a business meeting, not precisely understanding whether or not the people *to whom or with whom* he or she is talking is a professional employee or a personal relation is deadly stupid, totally lacking in common sense.

The commonsense need to understand time availability and limits related to different species of human conversation.

Such being the case, self-understanding, as well as understanding right emotional attitude during serious conversations has an impact upon commonsensically measuring the proper amount of time, effort, and energy we need to devote to them to maximize their effectiveness, profitability, and pleasure. In general, as Adler well understood, saying what we mean "is one of the hardest things in the world to do." (139) And equally hard is listening to what other people say to determine precisely what they mean. In fact, it tends to be more difficult because many of us prefer talking *to*, or—often negatively—*about* others, instead of listening *to* them or talking *with* them.

According to Adler, people who have not been well trained to enjoy listening to what others say to understand precisely what they mean tend to become "lazy or indolent talkers." He adds that "their intellectual sloth is one of the cardinal sins that, unrepented and uncorrected, bars the way to achieve and the goods that energetically conducted conversation can bestow." (139) In addition, he states that, if most of us made the same amount of effort and spent the same amount of time to achieve a meeting the minds as we do running after "love or money," we might expend the proper measure of effort needed to engage in the thoughtful kind of conversation demanded to secure mutual understanding and some amount of agreement or understood disagreement. (139)

Eleven commonsense rules applicable to all species of serious conversation, as well as to playful and other forms of informal talk.

After completing his discussion of emotional issues related to effective and profitable, impersonal and serious conversations, Adler turns his attention to the following eleven rules universally applicable to all species of serious conversation and a few forms of personal discussion:

1) Select the right place and occasion for a conversation.

2) Know in advance the species of conversation in which you want to engage: precisely what you want to talk about and precisely the way you want to talk about it.

3) Select the right people with whom you want to have your conversation, paying special attention to the nature of the conversation involved.

4) Avoid discussion of irrelevant subjects.

5) Avoid talking and listening only to yourself, as if you were talking to an empty room.

6) Before answering a question, make sure you listen carefully to the question with an effort as precisely as possible to understand it.

7) Do not be a lazy questioner. If you are asking, not answering, a question, ask your question as clearly and intelligibly as you can; and, if you have not been able to do so the first time, do so in as many different ways as allowable to get your point across clearly and intelligibly to others. Do not assume that, because you understand the question you are asking in the way you are asking it, others will also understand it that way.

8) Do not monopolize the conversation with questions, as if you are the only one in the room asking them. Do not pepper a speaker with questions one after the other without allowing him or her time adequately and comfortably, clearly and intelligibly to reply to the one asked.

9) Do not interrupt someone else when he or she or speaking, even if you think you know what he or she is going to say. Ignoring this rule is rude.

10) Avoid the extremes of engaging in side conversations and being too polite. The first way of behaving is rude, while the second tends not to challenge the speaker—which is something a serious conversation should always involve.

11) Allow for the three essential parts of a talk (introduction, middle, conclusion) to have proportionately appropriate amounts of time for them adequately and comfortably (not in a rushed way) to explore and answer issues essentially related to the topic at hand. (140–146)

A summary of nine commonsense rules Adler gives about what to do and avoid doing to make an informal conversation as interesting and pleasant as possible for as many people as possible.

1) Agree on a topic of mutual interest to all the participants.

2) Avoid use of cursing, swearing, blasphemy; jokes about ethnicity (to which I would add religion); unfamiliar and uncommon words and clichés of all types, from native and foreign languages; and rehashing old stories and topics,

Chapter 11: Some Commonsense Rules

especially ones familiar to pretty much all participants involved.

3) If the discussion is going well, stick to the topic at hand. Do not change, or digress from, it in any way.

4) Do not: pry into someone else's private life; ask questions of a person that are too intimate, none of your business; maliciously gossip; discuss confidential information you do not expect someone else to make public; include in your conversation repetitious, needless, expressions, colloquialisms that add nothing to the conversation's content and detract from its aesthetic nature; and do not "say 'Look' when you mean 'Please listen.'"

5) Avoid talking about yourself; instead, tend to ask other people about themselves.

6) Try to speak in a pleasantly-sounding way, not too softly or loudly, or in a way that most psychologically-healthy and/or unhealthy people might find irritating.

7) When someone else is speaking, fix your eyes on him on her to make apparent that you are paying attention to what he or she is saying.

8) If someone else enters the conversation, as briefly as possible tell him or her what the other participants had been discussing up to that point and encourage him or her to join in conversation.

9) "At dinner parties, break the ice by turning to the person sitting next to you and asking some question that is calculated to elicit an answer that can then become the subject of conversation. It does not make much difference what you ask if it succeeds in getting the other person to speak." (147–149)

In short, use common sense. Try to be as polite and amiable as possible as the occasion and situation allows.

A summary of twelve commonsense recommendations related to intellectual and emotional rules that Adler gives for conducting mind-to-mind, impersonal, serious conversations whose aim is chiefly theoretical or practical:

While Adler has already commented elsewhere in his monograph about how profitably and effectively to use one's intellect and control one's emotions in general and specifically in relation to instructive and/or persuasive speech, he returns to these issues in Chapter 11 in the form of eleven *commonsensical intellectual rules related to impersonal, serious conversations as summarized below*:

Chapter 11: Some Commonsense Rules

1) Every active participant in a serious conversation or discussion has a first obligation to focus on the chief question under consideration. If the subject is complicated in nature, Adler recommends the participant to analyze it into its constituent parts, and then label and order them. In this way he or she knows which to consider and when—first, second, third, up to the last. (149)

2) Stick to the plan, the tactics, for solving the problem at hand. Do not deviate, digress, wander off from it, and start to talk about some issue irrelevant to the topic at hand. "In short, be relevant, first, last, and always." (150)

3) While sticking to the plan, issue at hand, do not "beat it to death"; do not "stay on it forever. Keep moving on to the next point when this one has been sufficiently explored or discussed. Repetition can be deadly. Conversation can falter and fade if persons engaged in it are unable to pass on from one point to another, if they get stalled by someone's being unable to recognize that enough has been said on a certain point." (151)

4) Avoid bringing your own unacknowledged assumptions and intellectual blind spots—issues concerning which you lack understanding and that you have difficulty comprehending—into a conversation in which you are engaged. (151)

5) To avoid these obstacles, Adler's only recommendation is:

> You should be on the alert to recognize when you are failing to understand something and press for help in understanding it. You should be aware that you have certain preconceptions and assumptions, and try to dredge them up from the recesses of your mind and leave them on the table for everyone to examine. (151)
>
> Since few conversations begin at the beginning and different things are taken for granted by the persons talking with one another, the rule might better be stated as follows. Ask your companions to grant the assumptions you wish to make, and state your own assumptions when it comes to their turn to ask you for them.

In such a situation, he states, "The best cure is for everyone to try to make his own assumptions explicit and beg the others to accept them pro tem." (152)

6) "Never argue about facts; look them up if you wish to settle a difference of opinion about them." (152)

7) Avoid committing the most evident logical fallacies. (152)

Chapter 11: Some Commonsense Rules

8) Never cite authorities, unless you think that doing so will actually make some contribution to what is being said, that the person you are citing is going to be someone well received as an authority by the participants with whom you are engaging in conversation. (152-153)

9) Avoid indirect *ad hominem* attacks on other participants by making them against authorities other participants might cite. (153)

10) Avoid direct *ad hominem* attacks on other participants by maliciously making irrelevant references to their nationality, grandmother, political or business associates, professional occupation, personal habits, and so on. Among these, Adler admonishes: "The most exasperating form of this fallacy is the *bedfellow* (my italics) argument. You say to someone, 'So you agree with Hitler,' as if this suffices to discredit the point he is trying to make. Hitler may be in ill repute with everyone present, but that does not mean he is necessarily wrong about everything." (153)

11) Never take a vote when a conversation in which you are involved—such as a theoretical one—is not essentially related to taking some action, when no decision has to be made. (154)

12) Do not use examples unless you know how to do so relevantly, profitably, and effectively to the topic under discussion. Otherwise, a conversation will often start to go off on a tangent or around in circles. (154-155)

To be relevant, examples "should be well chosen for the purpose of making a general statement of your point more intelligible." To be relevant, you should treat them the way you do assumptions. "Just as assumptions should be allowed to exert whatever force they have only with everyone's explicit acknowledgment and consent, so examples should stand only if everyone sees their relevance and is aware that they are being used to illustrate a point, not to prove it."

Five commonsense emotional rules that Adler wants to add about controlling negative emotions in the course of conversations, plus one from me:

1) Catch yourself or someone else at the first sign that any participant, including yourself, is starting to get annoyed, over-excited, or angry.

2) If you see this starting to happen, take time out for a participant to leave the room and cool off.

3) If a participant "gets fighting mad," Adler maintains only two alternatives exist:

"Try to soothe him or placate him in a friendly way. If that does not work, change the subject for a while. He's probably just as nice as you are, but something happened to hit him in a tender spot. The barkeeper's advice, 'If you want to fight, go outside to do it,' should be followed. Suspend the conversation when it ceases to be an impersonal mind-to-mind to talk and turns into a passionate conflict."

4) "Do not allow an impersonal discussion to become a personal quarrel. Argument is not aggression. There is no point at all and trying to win an argument simply by putting your opponent down or beating him up."

5) Finally, pay special attention to emotional self-understanding, especially related to any negative impact it might have on your ability intellectually to support your case. (156)

6) If all else fails, while Adler does not suggest this, like Santiago, commonsensically ask yourself, "What would Joe DiMaggio do in this situation?" In addition, ask, "How might Tony Anastasia resolve this?" Doing so might help you understand the precise genus within which you find yourself talking and how most commonsensically and profitably for all concerned to converse within it. (155-157)

—CHAPTER TWELVE—

Lesson 12—Commonsense Gateways to Achieving Partial and Total Agreement in Two-Way Talks

Conversations as essential gateways to a meeting of minds—General assumptions about complete or partial meeting of minds in impersonal conversations that have a theoretical or practical aim.

Mortimer Adler begins his Chapter 12 (entitled "The Meeting of Minds") by making three *commonsense assumptions* (which, being the excellent rhetorician he was, he did not specifically label as such!) about how, whether or not participants in a meeting have actually thought about achieving a theoretical or practical goal as their chief aim, nonetheless, a group involved in impersonal conversations can reach one in a complete or partial way.

To do this, Adler's first observation is that, before they start a meeting, the participants in it should decide whether or not they have that the goal of their conversation should be to achieve some measure of complete or partial meeting of minds. To this, I would add, *make sure all the participants are on the same page about the subject under discussion, the way it will be discussed, and whether or not the discussion has a specific aim other than mutual enjoyment.* If they do not do this, common sense dictates that their conversation will be more or less aimless (a conversational taffy-pull) and will achieve no specific or individual goal, other than mostly, purposely, aimlessly talking for whatever pleasure and/or pain this might bring them, given their then-present situation.

Since a partial or complete meeting of the minds can only be achieved by two people sharing a common understanding, commonsensically evident to anyone and everyone intending to achieve this psychological end as a shared conversational goal is that they must avoid the universal pitfall to every species of mind-to-mind understanding: *common misunderstanding*—not being on the same page about the subject under discussion, the way it will be discussed, and whether or not the discussion has a specific aim other than mutual enjoyment. Because achieving a meeting of minds is an essential aim of every species of sales talk, *this is a caveat of which salespeople should take special note!*

Hence, Adler's second observation—commonsense assumption—is a commonsense no-brainer: "Practical conversations are often unsuccessful because misunderstanding prevents them from reaching a decision. Even with sufficient understanding present, disagreement can block the way to action." (158)

Chapter 12: Commonsense Gateways   269

Whatever the case related to success or lack thereof, once again, this appears to be essentially a commonsense nobrainer—an evidently true statement/assumption. If it were not true, practical conversation would not be practical. And the same goes for a productive conversation in the sense of making a product or reaching some goal, even if that goal be something as simple as securing mutual enjoyment or avoiding mutual pain.

Turning to theoretical conversations, Adler states that, while achieving a meeting of minds—common agreement—about some universal truth related to some matter might not be a pre-agreed aim made by participants in a meeting, such a meeting can still be profitable for everyone involved. The reason he gives for this is the evident truth that pursuing such truth "is a long, arduous, and difficult enterprise"—one that is seldom completely reached solely by pleasant conversation alone. (158)

Related to any species of mind-independent truth sought to be achieved by members of the same meeting for its own sake, as Adler notes, universal agreement is its chief aim. (159) Again, this observation is simply a commonsense nobrainer. Its truth "goes without saying," as Americans often say—is *a granted assumption* which, given what Adler had recently said in his previous chapter about making our assumptions clear to other people before attempting to engage in a profitable conversation with them, Adler shrewdly expects his readers already somewhat to have forgotten and to agree with him, no questions asked!

Having gotten these assumptions out of the way, Adler then states his next one: "Individuals may engage in conversation after conversation about a certain subject, the truth about which concerns them. Each of these conversations may constitute a progressive stage in their pursuit of truth. The fact that none achieves a state of mutual understanding and complete agreement that is final, conclusive, and incorrigible does not render any of them unprofitable if some advance toward the goal is made." (159)

Having gotten out of the way all these commonsense assumptions (shrewdly calling them "general observations," which he hopes his readers will not notice to be assumptions and will unquestionably accept), Adler concludes his proem to Chapter 12 by saying, "With these *general observations* (*unquestioned assumptions!*) noted and heeded, let us consider how persons engaged in such conversations or discussions should proceed with regard to achieving understanding and agreement, at least pro tem, if not for all time." (159/my parenthetical addition)

Adler's 1 rule for, at least temporarily, achieving a meeting of the minds in all impersonal conversations.

Rule 1:

"Unless you are sure you understand the position the other person is taking," Adler admonishes, "do not disagree—or, for that matter, do not agree—with anyone." While he does not explicitly say so, by the phrase "the position the other person is taking," Adler means, "What the other person thinks, or understands, himself or herself to be saying, or trying to say, in his native language, as a professional or non-professional."

In this rule, he is calling to attention of his readers the distinction between *saying something* and *meaning something*—the fact that sometimes what we say is not what we mean, can in fact be the contrary opposite of what we mean. For example, one person states the action another person has just committed was *brilliant*, but means it was *exceptionally stupid.*

In doing this, Adler is calling attention to his readers that no conversation starts with reasoning. All conversation starts with induction of a common understanding. This induction is immediate, evident, and commonsensical to the participants really involved in the discussion. To anyone to whom it is not immediately evident, that person is not, can never actually be, a member of, participant in, a conversation or discussion. Such a person can never be *on the same page* with other members of a discussion, participants in a meeting; and engage in profitable conversation with them, because he or she does not precisely understand what it is that they are talking about, how they are discussing it, and why they are chiefly doing so.

Precisely because they are not members of the same real genus as are the other people involved, people with no immediate, commonsense understanding of the subject of a discussion, and the chief aim related to which the subject is being discussed, can never enter into it at all, profitably add to it conversationally. For this reason, Aristotle and Saint Thomas Aquinas repeatedly say that the knower and the thing known belong to the same genus. For example, firefighters belong to the same genus (organizational whole) as the subject about which firefighters chiefly talk: fires and how to fight them; and baseball players belong to the same real genus as the subject about which they chiefly talk: the sports activity of baseball, and how to play it. Someone who understands nothing about firefighting and nothing about playing baseball can never profitably enter into discussions with others who do know something about these subjects.

The reason for this is that the only subject about which any and every human being can intelligibly enter into any sort of discussion, conversation—and especially into a profitable one—is about some organizational whole that, partially or completely, they conceptually understand. The only subject human beings are capable of knowing, conceptualizing, or even imagining, is an organizational whole, part of such a whole, or something that is totally simple (has no parts), but is conceived and imagined to be—analogously thought about as if it were—an organizational whole. For example, Almighty God or nothing (thought about as if it were a something, or part of something: like a hole in the roof).

Anyone who thinks I am wrong about making this claim can easily disprove it, or prove its evident truth, by actually trying to conceptualize and imagine some subject I have just said cannot possibly be conceptualized and imagined—defined in terms of its proximate genus and species and imagined as such.

Such being the case, Adler is totally correct to caution his reader never to agree or disagree with what someone else says unless he or she precisely understands what that person is saying. This first rule is an essential, commonsense first principle of any, and all, profitable conversations. For this reason, Adler is totally correct to maintain, "To disagree before you understand is impertinent. To agree, inane." (159)

Consequently, before you agree or disagree with someone about some subject, as Adler recommends, asking him or her something along the lines of "the following question: 'Do I understand you to say that . . . ?'" is eminently prudent, commonsensical, and personally polite. Only after you and the other person have gone back-and-forth about precisely what each of you understands each other to be saying will you, as Adler states, "have the grounds indispensable for intelligent and reasonable disagreement or agreement"—and consequently, for really profitable conversation. (160) While this procedure is time consuming and requires persistence and patience, it is far less time consuming and demanding of patience and persistence than is attempting to engage in a profitable discussion without first following it.

Adler continues:

> Real as opposed to apparent disagreement occurs when two persons, concerned with a certain question to be answered, understand that question in exactly the same way yet give incompatible answers to the question on which their minds meet in mutual understanding.
>
> Apparent as opposed to real disagreement occurs when two persons, concerned with a certain question, do not understand that question in exactly the same way. When their minds have not met in mutual understanding of the question, the incompatible answers they give to it constitute a difference of opinion that is not a genuine dis-agreement, even though it may appear to be such. Real disagreement occurs only when, with their minds meeting in mutual understanding of the question, they then give incompatible answers to it. (160)

Chapter 12: Commonsense Gateways

I disagree! Adler and I are not of a mutual meeting of minds related to the precise point at which real and apparent agreement—an actual, not apparent, meeting of minds—occurs between two human beings. Years ago, I would have agreed with him, just as I had agreed with Étienne Gilson when he had maintained that most philosophical mistakes start from badly framed questions.

What started my disagreement with Gilson and is at the root of my disagreement presently with Adler is that the starting point for agreement involving a real meeting of minds about understanding a subject does not start with a question about the subject. It begins with mutual agreement about the subject about which a question is being asked. Most philosophical mistakes—in fact, all philosophical, scientific, or any other species of conversational mistake, starts with not sharing a common understanding of the subject genus about which two people are talking, conversing—not being on the same page about what is the subject that participants in the discussion are chiefly talking.

Asking questions about a subject when the participants talking do not commonly understand the subject about which they are talking makes no common, or any, sense at all; and can never be profitable. It always tends to cause conversations to go around in circles or off on a tangent.

And this is a more serious mistake than is asking the wrong question. This second mistake leads to conversational circles and tangents of their own unique nature that waste enormous amounts of time. What tends to waste even more time is the fact that participants in a discussion do not first understand that they are not talking about the same subject—not talking about it precisely enough, or talking about it in different ways with different chief aims, or talking about it in the same way with different chief aims. *Such a waste of time can go on for centuries, or longer*!

Like Gilson, Adler is making the mistake of putting the cart before the horse: beginning by starting to correct the second—not the first—mistake most people make when attempting to enter into profitable conversations about anything. In so doing, because they obscure to their readers' understanding The Mother Of All Conversational Mistakes—the MOACM—both give their readers terrible advice about how to ensure they start off engaging in a discussion that will eventually lead to a meeting of minds when it concludes. As Aristotle cautions, small mistakes at the beginning of an investigation quickly tend to multiply as the inquiry proceeds!

Despite making such a mistake, Adler is totally correct to recommend to participants in a discussion that, when two people discover themselves to be in real disagreement about some issue standing in the way of their achieving a meeting minds, each has to adopt "a kind of impartiality with respect to the position taken by the other person." (161) By this, he means each person should attempt "to understand why the other individual holds the view he or she does. Each person should not only be able to state the position of the other in a manner that the other approves, he should be able to state the other person's reasons for holding that view." (161) The evident reason Adler makes this second point is because the only way in which a person can *understand the view* another person is taking is if he or she can understand this other person's reasons for so doing—at least reach a minimum meeting of minds about that understanding.

By sympathetically entertaining a position with which a person does not agree, "at least fully understands the view not agreed to," a person has entered into what Adler calls "a *minimal* meeting of the minds" with another. In so doing, he or she has opened the door to the most complete meeting of the minds humanly possible—which Adler maintains consists in "fully understood agreement." (161/my italics added)

While some, perhaps most, participants in a theoretical or practical discussion related to understanding some real truth, or truths, about some topic might not realize this about such a conversation, Adler maintains it places a "moral obligation" upon those who freely choose to engage in it. (161) In such a situation, he would agree that, if, at some point in the conversation, the participants have a disagreement, they should "be tireless" in their "effort to resolve." He goes so far as to claim we should *never* stop trying to overcome and reach agreement.

> If one conversation does not succeed in doing this, then we should try again at some other time, and we should keep on trying no matter how protracted and difficult the process may be. We should never discontinue the argument as profitless.
>
> To do so is to abandon the pursuit of truth and to treat the matter in question as if it belongs to the sphere of taste. That means treating it as if the disagreement or conflict were between purely personal and unsupportable opinions, purely subjective prejudices or preferences, about which agreement should not be sought and about which one should not engage in argument. (161–162)

While, abstractly considered outside any time or place, in some utopian universe, what Adler says might be true, concretely considered in the real universe all human beings inhabit in which we live our everyday lives, *I disagree*. Such hyperbolic claims are false, defy common sense, tend to be imprudent and quixotic.

And I think one reason Adler made them is precisely because he started his rules about hopefully advancing in, and eventually achieving, a meeting of the minds with some individual or another with step two of commonsense discussion-making, instead of with step one: understanding that the participants involved are talking about the same subject genus, doing it in the same way, with the same chief aim, and so on.

At times, people can enter into a conversation with other people who, at first, appear to be totally rational, appear to have some familiarity with a subject matter and to be able to enter into profitable conversation with others related to it. After a while, however, a person can discover that the person with whom he or she is speaking is an idiot (someone totally lacking common sense)—perhaps even, like Adler is in this instance, an encyclopedia open to the wrong page; or someone mentally unstable, a drug addict, or someone morally depraved. From practical experience, I know that this is the case. I have discovered this on more than one occasion with all such individuals! People tend to be conversationally persuaded by understanding—immediate induction—not by endless argument.

To engage in endless conversations with people who, for example, are theoretically intelligent in one way, but lack practical experience or moral prudence in a subject in another way, is fruitless, hopeless. I have spent decades attempting to do this with university colleagues, inmates, investment bankers, alcoholics, cocaine addicts, and assorted hoodlums, criminals, murderers, mafia characters, thieves, clerics, and politicians. And recommending anyone do so is bad advice, imprudent—even when advised to do so by the great Mortimer J. Adler.

None of these individuals—such as a loan shark to whom he or she owes a *Vig*, or one or another species of fanatic or mentally unstable person, psychopath or sociopath—is going to be persuaded, or emotionally moved in a positive way, by the four recommendations Adler makes below about what a person should say to overcome disagreement with the position taken by another person with whom he or she is having a discussion:

1) "I think you hold that position because you are uninformed about certain facts the reasons that have a critical bearing on it."

2) "I think you hold that position because you are misinformed about matters that are critically relevant."

3) "I think you are sufficiently well informed and have a firm grasp of the evidence and reasons that support your position, but you have drawn the wrong conclusions from your premises because you have made mistakes in reasoning. You have made fallacious inferences."

4) "I think you have made none of the foregoing errors and that you have proceeded by sound reasoning from out of the grounds for the conclusion you have reached, But I also think that you're thinking about the subject is incomplete. You should have gone further than you did and reached

other conclusions that someone alter or qualify the one you did reach." (162)

Had Adler attempted to explain the grounds for his disagreement about paying union dues to my grammar-school, Brooklyn friend *Paulie Walnuts*—who used to collect these monies for the *Longshoreman's Association*—or his friend and elementary and high school associate of mine, *Vinny Ocean*, I doubt he would have gotten to 'recommendation 2' before both of them would have broken his legs, or thrown him down a flight of stairs!

Three rules especially applicable to practical mind-to-mind, two-way, talks.

1) Practical conversations that aim at achieving mind-to-mind, practical agreement before some action can be executed must end sometime!

After my recent critique of Adler's misconceived understanding of the most crucial of all rules for achieving any degree of mind-to-mind, much less total, agreement between or among participants in a conversation, most fitting is that that he address specific rules for practical conversations of such a nature in which, as he states "a decision must be reached for the sake of action"; and where no profitable advance can be made in discussion or action "unless there is a meeting of the minds in understood agreement or understood disagreement." (163)

Unlike theoretical conversations (which Adler appears to continue mistakenly to maintain—simply because they pursue truth—can be interminable in this or that actual situation), Adler states that, due to the nature of the practical urgency surrounding practical discussions to solve practical problems, such discussions cannot be unending. In some cases—such as "whatever benefit they confer upon future attempts to solve similar problems," he says discussions might have to be put to an end by taking "a majority vote, accompanied by the upholding and dissenting views concerning the decision laid down." (163)

2) A need exists to recognize that thinking and talking about practical problems can and should occur at three different levels:

A highest one that is furthest removed from final, practical decision-making and subsequent action.

Adler states that this level is concerned with universal principles that apply to the problem being considered in its respectively applicable and really possible, realizable situations and times of execution.

On the second level—nearer to final, practical decision-making and subsequent action–exist "general rules or policies that represent the application of universal principles to different sets of contingent circumstances varying with time and place." (163)

On this and third the next level, at which a decision will finally be made for some action to be implemented or not implemented, Adler states that reasonable people may disagree and, for one reason or another, their disagreement might be incapable of being resolved. (163–164)

3) At this point, Adler's Rule Three kicks in. If the above problem on Level Two or Three ever happens, Adler recommends participants in the discussion should never make the mistake of thinking that, because appearances at the time suggests to them that they will never be able to reach a meeting-of-minds about the general rules or policies they need to adapt and apply to some particular case, they should abandon any further attempts to reach mutual agreement about common principles. These should just be dismissed, and action should be taken anyway.

Because the reasonableness of their action was predicated upon their common agreement about the universal truth and efficacy of the principles they were using, Adler claims that abandoning this common agreement and these principles and acting without these controlling causes would not be prudent. They should not think doing so will have no practical effect, or be reasonable.

Before finally acting, they should rethink and understand the precise nature of the disagreement that is precluding their ability to execute action as a rational, organizational whole: as precisely as possible understand the nature of their disagreement, rethink their principles, and try to reach a common agreement that will make these suitable relative to the situation at hand.

Four final, cautionary, remarks about moving beyond resolving understood disagreement to achieving understood agreement in all species of impersonal conversations.

Since achieving understood agreement is a greater and more efficacious good than achieving understood disagreement, Adler concludes examination about how to achieve total agreement in all species of impersonal conversations by adding four, final, cautionary remarks:

1) Because we human beings are, by nature, rational, through laziness or excessive skepticism about the nature of some real good we are pursuing and wish to obtain, we should never be deterred from following sound rules or recommendations for making our conversations or discussions as perfect as they can really be.

2) At the same time, because we are emotional and intellectual beings with minds that passions and other human failings sometimes obscure, we have to be satisfied if

Chapter 12: Commonsense Gateways

we never reach actual perfection in this or that conversation "and not inordinately seek its complete realization, at least not at any given time or place." (166)

3) If a discussion in which someone has been engaged reaches an impasse that he or she cannot resolve at some particular time or place, another time or place in the future might arise in which he or she might be able to revisit it and make progress related to it.

From personal experience, I can attest to the commonsense wisdom of this cautionary remark of Adler. Having reached the age of 75, after many decades reflecting upon and discussing with students and colleagues issues that had puzzled me for decades, within the past few years I have made exceptional progress beyond my wildest expectations in achieving improved understanding of, and even resolving, many of them.

4) "Finally," Adler commonsensically cautions his readers that, while they might never have thought this to be the case, "good conversation calls for an exercise of moral virtue. It requires the fortitude needed to take pains necessary to make it good. It requires the temperance needed for a moderation of one's passions. Above all, it requires the justice needed to give the other person his due." (166)

And, over and above all these, Adler should have added that good conversation can fulfill none of these requirements without its participants possessing the prudence and common sense to know: 1) that these are all necessary conditions for executing really profitable, pleasurable, and effective discussions and 2) precisely when, where, and how they should be realized! Do not, like a young friend of mine once did, try to strike up a conversation with men sitting outside an Italian Social Club in Bensonhurst, Brooklyn by asking whether or not you can take their photo!

—CHAPTER THIRTEEN—

Lesson 13—Commonsense Advice for Understanding How to Succeed at the 3 Species of Teaching and Learning

The three kinds of teaching and learning.

Mortimer Adler begins his Chapter 13 by distinguishing among three kinds of teaching and learning:

1) Didactic, which he calls *teaching by telling*. This involves one-way teaching and learning that best relates to instructing someone who tends to have close-to-no understanding, commonsense awareness/common wisdom of a subject he or she is about to learn.

Adler maintains that "acquisition of organized knowledge" in the basics—that is, in the essential, commonsense principles, understanding, and wisdom related to some subject genus—is the species of learning for which didactic teaching is best suited. Its method essentially involves one-way teaching *through different species of telling*, including lectures and textbooks. (167)

While Adler does not state so specifically, this is the form of teaching essential to training infants and novices in the essential commonsense principles of understanding and wisdom—understanding what everyone who knows anything about something understands about it—which the more highly developed forms of adolescent and adult learning essentially require. Such being the case, common, common sense indicates that application of this method of instruction for advanced students—students who have some commonsense understanding of the subject genus in which they seek to be instructed in a further, advanced, way—is imprudent, makes no common sense.

Advanced students reasonably interpret such instructors to be insulting them—treating them like children, or people with no commonsense understanding of what they are learning. Good reason exists for this method of instruction to bore them and for them to consider their instructor not to know what he or she is doing, to be somewhat incompetent, lacking in common sense.

2) Socratic, which Adler asserts is best suited for instructing relatively small groups of students in two-way question and answer discussion during which answers are often debated among students who have some prior familiarity with a subject area—similar to the species of conversations in which Socrates had engaged in the Agora in Ancient Athens.

Because this second, and the third, form of learning essentially involve different ways of applying commonsense first principles of understanding (widely possessed species of commonsense wisdom) to develop qualitatively advanced, improved, more perfect, and not widely, or commonly, possessed understanding—that is, to inculcate somewhat uncommon and more perfect habits of commonsense understanding and wisdom (psychological intellectual and moral virtues: uncommon, common sense in habitual intellectual and ethical perfection in judgment, choice, and action) related to diverse and multiple species of things already understood, Adler states that this method of teaching, and not didactic, "facilitates the kind of learning that is an enlargement of the understanding of basic ideas and values." (168) That is, it helps quantitatively and qualitatively to lengthen, broaden, and deepen in strength and intensity of perfection of having some commonsense understanding that a person already possesses of a subject genus and its contents. Simply put in the way many people would express this today, it helps a person master the basics, mechanics, of a field of learning, or of doing or making something, with which a person is already somewhat familiar.

That being the case, *since it is an essential gateway* to all genera and species of higher learning and to uncommon, common sense in all its genera and species, Adler maintains that the Socratic method of learning is the qualitatively most suitable one through which most students first, and should, tend to advance and acquire uncommon, commonsense mastery of the gateway—liberal arts—communication "skills of reading and writing, of speaking and listening, and observing calculating, measuring and estimating." (167) Being more advanced and presupposing the basics, the didactic method of teaching is poorly suited to inculcate these. Attempting to use it to do so is like a carpenter attempting effectively to drill something with a hammer.

The just-mentioned liberal arts communication skills are the exact ones essentially needed to secure the qualitatively highest species of human communication skills and qualitatively highest and most uncommon forms of common sense, and commonsense wisdom: science and perfection in human science/philosophy related to physical, mathematical, and metaphysical wisdom and moral and political prudence.

Liberal arts communication skills exist in-between basic training in commonsense principles that are the essential enabling means required to be applied to diverse subjects of study for someone to achieve more advanced learning and teaching through specialized coaching. This is the species of instruction in which contemporary students tend to engage at the graduate level in a university or in post-graduate studies. It tends to involve coaching by a grand master of a subject area, or an executive coach working in a supervisory, executive-consultant manner with top professionals within an area of specialization—such as highest-level corporate executives. For this reason, Adler states, "the skills of reading and writing, of speaking and listening, and observing, calculating, measuring, and estimating, cannot be inculcated by means of didactic instruction." (167) For the same reason, neither can highly-advanced and specialized executive-level training.

3) Coaching, a species of supervisory teaching and learning analogous to athletic coaching in which skilled habits are developed through practice under observation by "a coach who corrects wrong moves and requires the right ones to be made." (167)

Because, in a preliminary form, instruction through coaching and Socratic method have totally disappeared from elementary and high school liberal arts instruction nationally and internationally, Adler maintains, "Their absence leaves a large and deplorable gap in the development of the growing mind. From long experience with it, I also know that the seminar kind of teaching and learning makes the most fruitful contribution to the continued growth of the mature mind." (168)

And the chief reason it does so—which Adler neglects to mention—is precisely because, by communicating qualitatively higher, more perfect ways, and subjects, of learning, teaching communicates highest species of common and uncommon sense and common-and-uncommon, commonsense wisdom—essential elements for leadership in every species, and especially, in its highest, executive form: global leadership of international organizations!

No wonder should exist, then, why, today, throughout the world, nations are scrambling as quickly as possible to institute educational programs in the form of leadership studies and common sense. Nor should any wonder exist why the leaders of such movements are totally incapable of achieving the goals they seek to reach. Their educational institutions are the chief perpetrators of the intellectual and moral diseases they are now seeking to cure. Attempting to have the perpetrators of the disease be chiefly the ones to solve it so makes no common sense!

At the time Adler had written his monograph *How to Speak. How to Listen*, he had been conducting Socratic seminars for sixty years. Long experience using this teaching method with high school and college students—and with adults who had participated in his Aspen Executive Seminars—had convinced him that seminar teaching using this method, not what he called "the German one"—*by which he had meant the Enlightenment method of teaching*—belongs in high schools and colleges, and is suitable for life-long learning by adults.

I concur!

Chapter 13: Commonsense Advice

Some suggestions and recommendations Adler makes about how to moderate and participate in a Socratic seminar

In the remainder of his chapter, Adler attempts to distill and formulate from his lengthy seminar teaching experiences, under widely different circumstances with widely different groups, some suggestions and recommendations about precisely how to conduct them. In addition to these formulations, he states, "All the rules and recommendations set forth in the two preceding chapters, intended to provide guidance for making conversations of every sort more profitable and pleasurable, apply, of course, to the kind of conversation that takes place in a seminar. Seminar discussion is simply that special kind of conversation or two-way talk in which a moderator, or sometimes a pair of moderators, exercises some control over the course of the conversation and the direction it takes from beginning to end." (171–172) Beyond this, Adler remarks that the recommendations or rules he will add mainly concern helping readers understand the role moderators should play in conducting seminars and the way participants should try to respond the moderators so that both might "make the seminars fruitful." (172)

He starts to do this in a positive way by remarking that the goal of such learning should ideally be "discussable subject matter" suitable to the Seminar's two-way nature:

"basic ideas, issues, or values proposed by the moderator either on the basis of reading done or without such reading." (172–173) In other words, the subject matter should be great ideas—ideas that have some uncommon, commonsense theoretical or practical weight, *heft*, to them, which can provoke pleasurable and profitable discussion about the participants.

To guarantee this happens, based upon his prior experience conducting them, Adler asserts that three other requirements exist:

1) "At least an hour and a half, more often two hours or more" for them to last. (173)

2) A suitable seminar room space and seminar furniture—by which he means the kind of room in which something like "a large hexagonal table" can easily fit, "around which the participants sit, able to face one another as they talk." (173) To this he should have added: comfortable chairs, suitable air-conditioning or heating (as the season might demand); suitable acoustics; pens and notepads; name tags; location of the room in a building with lunch or dinner provided within it or close by; as well as bottled water and availability of other refreshments in the form of coffee, tea, snacks easily accessible during short breaks; plus a general meeting venue easily accessible by readily available transportation means.

3) All participants, including the moderator, should possess "the virtue of the docility." (173)

The moderator's main tasks

According to Adler, "The task of the moderator is threefold: 1) to ask a series of questions that control the discussion and give it direction; 2) to examine the answers by trying to evoke the reasons for them or the implications they have; and 3) to engage the participants in two-way talk with one another when the views they have advanced appear to be in conflict." (174) In a nutshell, his or her job is to guarantee that, in a way as suitable as possible to its conversational nature (including its being clearly audible), the seminar begins, continues, and concludes on time and profitably and pleasurably for all the participants involved in it. To achieve this end, common sense dictates that the moderator be well familiar with the participants and will have ensured that all of them have well understood before coming to the meeting all the rules and regulations about profitable and pleasurable two-way talk that Adler has articulated in his monograph *How to Speak. How to Listen.*

In addition, Adler should have added that the moderator should know the minimum and maximum number of participants invited to this meeting. Given its nature of the way Adler has described it, based upon lengthy experience I have had organizing such meetings, the minimum number should be fifteen and the maximum twenty-five.

As Adler's rightly observes, at the meeting, a moderator's most important obligation and the one most difficult to discharge well is to "be as active in listening as in questioning," especially in relation to tasks two and three given above. This requires energetic, often exhausting, effort on the moderator's part in relation to both these activities.

This job is even worse when the moderator is also the organizer of the meeting and has to account for selecting the meeting site; helping participants make reservations for local room, board, and transportation—not to mention such issues as insurance coverage, special dietary and medical issues related to this or that participant, and what to do and where to go if someone becomes sick or hurt.

—CHAPTER FOURTEEN—

Lesson 14—The Crucial Importance of Two-Way Conversation for Human Happiness

Two-way talk as the most characteristically human thing human beings do.

Mortimer J. Adler begins the concluding Chapter 14 of his masterful monograph *How to Speak. How to Listen* by making one more claim with which, at least partly, I disagree: "Of all the things that human beings do, conversing with one another is the most characteristically human. It may be in the long run the only human activity the performance of which will ultimately preserve the radical distinction between humans and brutes and between men and machines." (181)

I agree with Saint Thomas Aquinas that human nature is specified chiefly through activities of the faculty of reason existing in the animal part of the human soul; and that this mode of specification is essentially responsible in human beings for our possessing self-consciously, self-determined free choice and common sense. (*Summa theologiae*, 1, q. 77, a. 3, *respondeo*). These are activities we essentially cause through a self-understood, co-operative free choice of human intellect, will, and emotions that terminate in uniquely wise or foolish human acts—acts that make some, or no, common sense to us in this or that individual situation.

Contrary to human beings, according to its own natural abilities and left to its own resources, maturely developed, brute, animal intelligence appears to be totally practical, productive, and wild—completely without common sense of any extremes of kind or quality. Through its own species, endowed and innate abilities and resources, brute animal nature *evinces to me* no abstractly observational and contemplative abilities emotionally to abstract from and—through some qualitatively higher internal command and control faculty—be able to initiate some cause of self-control and self-restraint that prevents it from immediately and emotionally jumping to conclusions and executing choices that are, like those of human beings, commonsensically brilliant or dumb. It appears to have no internal faculty, other than brute animal instinct, whereby it exercises, or is even capable of exercising, emotional self-restraint and emotionally and abstractly observational and contemplative common sense.

Aquinas had maintained that both human beings and brute animals are innately born with some species and qualitative amount, intensity, of common sense, or commonsense wisdom and prudence, *analogously so-called*. And he located both within the soul, within an animal sense faculty where both are specified. In other, higher species of animals apart from human, he called this sense faculty that of natural estimation (*aestimativa naturalis*—meaning something like what, today, we might call *estimative intelligence*—to which, presently, we generally refer as animal *instinct*). In human beings, following the lead of the Islamic scholar Avicenna (Ibn Sina; b. 980/d. 1037), Thomas referred to this as *cogitative*, or *particular, reason*. (*Summa theologiae*, 1, q. 78, a. 4, *respondeo*)

He describes this as a knowing faculty within animals necessary for them to have in order to move toward or away from some external stimulus (formal object); and not simply because—like every external sense power naturally inclines to do—what it perceives actively stimulates the faculty and causes an animal immediately to perceive this stimulus as pleasant or painful: such as the external sense faculty of hearing perceives some sound, within a specific, qualitative range of loudness and softness, pleasing or painful and immediately moves an animal toward or away from it. He depicts this as an external stimulus naturally inimical (*inimicum naturae*, naturally unfriendly), an enemy to its natural needs, or self-preservation, as this or that species of animal. (*Summa theologiae*, 1, q. 78, a. 4, *respondeo*)

Saint Thomas, then, gives two examples of such stimuli, and the chief reason they cause different animals to react the way they do to it.

The first is that of a lamb which, when it sees a wolf coming toward it, flees from the wolf. According to Aquinas, the lamb runs away from the wolf because it perceives the wolf to be a natural enemy (*inimicum naturae*). He states it does not do so because it finds the wolf's color or figure unpleasant, painful. (*The sheep is not an anti-wolf bigot or racist.*) It does so because it possesses an internal, *natural-law related*, sense faculty of self-preservation and healthy animal development that enables it to perceive things necessary for it to recognize as helpful or harmful to it as the species of animal it is.

The second example Thomas gives is of a bird that collects straw. He says it does not do so because it finds straw *pleasing* to it. It does so because it perceives straw as *useful* for a building its nest. Like the wolf, it possesses an internal, *natural-law related*, sense faculty that enables it to perceive incoming stimuli that no exterior sense faculty is capable of apprehending. (*Summa theologiae*, 1, q. 78, a. 4, *respondeo*)

In relation to these two examples, Thomas is evidently behaving like an impartial social scientist and commonsense, behavioral organizational psychologist. Unlike the wolf and the bird, he is not immediately and emotionally jumping to a conclusion that what each is doing is the commonsense choice to make within the species-specific, self-preservation situation each perceives itself to be existing at this time or place.

Aquinas is doing so as a qualitatively more perfect member of the animal species than is either the wolf or the bird—as an impartial, observational social scientist and behavioral psychologist. Anyone familiar with the classical emotional psychology of Plato and Aristotle can easily recognize that Saint Thomas is attributing to species of higher animal life—animals that possess faculties of sight, hearing, imagination, and sense memory—the internal sense faculties Platonic scholars generally translate as *higher and lower emotions* and Aristotelian/Thomistic scholars tend respectively to name the *irascible and concupiscible appetites*.

The higher/irascible emotional faculty naturally inclines to take orders/directions from the human intellect and act *as a commonsense command and control principle* communicating—in the form of immediate, knee-jerk, commonsense choices to make in particular situations—to the lower, concupiscible appetite. This higher psychological faculty contains contrary opposite passions (motivating principles/causes) related to external stimuli perceived as being useful or useless, safe or dangerous for human beings. All these motivating causes activate species of internal passions of hope and fear unobservable to the lower, pleasure-seeking/pain-avoiding concupiscible appetite.

For an animal to be able to survive and develop for any extent of time, this psychological faculty has to communicate these *useful, species-specific, commonsensical* command and control directives to the lower emotional faculty precisely because, in and of itself, this lower faculty has *no rational* common sense akin to animal instinct. It is incapable of perceiving sensible reality in the form of commonsense utility and safety. *Utility- and safety-wise, it is just plain damn rationally dumb!* All it is able to do is to report the way it is being stimulated as being pleasant or not pleasant to it according to its own limited abilities. It has no ability on its own to recognize or report sensory stimuli that are real signs of real utility or lack of utility, safety or danger to an animal as the species of animal it is.

According to Thomas Aquinas, human rationality is specifically a human perfection because it makes human beings the most perfect of animals in the real species animal! And the reason he maintains this is because, as he states quite clearly and emphatically, not just any cause is the principle of specific diversification within a real genus. More perfect possession of a generic form is the chief cause of specific diversification within a genus. And most perfect possession of a generic form distinctive of the human animal is precisely due to our being *animally, not angelically or divinely, rational.*

Human rationality chiefly consists in human beings having uncommon commonsense animal understanding: animal wisdom and prudence—not in our having the lowest form of angelic understanding or any form of angelic wisdom, or the wisdom of Almighty God. Our uncommon commonsense animal understanding—not our ability to reason or our ability think as a bodily-separated mind—makes us the highest and smartest of animals. Being the qualitatively lowest and dumbest of angels, or being God, does not specifically make us who and what we are.

All this being said and adequately understood, my chief area of disagreement with Adler above is not about what I think he actually *meant*. It is with the way he chose to say what I think he really meant, what many readers might mistakenly conclude he was actually saying, or mainly saying.

If, in stating that "conversing with one another"—by which he indicates he clearly meant two-way talk between human beings that "seeks to achieve a meeting of minds, a sharing of understandings and thoughts, of feelings and wishes" (an identity of personal psychologies as if they were possessed by one in the same mind)—"is the most characteristically human," he meant that this is the activity in which most human beings most frequently engage on a daily basis, I totally agree with him! (And this is actually what I think he did mean!) Even as individuals, we tend to talk to ourselves in this way on a daily basis, as if we were talking to someone else to make something intelligible to ourselves.

And if he meant that, long-term, this sort of two-way talk might be the only means we human beings can use that ultimately will enable us to preserve the radical distinction between the qualitatively higher and more perfect, uncommon commonsense animal wisdom of human beings from that of lower species of animal life and the non-existent common sense, or prudence, sometimes mistakenly and analogously attributed to machines, I also tend totally to agree with him. And, again, *this is what I think he actually did mean.*

My criticism of him, once again, is not about what he said as I understood him to mean it. *It is about the way he said it*; and precisely because the way he said what he meant is likely to incline some readers to misinterpret what he meant and to be unable fully, or in no way, to profit from it if properly understood.

Moving on to the remainder of Adler's Chapter 14, to help explain why two-way talk might be the only means we human beings will be able ultimately to use to preserve the real distinction between our specifically different uncommon common sense wisdom from the commonsense wisdom of other animals and the non-existent, *analogously and falsely said wisdom if actually attributed to machines*, Adler spends several pages discussing the difference between human communication by means of signs as these are employed by other animals. Because he devotes a lengthy discussion to this issue in "Appendix 1" of his "Epilogue," considered in itself, the only mention he makes of it in this chapter is one paragraph in which he states:

> This century (meaning the twentieth/my addition) has also seen the production of computer-like machines

that are eulogistically referred to as artificial-intelligence machines. Their inventors and exponents claim for them that they will soon be able to do everything that the mind enables human beings to do. The claim goes further than predicting that these machines will someday stimulate characteristically human performances of all sorts, such as reading and writing, listening and speaking, as well as calculating, problem-solving, and decision making. It predicts that the machine performance of these operations will be indistinguishable from the human performance of them. (182)

Nowhere in his Chapter 14 does Adler go into a criticism of this claim and of 'artificial intelligence' (*AI*). He considers them too hyperbolic and essentially unrelated to the chief aims of his text as a whole and to the content of Chapter 14 to do so. He leaves them for his appendix to examine and refute; and, even in relation to that discussion, he states, "I think I have demonstrated that machines will never—never in the whole of future time—be able to engage in anything like human conversation. Instead of repeating the argument here, I refer the reader to Appendix 1 for that demonstration." (184—185)

Even though the subject of *AI* is quite important to consider in many respects today, because it is not crucially germane to the chief goals I am pursuing in my monograph, or even those Adler was considering within his, and because

Adler did not think it especially essential to his, I will not go into it in depth in my monograph. Suffice it for me to say that *AI* machines are not, and never will be, alive; and they communicate by means of non-living, electrical signals, not by living, psychological signs. *They have no soul, and never will have—even if metaphysically-challenged, Silicon Valley, fundamentalist, religious gurus and media elites think they will someday be able to upload their souls into computers!* For this reason, strictly speaking, *AI* machines have no common sense, and never will have, human or otherwise. The closest they will have to this is some form of prudence programmed by human beings into their electronically commanded and controlled reactions to situations—such as those as an airplane's automatic pilot and submarine radar.

Turning to non-human animal communication, Adler states:

> Shared thoughts and feelings, understood agreements and disagreements, make humans the only animals that genuinely *commune* with one another. Even though they signal their emotions or impulses to one another, other animals remain shut out from each other. They do not commune with one another when they communicate. The human community would not exist without such communion, which would not exist without human conversation. (182)

Chapter 14: The Crucial Importance of 2-Way Conversation

I disagree. Non-human animals genuinely *commune* with one another. They are not machines. But they commune in a non-human way, somewhat like slaves were conceived to do by some ancient Greeks. And they are not totally shut off from each other or from human beings. Human beings often communicate with animals as pets, sometimes as beasts of burden—which might also be a pet (like some farm animals), and in many other ways. Some human beings often communicate and commune with their pets better than they communicate and commune with other human beings; but they can never do so as two-way talk partners existing within a liberal arts or scientific educational commune, or community considered in itself, or considered as an enabling means for becoming self-providers and building an educational culture.

While, in this chapter, Adler more fully considers possible development of *AI* machines, he does so in relationship to a counter-prediction of their success made by the "famous French philosopher René Descartes." (182) And he does so by: 1) contrasting the way in which brute animals (whom Descartes had essentially reduced to the status of machines, robots) use signs; 2) focusing on the difference between the way in which human beings conversationally communicate emotions and impulses to each other by means of signs, with human beings doing this chiefly through use of concepts and other animals doing this chiefly through perceptions and images. (182–184)

Related to this discussion, Adler concentrates his attention on Descartes's observation that, because they lack the powers of "intellect, reason, and conceptual thought," no brute animals could ever be able to: 1) "use speech or other signs as we do when placing our thought on record for the benefit of others"; or 2) be able to "arrange his speech in various ways, in order to reply appropriately to everything that may be said in its presence, as even the lowest type of man can do." (184)

On the basis of his study of what Descartes had said, Adler had understood him to stress that, given the close-to-infinite flexibility of human language, the different nuances of meaning its words can signify at this or that time in this or that situation (such as, recently predicting a U.S. presidential election) had caused him to: 1) conclude that "programmed machinery will never be able to simulate" the unpredictability human conversation can take; and 2) predict that "the wizardry of man's technology will never be able to shape unthinking matter into truly thinking machines." (184)

All these points having, hopefully, persuaded his readers that: 1) only human minds, and intellects, with the power of conceptual thought can engage in conversation with one another; and 2) two-way talk that ends in a meeting of minds will always remain the irrefutable evidence that man is radically different in kind from brute animals and *AI* machines, Adler finally feels comfortable enough taking up the main topic of his Chapter 14, for which he thinks the prior discussion has essentially paved the way.

The great significance for achievable human communion (getting along with other people) two-way conversation has for private life.

Adler starts his analysis of the great significance of two-way conversation for human life by doing three things. First, while he does not explicitly verbally express what he is doing in the following way, he essentially unites this significance to the *metaphysical principle of unity*. He says that two-way conversation is significant precisely because of the achievable *union* in the form of *communion* between two or more human beings it has the power to cause.

Evident to me is that Adler begins his analysis in this way precisely because he has some understanding of the essential connection between unity considered as a metaphysical principle and enrichment or impoverishment of human life, and all forms of existence, in particular and general. Hence, he immediately emphasizes a crucial *unifying property* two-way conversation causes in particular: "It *unites* members of a family—husband and wives, parents and children. It is the spiritual parallel of the physical union by which lovers try to become *one*." (185/my italics added) That is, unity can be analogously predicated, said of, physical and spiritual subjects—such as lovers—to signify meanings that are somewhat the same and somewhat different.

Using the analogy of the metaphysical principle of unity, note how intensely strong, when it is achieved, Adler considers two-way conversation to be. Not only does it *unite* the relationally-closest of human beings (family members) so as to enable them *to get along with each other*. It does so in the closest way—psychologically, as *one soul*, analogous to the physical *union* of lovers attempting to become *one living body*. In doing this, Adler assumes the existence of some sort of spiritual reality, that it is superior in qualitative greatness, intensity, unifying bond, strength, to physical reality; and, in so doing, that it is psychological—that its psychological, metaphysical/spiritual, quality makes it great *as a unifying cause*, even greater in kind than a living, material cause effecting material greatness!

Immediately after doing this, however, he qualifies this *unifying power* of human conversation by stressing its potential to fail, and the consequences to human life when this happens. Hence, his second point: "Please note that I did not say 'the communion achieved by the conversation.' I said rather "the communion that *can be achieved*." (185)

And, his third point, which he immediately adds, is that:

> Human beings sometimes—in fact, too often—fail to achieve it by their failures as speakers and listeners in two-way talk, especially in personal heart-to-heart talk.

When they fail, the sexual bond that unites husband and wife, unaccompanied by spiritual communion, usually fails to preserve their marriage. Divorce as frequently results from failure to communicate intimately and heart-to-heart talks as it does from the weakening of sexual attraction.

One kind of intercourse without the other kind of interchange between spouses is less than completely human. Nor is it enough for them to be able to converse intimately about personal or emotional matters. (185) A marriage not enlivened by sustain conversations about a wide variety of subjects, from which there results a meeting of the minds in understood agreements or disagreements, has vacuums or voids in it that need to be filled to give it vitality. (185–186)

Having concluded making these sober, sage, and uncommon commonsensical, metaphysical points, Adler analogously transposes and expands them to the other most private and personal genus of human relations—that between parents and children. He speaks about "the so-called generation gap" and the "estrangement" caused by lack of effective and profitable two-way talk between parents and children it can cause, saying, "The broken home, the split-up family, whether it occurs through the divorce of husband and wife on estrangement between parents and children, testifies that conversation has completely deteriorated, if it ever truly existed." (186)

Having extended the *analogy of unity* beyond husband and wife to parents and children, he then further extends it, and transposes it, into genera beyond the *bonds* of family life, friends, and lovers—to public life in all its different genera. And, before doing this, he makes evident the influence Aristotle has had upon everything he has said up to this point in this part of his chapter:

> Friendship and love endure as a genuine communion only as long as they are both able, and also persist in their effort, to engage in profitable and pleasurable conversation with one another.
>
> Aristotle defined the highest form of friendship as that which involves the communion of persons of like character, two persons alike in their moral virtue. I would add that it also involves the existence of intellectual communion through conversation that achieves a meeting of minds. (186)

And I would add, beyond Adler, this also involves intellectual communion in a meeting of personal psychologies that essentially shares a common understanding of *common sense—what goes without saying and needs not be said because it is taken for granted, already understood to be evident, between them.*

Beyond this, before he passes over into discussion of two-way conversation in public life, I would add that some concluding remarks Adler makes related to the closest forms of private and personal, heart-to-heart conversation all of us should take as most sage, commonsense, observations as social lockdowns related to conversations between and among human beings become increasingly popular in our contemporary age:

> However effective human conversation may be in achieving the communion of hearts and minds, it can never be so perfect that the solitariness of the individual is ever completely overcome. All of us are somewhat imprisoned in the solitude of our own minds and hearts. There always remain thoughts and feelings that we never do succeed in sharing and completely with others.
>
> We may never be as completely locked out from one another as other animals are, but we also never fully overcome the barriers to communion. We never achieve on earth that perfection of community which is attributed by theologians to the communion of saints in the company angels in heaven. (186–187)

That being so, common sense dictates we should never expect utopia, in any species, on Earth in private or public life.

The achievable profit and pleasure effective two-way conversations can make to business dealings with each other.

Adler starts his examination of the achievable, profitable and pleasurable benefits effective two-way conversation can contribute to business activities by observing that few business organizations are actually conducted without excessive numbers of excessively frequent, overly long conferences that waste too much valuable time, energy, talent, and money "when they are measured by the benefits they confer." (187)

The three chief reasons he maintains for this happening are commonsensical to pretty much any corporate executive—poor communication, planning, and execution. Also commonsensical to such people is that the first tends to be main cause of the second and third. For example, because business personnel involved in organizing conferences often tend not to consider beforehand precisely what should be discussed, the day of a conference the participants tend not to know precisely how to talk to each other and to achieve maximum benefits from their conversation. Consequently, Adler states:

> The agenda laid down are often poorly constructed. The discussion often wanders from the point at issue. The interchanges often exhibit inattention and failure to

listen well enough to produce relevant responses to what others have said, and what others have said may often be too poorly expressed to elicit or deserve careful listening. This discussion too often fails to move on from point to point, making progress toward the decision aimed at. (187)

In other words, the participants often do not understand precisely: 1) where they chiefly want to go; 2) how most effectively they can get there; and 3) how most effectively they can talk to each other about most profitably getting where they mainly want to go without wasting a lot of time, talent, energy, and money. They do not understand the commonsense *KISS* principle when applied to business conferences.

As Aristotle cautioned centuries ago, the net result of not starting off your investigation correctly—by which he meant *prudently, commonsensically*—is that you tend to get sidetracked down the road, running into increasingly greater numbers of detours and rabbit holes until you finally wind up running around in circles like a dog chasing its own tail, or hitting a brick wall. First principles of business are not logical abstractions. They are practical, commonsense principles of organizational self-understanding and foresight precisely and essentially related to organizationally doable and undoable deeds!: 1) what you chiefly understand yourself organizationally to be; 2) what you chiefly want to do organizationally in the long term and the here and now; and 3) whether this or that action you propose to execute organizationally at this or that time is something really doable where you are organizationally at this time, in this situation with the team and other resources you have available to you now and in the long term.

In his Chapter 14, Adler gives examples of the application of such prudential, commonsense principles I have just mentioned to different organizations, including a job offering once made to him from R. H. Macy and Company for him to become a chief conference planner for them. (188-190) Since these principles apply to all genera of cultural organizations—such as medical, educational, athletic, religious, and so on—no need exists to go into detail related to them all. Just as the principles of two-way, heart-to-heart conversation are analogously transferable to all genera of private, or personal, talks and life so, also, are the principles of two-way, professional conversation transferable to all genera of professional life. Not only do they make such life profitable in general, one of their great profits is that the discussions involved in them become increasingly more pleasurable, less boring and less physically and psychologically exhausting as they become more commonsensical!

Chapter 14: The Crucial Importance of 2-Way Conversation

The achievable profit and pleasure that effective two-way conversation can make to local, national, and international political life.

Because of a chief interest Mortimer Adler and some of his colleagues had had immediately after the international devastations of World War II, short-and long-term, of using two-way conversations as a political means to secure political peace in all its species—local, national, and international—he focuses attention in the rest of his concluding chapter of *How to Speak. How to Listen* on precisely this topic. In so doing, Adler makes commonsensically intelligible to anyone interested in maximizing the extent and quality of peace and prosperity in human life precisely why this topic is crucial to consider. No other area of practical human communication has as great, wide, and deep an influence on leading an enriching or impoverishing individual and/or social human life than does politics—especially international politics!

To drive home with special gusto this last point, Adler starts to give his readers a history and ethics lesson about the importance of political discussions in republican government. Given the widespread, impoverished, contemporary local, national, and international condition of politics, the importance of such a lesson seems hardly necessary to give to any commonsensical, contemporary reader. Nonetheless, as usual, what Adler says about these topics tends to be as generally pleasurable as it is profitable.

Just why Adler focuses his attention on two-way conversation in republican government might puzzle some readers, but the chief reason he does so is, once more, a credit to his uncommon common sense. Republican government is the only form of government in which two-way talk can exist in its most complete form. All species of totally despotic, or totalitarian, government politically allow only one form of talk: One-way. *The ruler talks. The ruled shut up, become conversationally isolated, and silently listen*! Under totally despotic forms of rule, all forms of two-way talk tend to be silenced, crushed. This action is an evident sign to anyone with common sense that he or she exists under this kind of rule.

In between this kind of rule and its contrary opposite of perfect republican rule exist extremes of more or less benevolent/malevolent despotic government—oligarchies, generally plutocracies, of one species or another in which only a few, privileged groups of citizens are actually citizens and permitted fully to engage in two-way talk.

For this reason Adler starts his discussion of political speech by saying:

> The public discussion of public issues, by the people at large as well as by those in public office or the candidates for such offices, is the lifeblood of the republic.

A republic in which there is no discussion of the res publica—the public things that we refer to as public affairs—is as much a caricature of its true self as would be a military organization in which there is no armament and no consideration of the strategy and tactics for the use of arms.

It makes no difference whether the republic involves direct participation of all its citizens or is a representative form of government in which both the people as a whole and elected or selected officials participate. The agoras and forums of the republics of antiquity in Greece and Rome testify to the role that public discussion played in their lives. (189)

To emphasize this point, in relation to the great discussions that had existed in the Roman Republic, Adler notes "the republic died when discussion ceased and the Caesars, with their praetorian guards, took over the reins of government." (190) Analogous political deaths that have occurred during the twentieth and twenty-first centuries will likely be ones some contemporary readers will easily be able to draw—especially at this historical moment. Hence, no need exists for me to supply any.

Especially noteworthy related to the crucial nature two-way conversation plays as the lifeblood of a politically free, or republican, people is the attention to which Adler directs his readers to pay to the etymology of the term "parliament" within modern republics: "Modern republics, most of them in the form of representative government, have their parliaments, congresses, diets, or otherwise named legislative assemblies, in place of the agoras and forums of the ancient republics. The word 'parliament' is the most significant of these various names because its etymology signifies that this branch of government involves speech or talk, the kind of speech or talk, of course, that is concerned with res publica"—*by which Adler evidently means two-way talk.* (190)

Consequently, he immediately adds that political protections—like constitutional amendments—of unfettered speech, and unfettered public assembly, for example—are signs of such two-way talk being a republic's lifeblood. Indeed, existence of these constitute real signs that a political society, in any species, is actually free! (190)

However, Adler cautions that no governmental act or constitutional enactment can guarantee the existence of free, political speech. Instead, he maintains that the best guarantee for the existence, and advancement, of political speech consists in "improvement in the quality of the schooling that the people as a whole receive." (191) And this must include, most of all, improvement of citizens "in their ability to speak and listen well enough to engage effectively in two-way talk, as well as an enlargement of their understanding of the basic political ideas and principles that underlie the framework of our government." (191)

To that end, among other things, Adler notes his own work; that of Robert Hutchins in composing the *Great Books of the Western World* and having it carry the title *The Great Conversation*; and the emphasis this entire series had placed upon dialogue, discussion, and the exchange of ideas. (192)

Focusing attention on international politics, Adler states that this is where, "the importance of conversation reaches its maximum." (193) The chief reason he gives for this is: "International wars begin when diplomatic conversations between nations fail. They are presaged by newspaper reports to the effect that 'conversations are deteriorating' or that they 'have broken down.' Then, if the conflict of interest between nations is sufficiently serious, there is nothing left for them to do but fight to secure their national interests." (193)

To support the commonsense truth of this observation Adler cites several thinkers from different times and political persuasions—including Cicero, Machiavelli, Locke, Hamilton, Madison, and Jay—expressing the same sentiment.

From such observations related to securing and maintaining political peace, Adler states he learned two lessons: 1) "Civil government provides the apparatus needed for maintaining conservation or discussion as a way of settling disputes. When the machinery of government operates as it should, it does not allow conversation to deteriorate to the point where individuals or nations must resort to the use of force—the method of brutes in the jungle, not the method of humans in civilized society"; and 2) as the only unit of human community capable of providing the apparatus for maintaining international, and global, peace—ongoing, two-way talk—"local civil peace requires enforceable world civil government." (195)

While maintaining conversation as a two-way method of settling disputes certainly appears to be a necessary condition for so doing, the claim, which Adler appears to be making, that the only way to ensure this happens is for an over-arching civil government to do so appears to me to be a glaringly non-commonsensical and logical *non-sequitur* conclusion on Adler's part.

First of all, endlessly engaging in conversations, even political ones, is not evidently essentially and universally prudent; for example, when one participant in a lengthy political dialogue uses this as a tactic to launch a sneak attack against the other participant. In such a situation, quickly ending dialogue and finding a different, just way of settling disputes, short of all-out war, appears to me to be prudent, commonsensical. Such being the case, Adler's second conclusion does not appear necessarily to follow as a matter of political justice, prudence, or common sense.

While recourse to global government to solve international problems related to global peace might have been the only available option justly, prudently, peacefully, and commonsensically to resolve them short of national or international conflict during Adler's time, this does not necessarily mean that is the case now, or will be even in the future. It could even be the greatest obstacle to it, especially because the best way to weaken power is sometimes widely to distribute it, not to concentrate it in the hands of a central government. *In every case, the answer needed would appear to require prudent, commonsensical, and just government,* whether or not this is, or is not, a world government.

A world, national, or local government led by morally unjust, despotic fools does not appear to be the commonsense, or any, solution to securing global, or any other species of, peace. And, secondly, it appears to be extremely odd and non-commonsensical for Mortimer Adler to have recommended at the conclusion of a book chiefly claiming that two-way talk is the best of all species of *human* conversation.

Human conversation is freely chosen dialogue characteristic of adults and political equals, not despotically demanded one-way speech and silent listening characteristic of adults talking to children, even if these adults might appear to politicians to be behaving like children. No enactment demanded by a civil, political government—even a global one claiming to be republican—trying, always and everywhere, to force unending two-way talk, can guarantee that such a decree is prudent, just, and commonsensical; and that it will necessarily ensure that civil peace will necessarily follow from it.

As Adler repeatedly maintained, advancement of just and prudential, commonsense political speech consists in improvement in the just, prudential, and commonsense quality of the schooling, especially of college and university education, the citizens as a whole and, especially the political leaders, of a political community, receive. (191) This must include, most of all, improvement of citizens and political leaders in their ability justly and prudentially—commonsensically—to speak and listen well enough to engage effectively in two-way talk, dialogue, or one-way lecture, as well as in enlargement of their understanding of the basic political, moral, and metaphysical ideas and principles that underlie the framework of just, prudential, commonsensical government. (192)

To suggest that citizens of the contemporary world, at this time in human history, submit to global governance determined by global political leaders who have been inculcated chiefly and almost totally under the influence of anarchic, nonsensical Western Enlightenment metaphysical and moral principles makes no common sense. And, since it essentially contradicts metaphysical and moral educational principles and decades of criticism Adler had leveled against the metaphysical and moral bankruptcy of Enlightenment colleges and universities and their leaders, concluding the final chapter of his otherwise largely masterful and commonsensical monograph appears to me to defy all forms of common sense, especially that of moral and political prudence. To me, the conclusion he should have reached is something essentially different—about which I will talk in my next, and concluding, chapter.

—CHAPTER FIFTEEN—

Lesson 15—Common sense: The Personal Meeting Point in and through which Providence First Touches an Animal Soul as that of a Human Person

Uniquely human common sense as a participation in Divine Wisdom that specifies an animal soul as essentially rational—The analogy of unity between God and human beings in right reason; providence; wisdom; prudence; common sense; all species of law and virtue, and conscience.

The chief aim of this concluding chapter is to defend and consider some implications for the contemporary world of the following thesis: According to Saint Thomas Aquinas, and in truth, human common sense—as distinct from brute animal common sense, or animal instinct—is the uniquely personal (in the sense of metaphysical and moral) way in which human persons enter into a *meeting of understandings—intellectual communion* and *communication*—with a qualitatively higher-than-human wisdom, *which I call God*. Thomas understood the latter to be Divine Wisdom. Implicit within this thesis is the claim that this unique manner of participating in this communion of wisdom is partially the product of the qualitatively unique human faculty that Aquinas calls *cogitative*, or *particular reason* in which natural law appears chiefly to exist as a concrete commanding principle; and out of which, to some extent, grow to maturity *all* human, natural and acquired habits (*habitus*) and virtues (*virtus*).

While the claims I make above might strike some readers as being exaggerated or, in one way or another, false, I stand by them. In fact, they necessarily flow out of what I have already reported about Saint Thomas's claim that human rationality locates our specific difference in an otherness within the sensitive, or animal, part of the intellectual soul! (*Summa theologiae*, 1, 77, a. 3, respondeo)

By generating the faculty of sensory reasoning, sentient, command-and-control *particular*, or *cogitative*, reason—which Thomas claims corresponds to "instinct" in brute animals (*Summa theologiae*, 1, q. 78, a. 4, respondeo])—Saint Thomas Aquinas maintains God creates in an animal soul a personally-human and immortal, *single rational principle* able to function abstractly in a non-sensory way and concretely in a sensory fashion. When not focusing attention on concrete, individual, animal activity, acting under direction from a human being, the intellectual soul causes its single faculty of reason, or understanding, intellectually to operate in an abstract and syllogistic way. When choosing to reason concretely to move animal faculties, under direction of this same human being, the intellectual soul causes its intellectual and reasoning power to *flow into and become activated within the sensory faculties that exist within the sensitive part of the single human soul.*

Particular, or cogitative, reason: The gateway, through natural law, to providence, human prudence, common sense, and pursuit of human and global perfection specifically and completely entering into the human soul and the physical universe.

Through concrete particular, or cogitative, reason harmoniously working in conjunction with syllogistic reason as two essential parts, or extremes, of one organizationally whole faculty of human reason, or human understanding, one existing person operates as a rational command and control principle moving rational—including freely-chosen wise and prudent, foolish and imprudent, commonsensical and non-commonsensical directions—into the sensitive faculties, appetites, passions, and all their activities. Through these activities moving the human body, in turn, the human person moves human reason as a directing principle into the whole of material creation and causes it to become more or less humanly rational, prudent or imprudent, commonsensical or not commonsensical, wise or foolish. (*Summa theologiae*, 1, 78, a. 4, ad 5)

In so doing, in a sense, through what Mortimer Adler would call *a meeting of minds* (but is better to call *a meeting of understandings*) between Divine Wisdom and animal human nature—the rational part of the soul enables the sensitive part to achieve its animal perfection as an acting, sensitive soul—an acting person. This is something no other animal soul can achieve: being a deliberative, metaphysical and moral (free) animal! In addition, through the sensory part of the soul, the rational part of the soul inclines the whole of the created, material order naturally to gravitate toward (become *docile* toward, not resist) being ruled by metaphysically and morally virtuous or vicious human directive. Simultaneously, it causes the morally and metaphysically virtuous or vicious person—*the person with or without common sense*—to become a first principle, cause, and measure, of healthy, wisely and prudentially guided, social life and personal rule within and throughout the material universe.

In maintaining these teachings, Aquinas is doing nothing more than applying to the relationship between God and human beings what Adler repeatedly refers to as a "meeting of minds," or "agreement of understanding." In addition, these teachings are simply analogous transpositions of teachings of Socrates, Plato, Aristotle, and Plotinus regarding the physical universe being rationally ordered by a Divine Wisdom, or the Good, in the sense of being the Absolutely Perfect in all respects.

How these preceding teachings had entered the behavioral psychology of Mortimer Adler and influenced his personal and professional life.

Recall that, in Chapter 3 of this monograph, I had referred to how Anaxagoras had failed to identify for Socrates a universal, *providentially guiding* cause that unequally relates and harmonizes a multitude of other causes to cooperate to become parts of one, ordered, whole acting unit. In so doing, he could not enable Socrates to understand how and why Socrates was doing what he was doing. As a result of this failure, Socrates had set about his famous *Second Voyage* in philosophy and developed his own famous "Theory of Forms."

In addition, in that Chapter, I had maintained that, in my opinion, for analogous reasons, while a graduate student in the Psychology Department at Columbia University, making a similar discovery, Mortimer Adler had decided he had to launch himself on a second philosophical voyage similar to that of Socrates. Once he had concluded that the behavioral psychologists, philosophers, and social scientists of his time were aping the materialistic and mechanistic scientific positivism prevalent during his time, he became increasingly aware that, in some way, he would have to reinterpret the nature of all three disciplines in relation to: 1) the human mind and 2) the order within things considered as composite wholes generated by harmonious cooperation of parts, and not by a mechanistic external union. That is, to make the universe commonsensically intelligible to himself, at least implicitly, Adler had decided he had to reinterpret his world order providentially.

I have no doubt that Adler's reading of Aristotle as interpreted by Aquinas had psychologically inclined him to set about his own second philosophical voyage. A chief reason it did so was because both Aristotle and Aquinas had located in the act of intellectual understanding the principles of right reason (*recta ratio*, or better, *rectus intellectus* [right understanding]; *orthos logos* in Greek) that *measure all intellectual acts as species of common sense*. In any and every species of human activity, the person with common sense in its most complete form rightly understands the proximate principles (beginning, means, and ends) that cause an organizational whole to exist and behave the way it does. According to Saint Thomas, these principles may be of starting points, conclusions, or of ways of moving from beginning principles to concluding ones (such as aims, ends, goals). He maintains that all principles of right reason everlastingly exist in their highest form in God's understanding as identical with God's *Divine Wisdom*, and substance. (*Summa theologiae*, 1, q. 22, a. 1)

How, according to Aquinas, these principles necessarily enter into the behavioral psychology of every human being, including every philosopher/scientist, and artist.

In addition, in his *Commentary on the Nicomachean Ethics of Aristotle* (bk. 6, lect. 6), Thomas refers to the *faculty of understanding* as containing *the habit of first principles.* Among these he includes all principles used as the highest measures of truth—whether these be known speculatively as immediately evident (*per se nota*, known directly through themselves) or practically or productively from human experience (*per aliud nota*, known indirectly through another). In other words, *this faculty of understanding contains all the commonsense principles of immediate induction and practical or productive experience that all human beings use*—the universal principles of commonsense wisdom and prudence that human beings apply to measure truth and virtue in understanding and in all forms of in-between and subsequent reasoning, art, and science!

The truth of the claims I make above is supported by what Saint Thomas says in his *Commentary on the Posterior Analytics of Aristotle* (bk. 1, lect. 14), where he states that the *conclusions* of scientific demonstration must be from *causes* that are *proper* and *per se*—ones that necessarily inhere in a subject. They cannot be from causes that, like Platonic forms, exist outside and are *remotely related* to the subject genus to which they are being referred. A scientific principle must be one immediately observed as *existing as a proximate cause within a many and said about it as a proximate cause existing within it.* (bk. 1, lect. 20) Hence, in his *Commentary on the Nicomachean Ethics of Aristotle* (bk. 6, lect. 5. n. 1183), Aquinas states that, in inferring the truth of conclusions from principles, we call human wisdom "science"; but when we immediately declare truth regarding principles, we call this wisdom "understanding."

When referred to as governing the entire created order toward harmonious organizational operation, Thomas calls such understanding, *orthos logos, divine wisdom, divine providence, eternal law*, and *prudence*—all of which are ways of talking about God entering into communion with and rightly ordering creation. In Latin, the term 'prudence' (*prudens/phronesis* in Greek) is simply a contraction of the word 'providence' (*providens/foresight* in English). Etymologically, both 'providence' and 'prudence' derive from the same Greek word: *pronoia*—foreknowledge, care, forethought, providence. In his famous *Treatise on Law*, Aquinas refers to all varieties of law as rational *rules and measures* of action, a rational plan of harmoniously regulating organizational operation—"an ordinance of reason toward a common good." (*Summa theologiae*, 1–2, q. 90, a. 4; and 1–2, q. 91, a. 1, respondeo; see also, *Commentary on the Nicomachean Ethics of Aristotle*, bk. 6, lects. 1–4) Considered as such, every species of law is a species of providence.

Hence, within the same treatise, in contrast to the way God governs brute animals by animal *instinct*, he calls 'natural law' the distinctive way in which human beings *as individual members of the human species* participate in God's providence, as rational beings. (*Summa theologiae*, 1–2, q. 91, a. 2) In saying this, Thomas is indicating that, by natural law's prudential rules, God inclines human beings to move toward human happiness in and through our species-specific faculties of particular and intellectual reason, and human virtue.

Since the prudential rules of natural law are an insufficient means to regulate individual human behavior commonsensically through individual prudence to enable an individual human being to become as perfectly happy as he or she can be as a rational animal, Aquinas claims that God supplements his providential guidance of human behavior through the natural human desire to become, as perfectly as humanly possible, disciplined through intellectual and moral virtue—including through self-educational acts of personal conscience. This natural desire inclines us qualitatively to transcend and replace animal instinct with *individual human discipline* (learning, education) *and industriousness* and to become *virtuous self-providers and providers for others!* (*Summa theologiae*, 1, q. 79, arts. 12–13; and 1–2, q. 91, a. 2; and q. 95, a. 1, respondeo)

How prudence causes a virtuous person to have a sound conscience and be psychologically healthy and lack of prudence causes a vicious person to have an unsound conscience and be psychologically unhealthy.

Before discussing the nature of conscience in Part 1, question 79, article 13 of his *Summa theologiae*, in his response to article 12 of the same part (considering the question whether conscience is a power [potency]), Saint Thomas identifies 'conscience' as *an act*—not a power or habit—*essentially connected to an innate habitus and virtus* (what Adler would call *a natural endowment*, and many Americans today would call *a native ability/talent*) of *immediately understanding, inducing,* principles: the habit of *synderesis*. When the human intellect functions theoretically, practically, or productively, this habit moves us toward inducing principles that *command us* to apply principles in an individual situation in such a way that we follow, or stick to, the plan of providence. They move us toward applying them rightly—in accord with right reason, wisdom, prudence, and commonsense—to acting well and away from applying them incorrectly, in an organizationally unhealthy fashion: contrary to right reason, unwisely, imprudently, and not commonsensically.

As organizational beings (living, physical substances), right reason inclines all human beings to move toward operating as perfectly as humanly possible—living as best, perfectly, as we can. The reason it does so is because this is the way eternal reason inclines all organizational beings to operate. *The good is an organizational principle that naturally inclines organizational parts to move toward perfect organizational operation and organizational perfection.* (*Summa theologiae*, 1, q. 5, a. 1, ad 1)

Since good and evil are real qualities that cause realities that can really hurt and help human existence, denying the reality of the real perfections—such as someone being the best of all football players at this or that time—would rationally require a psychologically healthy human being to conclude that no good or bad football player could exist. It would also require a psychologically healthy human being to conclude that: 1) *nothing* can ever really help or hurt a human being; 2) *nothing* really exists that can make human life qualitatively better or worse; 3) *nothing* really exists to hope for or fear; 4) *nothing* really exists that causes cowards and courageous, just and unjust, prudent and imprudent people essentially to exist and to differ; and 5) *nothing* exists that can specifically differentiate people with common sense from people with no common sense, wise men from fools; happiness from misery; truth from falsity; scientists from idiots; and psychologically healthy human beings from psychologically unhealthy ones.

Organizational pursuit of organizational perfection and human pursuit of human perfection are so widespread and evident that attempts to deny their reality tend to verify their existence as commonsensically observable and actually observed truths. Simple observation of everyday human behavior confirms the evident truth of what I am saying. We human beings tend to hate being wrong, making mistakes. Psychologically, we tend to get annoyed, sometimes angry, with ourselves when we do so. At times, this desire to do things perfectly inclines us to experience *angst*, lie to ourselves, pretend that we are perfect, and to dislike people who point out imperfections in our behavior, especially when we are lying to ourselves.

Professionally, psychologically healthy human beings tend to admire excellent performances and talent; and love virtue, hate vice; seek to do business with organizational professionals and avoid doing business with professional incompetents. They do not tend to frequent restaurants that have rotten cooks and waiters, auto mechanics who cannot repair cars. And they tend to criticize organizations that do not operate harmoniously, smoothly, like well-oiled machines. In fact, psychologically undeniable to any psychologically healthy human being is that no totally unharmoniously operated organization could ever be healthy, that anything organizationally unhealthy could be organizationally good; and that something run in a totally unharmonious, unhealthy way could be an organization at all.

I mention all these points about organizations and the way they naturally incline to operate because they are essentially connected to understanding the nature of conscience and the way it operates to measure our common sense—our healthy and unhealthy human behavior, the extent to which we admit or deny ownership of our own acts and are in, or out, of touch with reality. Thomas notes that, etymologically and *properly speaking*, the word 'con-science' imports an understanding of being a knowledge related to something (importat ordinem scientiae ad aliquid), of being a *cum alio scientia* (with other knowledge). Etymologically, Thomas understands this to mean that conscience essentially refers to applied knowledge—application of knowledge through which some act is done (*applicatio autem scientiae ad aliquid fit per aliquem actum*). This is knowledge being used as a means to realize some action as an end or goal. For this reason, Aquinas states that conscience has the following six judicial and legislative, *psychological attributes*: 1) *testificari* (to witness); 2) *ligare* (to bind); 3) *instigare* (to incite); 4) *accusare* (to accuse); 5) *remordere* (to torment); and 6) *reprehendere* (to blame).

In and of themselves, these qualities are not those of *synderesis*. They come into existence when *synderesis* is wisely or unwisely, prudently or imprudently, applied to individual action considered as organizational action in an individual situation. When applied in the form of conscience (which consists in a conflation of *synderesis* and prudence or lack of prudence, common sense or lack of common sense), using these six attributes of a complete judicial, or courtroom, proceeding (consisting of a judge, jury, and prosecuting and defending counsels), *the psychological disposition of a person sits in judgment* of his or her psychological behavior in order to analyze, measure, and praise or blame, reward or punish himself or herself for it! In short, conscience largely consists in prudence, or common sense, as judge, jury, and prosecuting and defending attorneys measuring, evaluating, our prior behavior as good or evil and, depending upon the final verdict, psychologically rewarding or punishing, even torturing, us for seeing ourselves in our own psychological mirror and liking or not liking what we observe.

How the moral virtue of prudence becomes a necessary condition for acquiring all forms of education through learning, socializing us, and enabling us to become as humanly perfect as we can be as an organizational whole and completely happy.

According to Saint Thomas, because no one human being is entirely self-sufficient in complete human virtue (the means to becoming totally educated in human virtue and, through so doing, becoming able to become as humanly perfect as we can be, and, thereby, completely happy), this lack of instinctive, brute animal self-sufficiency inclines us to seek social life and educational discipline in complete human virtue. Thomas recognizes that most human beings first tend to receive this discipline at home. As this happens, some children are naturally inclined toward docility in taking parental directions. By a divine gift, good natural disposition, or custom, Aquinas says a little *fatherly discipline* in the form of a warning is all we need to be inclined to act virtuously (Et quidem quantum ad illos iuvenes qui sunt proni ad actus virtutum, ex bona dispositione naturae, vel consuetudine, vel magis divino munere, sufficit disciplina paterna, quae est per monitione). (*Summa theologiae*, 1–2, q. 95, a. 1, respondeo)

Unhappily, as Thomas says, such a docile natural or acquired disposition is not universal to all youth. Some are not naturally docile, easily persuaded by words to behave virtuously. Some are naturally inclined to do evil deeds. Not being inclined toward doing virtuous acts, fear and force have to be used against them to cause them to desist from such activities and, at least, leave other people in peace. They need the discipline of punishment, which is discipline meted out by law (Huiusmodi autem disciplina cogens metu poenae, est disciplina legum). (*Summa theologiae*, respondeo) For this reason, to make up for the inadequacy of natural law to bring human beings to complete human virtue, beyond natural law, as part of the eternal law through which he governs all created orders of being, God included human/positive law within the order of human providence.

In such education, especially when dealing with particular and contingent, practical and productive *actions*, not general meanings and truths, Aquinas tells us that starting reasoning solely from principles immediately understood *per se* (from an immediate induction of general meaning and truth—such as that a triangle has three sides) makes no common sense. Because of their almost infinite multitude and diversity, even given a close to infinite, not a little, time, one person could not possibly sufficiently consider all of them. In such matters, from its start, education needs to include principles of practical and productive common sense, which are the concern of *experiential* (*per aliud notum* [known through another], not *per se notum* [known through itself], *commonsense understandings*, or first principles of common sense).

Actionable prudence is specifically different from *observational*, or *speculative*, *prudence*. It involves coordinated synthesis of observational and actionable understanding of abstract, universal, reason and concrete, particular reason—of abstract, speculative prudence, and concrete practical prudence. Hence, Thomas states that, in such matters, "a human being stands most in need of being educated by others, especially by elderly people who have acquired a sound understanding of actually achievable goals." (*Summa theologiae*, 1–2, q. 95, a. 1, respondeo; see also, *Commentary on the Nicomachean Ethics of Aristotle*, bk. 6nn. 1252–1254)

Beyond this, he quotes Aristotle's sage observation from Chapter 2, Book 2 of his *Nicomachean Ethics*, "Because

Chapter 15: Common Sense: The Personal Meeting Point

experience enables them to see principles, it is necessary to pay attention to the indemonstrable assertions and opinions of experts, the elderly, and prudent people, no less than to those who provide demonstrations." He immediately follows up this authoritative support with the following quotes from the biblical book of Proverbs (3:5): "Do not lean on your prudence"; and Ecclesiastes (6:35): "Prudence exists in the multitude of the priests; from your heart join yourself to their wisdom." From which, Thomas concludes that "Receptivity to being well disciplined pertains to prudence. Hence, docility is posited as a part of prudence." (*Summa theologiae*, 2–2, q. 49, a. 3, respondeo)

Precisely because of the essential connection Thomas understood to exist between the moral virtue of prudence and human teachability (docility/*docilitas*) and natural and acquired insufficiency of individual human beings, even with the help of law, to succeed in becoming perfect, or even close to perfect, self-providers and totally happy, beyond natural law (regulated by species prudence) and positive law (regulated chiefly by the virtue of civic prudence), he maintained that complete human *education in virtue* required for human beings to achieve human happiness in this life or the next demands more. It needs as part of eternal law's governance of the created order *individual virtue totally measured by the form of all moral virtue*: all the preceding forms of naturally knowable legal principles and the *supernaturally revealed divine law and its principles* embodied in the commandments of the Old Law, which focused chiefly on changing human behavior through acts of justice and fear; and the New Law, which concentrated on altering human behavior mainly through keeping commandments out of love of God and hope of eternal reward. (*Summa theologiae*, 1–2, q. 91, a. 5, respondeo)

According to Saint Thomas, wherever science is at work, right reason is at work. Intellectual and moral virtue essentially consist in application of right reason (evidently true, *per se*, or *per aliud*, *principles of right understanding* [common sense] rightly to order some organizational multitude in relation to realizing some essentially healthy, real human good). (*Commentary on the Nicomachean Ethics of Aristotle*, bk. 6, lect. 1. n. 1109) Considered as principles of understanding, all intellectual and moral virtue consists in applying principles of divinely and providentially implanted (what Adler repeatedly calls "endowed") commonsense wisdom and prudence (what we know best!) to speculative judgment or practical or productive choice. In doing this, we are simply applying to this or that genus and situation specific principles received by human participation in Divine Wisdom, through what Thomas calls *synderesis*—the first principle of natural law. (*Summa theologiae*, 1–2, q. 94, a. 2, ad 2)

Regarding the claim I make above about the analogous unity in the teaching of Saint Thomas and in truth of *right reason; providence; wisdom; prudence; common sense; all species of law and virtue, and conscience*, while I might not have appeared to some readers to have done so, at least by implication, I have already rationally defended this assertion in relation to all these subjects. However, because some readers might not realize precisely how I have done this, I will explain in some detail why I say I have done it.

As I have shown, in the teachings of Aquinas right reason is analogously identical with divine providence, or God's prudence. Human prudence exists within human rationality as the difference that specifies human beings as other than brute animals. Human reason contains human wisdom, which is analogously identical to human prudence. Virtue in all its species is a psychological habit that perfects human beings considered as organizational wholes in natural and acquired facultative acts to be able to provide for ourselves—*to be self-providers*. In fact, Thomas says, that rational creatures are ranked as being qualitatively more or less excellent, or perfect, through our ability to provide for ourselves and for others. This is precisely the way in which every rational being participates in eternal reason (*aeterna ratio*), which is the principle of eternal law.

Through eternal law, in turn, he maintains human beings have our natural-law inclination to exercise our specifically human activities to pursue complete virtue so as to achieve our human end—human happiness. He calls "natural law" this participation in eternal law by a rational creature: "Inter caetera autem rationalis creatura excellentiori quodam modo divinae providentiae subiacet, inquantum et ipsa fit providential participeps, sibi ipsi et aliis providens. Unde et in ipsa participature ratio aeterna per quam habet naturalem inclinationem ad debitum actum et finem, et talis participatio legis aeternae in rationali creatura 'lex naturalis' dicitur." (*Summa theologiae*, 1–2, q. 91, a. 2, respondeo)

Divine providence inclines human beings to become educated, including self-educated by conscience, to acquire any and every virtue and become perfect self-providers. Wisdom is the highest of all intellectual virtues. Prudence is the highest of all practical virtues. Just as wisdom is the form of all intellectual virtues, in practical activities Saint Thomas maintains prudence is the form of all virtue; and that the prudent man is this the measure of all moral virtue. (*Summa theologiae*, 1–2, q. 66, a. 5, respondeo/*Commentary on the Nicomachean Ethics of Aristotle*, bk. 6) Considered in and of themselves, all virtues are species of providential behavior, perfecting qualities of self-sufficiency and self-providing. This includes every species of art, science, and even poetic imagination, through which, we stretch the philosophical/ scientific intellect.

As Aristotle recognized, poetic understanding is a habit of wondering about causes. Wondering about causes is distinctively human, and, as Aristotle notes (*Metaphysics*, bk. 1, ch. 1, 982b10–27), a specifically metaphysical, activity. The epic, metaphysical, poet is first among professional teachers in any and every culture in which the written word is not the main form of cultural education.

In addition, possession of a great sense memory is an essential condition for such great poetic ability. Aquinas locates the specifically rational ability to engage in sense wondering and possession of sense memory in cogitative, or particular, reason. Hence, poetic imagination, and especially the liberal art of poetic imagining, with its ability to *stretch the imagination to wonder about qualitatively new and higher things*, must exist in particular, or cogitative reason—which is precisely where Thomas locates moral prudence as a species of commonsense shrewdness (*solers* in Latin) and teachability! In exercising the activity of moral prudence, following Aristotle, Aquinas understands a human being to possess psychological investigative, judgmental, and commanding perfections, five *qualities* of a good leader and judge 1) *synesis*, 2) *eubulia*, 3) *eustochia*, 4) *gnome* and 5) *solertia*. (*Commentary on the Nicomachean Ethics of Aristotle*, bk. 6, lects. 8–9)

Starting with the first, Thomas explains that it is the contradictory opposite of *asynesis* (being *asinine*, a fool) when making individual decisions. The person with *synesis* is the type of human being any person with common sense would want to appear before in a court room, pretty much identical to a person with *eusynesia*: someone with a lot of experience who exercises generally sound, shrewd judgment; a *commonsense judge*, one with benevolently disposes good sense about employing common rules of behavior regarding what decision to make related to particular cases: of which the prudent person would be a species in practical matters and the wise person in speculative ones.

Similar to this person are human beings possessing the psychological quality of *eubulia*—excelling at shrewd, slow, methodical, emotionless, discursive, rational deliberation that completely explores every aspect of an investigation *to induce* what is actually the real means, doable deed, to secure this or that desired goal; *eustochia*—excelling at quickly and accurately, without the need rationally and discursively to deliberate immediately to *induce, shrewdly sense, size up*, the right means, act, to choose to achieve a desired end in an individual situation; *gnome*—similar to *synesis*, but having the quality of a benevolent judge related to exceptional cases, where application of commonly applied standards of behavior will result in a foolish decision, such as those involving courtroom equity; and *solertia*—someone having a conflation of *solers* [shrewdness] and *citrus* [quick, inductive-judgment/understanding] all species of shrewdness in both practical and speculative matters). (*Summa theologiae*, 2–2, q. 48, a. 1, respondeo; q. 49, arts. 3 and 4; *Commentary on the Nicomachean Ethics of Aristotle*, bk. 6, lect. 9)

Chapter 15: Common Sense: The Personal Meeting Point

Perhaps the greatest discovery in the history of philosophy/science: Particular reason as the Archimedean-point and lever in the human soul that stretches human imagination and causes all Eureka!-moments of discovery and invention.

In making the observations in the section immediately above, Saint Thomas was building upon perhaps some of the most brilliant psychological observations ever made in the history of philosophy/science—by Aristotle, toward the end the Book 1 of his *Posterior Analytics*—about the nature of philosophy/science, about psychologically how philosophy/science operates. Therein, in specifically two different ways—1) as principles and conclusions and 2) as habits that zero in on a middle, or intermediate, cause—Aristotle starts to compare five different species/habits of knowledge, specifically related to truth: wisdom, science, understanding, art, and prudence.

Commenting on this passage, Saint Thomas notes that, in Book 6 of his *Nicomachean Ethics*, Aristotle discusses these same five habits, but adds two others—suspicion and opinion—concerned not only with truth, but also with falsity. Because the first five imply right reason—having no doubt about truth—in a sense, they are only, or mainly, concerned about, truth.

Of these five habits, three—wisdom, science, and understanding—imply right reason about necessary truths.

Science does this related to conclusions. Understanding does it regarding principles; and wisdom does so related to highest, divine, causes.

Regarding the two remaining habits—art and prudence—Saint Thomas states that art mainly implies having right reason about acts that do not terminate within the psyche of individual person (liberal arts would be an exception, for example). Having art implies having right reason about actions that terminate in some external receiver/subject. As examples, Thomas gives cutting and other activities that human art directs. Regarding prudence, Aquinas states it implies acts that remain within the person acting. As examples, he gives love, hate, choosing analogous acts—like prudence—that involve moral activity. Beyond this, he adds acts of reason—acts that essentially involve bringing logical principles to logical conclusions.

After making these psychological observations, following Aristotle, Saint Thomas turns his attention toward: 1) the nature of wisdom—what it is and how it operates; and 2) science, understanding, and art and how, in some way (analogously), they relate to metaphysics; 3) prudence—how it relates to moral activity; and 4) understanding and reason, and how, inasmuch as they name powers of the soul, they involve natural mental activities.

After doing all the preceding, Thomas notes Aristotle mentions *one habit that specifically concerns itself with seeing and knowing middle, or intermediate, causes*—the habit of *solertia*. In his *Summa theologiae*, Thomas describes this habit as conflating within its single nature the qualities of shrewdness (*solers*) and quickness (*citrus*)—thereby causing to come into being the psychological quality of having the facile, quick-witted ability immediately to see, induce, middle, or intermediate, causes: such as, the middle term of a syllogism in speculative reasoning or the right means to an end in practical activities! (*Summa theologiae*, 2-2, q. 49, a. 4, respondeo)

In his *Commentary on the Posterior Analytics of Aristotle*, Thomas explains that this person possesses the psychological quality of *recta aestimatio* (right estimation)—immediately being able to surmise the reason why something happens, even when a person does not have a lot of time available to inspect or deliberate about a situation. As an example, Saint Thomas refers to a person's ability to infer from the fact that the Moon has all its brightness whenever it faces the Sun immediately to understand, jump to the conclusion, why this is so—because the Sun is illuminating it! (Lect. 44; in Aristotle, bk. 1, 89b10–b30; cf. *Summa theologiae*, 2-2, q. 49, a. 4, respondeo)

Turning his attention toward ethical matters, Aquinas gives the example of someone seeing a poor person engaged in an argument with a rich person immediately rightly concluding that the rich man took something from him, and that the poor man wants it back. Or, if the same person, sees people who had formally been enemies now being friends, immediately and rightly concluding this is because they now have a common enemy.

After presenting these two examples Thomas explains how Aristotle shows two ways in which knowing a middle cause enables a person to know the reason why something is happening. He says Aristotle shows this by first explaining that the quick-witted person simultaneously induces all middle causes, the last or final effect they are generating, what is causing them to generate it—the reason why what is happening is happening.

Then Thomas says Aristotle reinforces his explanation through an example that he presents in the form of a syllogism, which I simplify in the following way:

Major premise: Whenever a celestial body faces the Sun, light from the Sun causes it to be illumined.

Minor premise: The Moon is a celestial body now facing the Sun.

Conclusion: The Sun is now causing the Moon's illumination.

From this syllogistic example, Saint Thomas maintains that a natural endowment or an ability acquired through training causes a person to be quick witted—to have the psychological quality of *solertia*, and with it the ability of

Chapter 15: Common Sense: The Personal Meeting Point 353

quickly being able—apparently in the form of an enthymeme, even a series of them—to apprehend middle causes that explain why something is happening. Thomas gives us another example of the nature of being quick witted by showing how this power is essentially connected to the ability to recognize, induce, what, in Book 6, Lecture 10, of his *Commentary on the Nicomachean Ethics of Aristotle*, he calls *ultimates, singulars,* and sometimes *singular ultimates* or *ultimate singulars*.

He does this within the context of explaining Aristotle's teaching about the nature of the habit of understanding. He says this innate *habitus* and act is present in both speculative and practical knowledge. It essentially relates to ultimates because ultimates are first principles—acts of understanding, not the act of reasoning; and understanding apprehends first principles. Reasoning starts by applying first principles that understanding discovers, induces. Thomas then adds that two species of understanding exist:

1) Understanding immutable and necessary first principles, or ultimates, used in speculative, syllogistic demonstrations. He states that, because they have to be known before such demonstrations can start, these principles are demonstrably unchangeable syllogistically, and must be first known prior to such demonstrations. They have to be known first because they are the starting points, necessary conditions, from which such a syllogistic demonstration proceeds through the middle term (cause/

principle) of its minor premise to its rationally induced and inferred conclusion (concluding principle). *Only after these first principles are, to some extent, known can such a demonstration begin!* And they are immutable because knowledge of them is innately endowed and can never be removed from the intellectual soul of a human being.

2) Understanding contingent and singular ultimates, first principles, used in practical, syllogistic demonstrations. Such demonstrations essentially relate to a qualitatively different kind of universal apprehended through a middle cause, middle term, or syllogistic minor premise. And they do so for a different chief end than the one that causes a speculative syllogism to order its beginning premise to its concluding premise—which is to execute a single action that a multitude of organizational parts unites together to cause to come into existence within an individual situation (at some individual time and place).

The principles of a practical or productive syllogism are proximate, concretely assembled causes being harmoniously united together and applied as a single means, middle cause, to effect a single chief end: *to effect, bring into being, numerically one action or product.* They are not proximate causes moving through abstract ideas and definitions harmoniously to join them together as a means to generate abstract intelligibility, explain why something is as it is. Their chief aim is not to cause/effect intelligibility, cause speculative understanding of the reason why. *Their chief goal is not*

Chapter 15: Common Sense: The Personal Meeting Point

to make intelligible, explain, the chief reason *why* John is an animal. It is to *explain how* to build a bridge, bake a cake, win a game, or cause someone to become courageous. *In the operational, practical and productive syllogism the reason how is the reason why!*

Practical and productive syllogisms are the *necessary means* for causing a contingent, situational, organizational action. They are essentially acts of understanding in the form of knowhow (applicational understanding, understanding chiefly aiming at causing action) concretely moving, uniting, specific parts of a generic, organizational whole into an operational organizational unit to cause numerically one chief action. In behaving in this way, an operational (practical or productive) syllogism acts analogously to the way an observational syllogism abstractly unites abstract, universal, ideas of animal and rational, generically and specifically to generate the abstract general and intelligible idea and understanding of the essential relationships that have to exist to make intelligible what causes some individual to be part of some genus—for example, what chiefly causes John to be an animal, what is the causal means in and through which John becomes an animal.

In both species of syllogism, some sought-after definition of the reason why or reason how causes the syllogism to move from major premise to concluding premise through a middle premise! In both species of syllogism, this definition takes its genus from its chief aim and its species from its middle term or minor premise! The middle term is the means to the end. However, because in the different species of syllogism the chief goals are different—explanation causing intelligibility (understanding the chief reason why) versus explanation by doing (showing how to make a product or perform an action), the middle terms function as a qualitatively different means and in qualitatively different causal ways.

Considered simply as a middle, or intermediary, cause, that leads human reasoning from its starting, major premise to its ultimate conclusion and final end, every act of understanding is an operation, a movement, that must pass through a middle term or minor premise as a proximate cause or proximate first principle capable of transporting human understanding from its starting principle to its concluding principle. This generic movement is involved in all species of syllogistic reasoning. Irrelevant to such reasoning is whether or not its terminating conclusion will be one of abstract understanding that terminates within the psyche of an observational knower or concrete understanding concluding in the form of doing or making outside the human soul in some action chosen or something built or made.

In both instances, the genus of the idea and definition that moves the reasoning is taken from the end and the species is taken from the means: the middle cause. The end exists in the beginning. The effect exists in the cause; and the effect itself is a first and final cause of moving reasoning from understanding's starting point of desiring, through a middle cause as an intermediary means, to understanding an end or cause an action or some thing. Both species of syllogistic reasoning are simply two different ways of using reasoning intellectually to move from one species of understanding (a beginning, qualitatively less perfect one) to another (a concluding, more perfect one) through an intermediary (more or less perfect) understanding that connects them together.

To explain the nature of such principles and how they are psychologically acquired, Saint Thomas first refers to the fact that both the principles of abstract, observational, or speculative, understanding and those of concrete, operational, or practical understanding must first be drawn from, abstracted out of, induced, from singulars. And they must include some single observational understanding of starting points and some understanding of some single, desired, chief goal. Then, he follows this with a concrete example. He states, from the observation that some herb has cured this or that ailment in some person, this effect signifies to some person possessed of *synesis* that this herb has some medicinal ability to cure him of her of the same disease.

For this reason, he maintains such people are said to have *common sense*. He adds that not just any person has this ability in practical matters. To have it, this person must have experience of these singulars, these principles and ultimates, by both some exterior and interior sense faculty. Then he recalls to his readers that Aristotle had previously said in Book 6 of his *Nicomachean Ethics* (nn. 1214–1215 in Aquinas's *Commentary*) that prudence is the property of an interior power of judging that Thomas calls "particular reason." He adds that, on the sense level, this faculty is called *understanding* and its formal object is the sensible and the singular—that is, *first principles sensed as such in and through the sense faculty of particular reason*. (n. 1249 in Aquinas's *Commentary*)

From this observation, in agreement with Aristotle, Thomas concludes that, *by nature, no human being is called, or can be, a philosopher. To become a philosopher, a person must first have common sense*. While, he says, some human beings are naturally more inclined to have common sense about first principles, common opinion tends to recognize that, if common sense ever comes to human beings, it does so in old age.

Indirectly, through Aristotle—evidently referring to the character of Cephalus in Book 1 of Plato's *Republic* (328b–331d) as that of an old man possessed of common sense—Thomas then discusses the fact that, because they have acquired a habit of right judgment in individual matters as a result of long, practical experience at living, elderly people tend to be more quick witted in recognizing principles. Since Thomas states "principles are more certain than conclusions of demonstration," nobody with a weak faculty of particular reason and the feeble commonsense understanding of first principles it brings with it to a human being can properly be called, or be, a philosopher. (nn. 1235–1255 in Aquinas's *Commentary*)

Because, as a moral virtue, 1) prudence exists within the prudent man's concrete cogitative reason, and 2) to exist therein precisely as a moral virtue, it must also simultaneously exist as a command and control principle within this person's abstract, syllogistic reason, Saint Thomas maintains that, within the individual circumstance, precisely what makes the prudent man the measure of moral activity is the fact that he is able to apprehend with precision universal and singular first principles of moral choice. Through abstract syllogistic reason, he is able to recognize the universal human good. Through concrete, cogitative, or particular, reason, he is able precisely to sense the enabling means to choose to move closer toward this end at this time and in this place. As a real end and real means, what is really good in the individual circumstance appears really good to the prudent man's cogitative and intellectual reason!

This radically distinguishes this person's judgment from that of the morally vicious person. *According to Aquinas, while both the morally virtuous and vicious person may be shrewd,* within even the viciously shrewd person, "moral vice perverts the judgment of reason and causes deception in the conception of practical principles, doable deeds, on the level of universal and particular reason. Since we cannot reason well when we are mistaken about principles, the moral psychology of imprudent, vicious people prevents them from being able habitually to reason well in practical matters. Their unhealthy moral psychology prevents them from being able habitually and precisely to conceive the human good, the good doable deed, or the means to it within the individual circumstance." (*The Moral Psychology of Saint Thomas Aquinas*, 370–371; and *Commentary on the Nicomachean Ethics of Aristotle*, bk. 6)

When we understand that wisdom and prudence are simply species of common sense and conscience in the way I have just described, the stupidity of the behavior of the morally vicious person, culture, society, or civilization becomes even more stark and dramatic. The more vicious he, she, or it becomes, the more out of touch with reality, lacking in common sense, he, she, or it gets.

At the extreme, all these totally lose a conscience; and if this psychological mindset comes to dominate a culture's, society's, civilization's educational and legal institutions, these will become akin to a mental prison camp in which the inmates run the asylum! *Is this the sort of mindset any psychologically healthy human being would choose to rule over himself or herself politically or otherwise?*

So what? What of It?

Whether or not a serious reader or audience member agrees, disagrees, or suspends judgment about the contents of any artistic performance to which he or she has taken the time and trouble to pay attention or witness, in Chapter 8 of his masterly monograph, *How to Speak. How to Listen*, Mortimer J. Adler recommends that, once it has concluded, in relation to it, he or she should ask the following question about it: "What of it?" Or, as I put the same question, "So what?" Today, we might say a reader or audience member should take a *Satisfaction Survey* or *Assessment* of the performance using the chief aims, means, and ends the performer has set for himself or herself. That is, what beneficial or harmful consequences result from the fact that you have agreed, disagreed, liked or disliked, or have suspended judgment about agreeing or disagreeing, or cannot figure out whether you have agreed or disagreed with or liked or disliked some performance and the way the performer might or might not have rationally justified them to you? (108)

According to Adler, and I agree with him, asking this final question involves a listener or observer thinking about the personal significance of a performance considered as a whole and in relation to all its parts. Using this assessment tool related to note taking, in Chapter 8, Adler had asked why bother following the cumbersome rules and recommendations Adler has given related to note taking unless a listener is convinced "that the character and substance of the speech is rich and important enough to deserve all the effort called for"? (108) The rational answer to such a question appears evidently to be that *doing so makes no common sense.*

For this reason, after asking this question, Adler immediately adds that the way a person answers it must be determined *by the precept of prudence*—which is what most of us, most of the time, understand to be identical with practical and productive common sense: "The precept of prudence in following the recommendations suggested is simply to make whatever adaptation or use of them the substance, style, and importance of the speech deserves, making the maximum effort for the best of speeches, less for those that are less worthy, and not at all for those that were not worth listening to in the first place." (108)

Analogously considered, to be logically consistent— which is something Adler always insisted upon being—I think Adler would use the same precept of prudence to measure the worth of both our books and use of your time and effort to have read them. I would do the same. Given the nature of my monograph I can think of no better way to end it than to recommend to the reader that he or she conclude his or her reading of my monograph than by using Adler's criterion to measure the worth of mine, considered in itself and according to your personal pleasure, overall psychological profit; and any advancement or lack thereof it might have contributed, or not contributed, to satisfaction of your natural pursuit of happiness.

To assist you in your ability easily to do this, I provide as follows *a Reader Satisfaction Survey* that includes a summary of the prudential, or commonsense, plan (consisting of a list of nine specific commonsense goals and corresponding means to realize them) for organizing this book that, in my Introduction, I had set out for myself to ensure it would be as pleasurable and profitable as I could make it for readers to take the time, effort, and bother to purchase and read. Each section includes questions for you to answer related to my success or failure to achieve what I had set out to do and reader recommendations for more perfectly realizing my goals.

Reader Satisfaction Survey consisting of nine main reasons the author wrote this book with each reason followed by three questions: Was the author totally, partially, or not at all partially successful in achieving these goals? Why or why not? In light of his success or failure to realize these goals, was this book worth the time, trouble, and bother for you to read?

Reason 1): As a chief means for enabling contemporary readers to come into contact with common and uncommon commonsense wisdom of past intellectual giants.

Questions for the reader: Was the author totally, partially, or not at all partially successful in achieving these goals? Why or why not? In light of his success or failure to realize these goals, was this book worth the time, trouble, and bother for you to read?

Reason 2): To foster world peace by enabling readers to enrich their own lives and that of others by acquiring some of this wisdom and putting it to use on a daily basis.

Questions for the reader: Was the author totally, partially, or not at all partially successful in achieving these goals? Why or why not? In light of his success or failure to realize these goals, was this book worth the time, trouble, and bother for you to read?

Reason 3): To help repair terrible contemporary damage that loss of common sense and commonsense wisdom from the West is causing to human, and other forms of, life today on a global scale.

Questions for the reader: Was the author totally, partially, or not at all partially successful in achieving these goals? Why or why not? In light of his success or failure to realize these goals, was this book worth the time, trouble, and bother for you to read?

Chapter 15: Common Sense: The Personal Meeting Point

Reason 4) To use Adler's book as a great introduction to a tradition of the uncommon commonsense metaphysical wisdom and moral prudence going back to the Ancient Greeks.

Questions for the reader: Was the author totally, partially, or not at all partially successful in achieving these goals? Why or why not? In light of his success or failure to realize these goals, was this book worth the time, trouble, and bother for you to read?

Reason 5): To use topics from Adler's *How to Listen and How to Speak* to transcend his book primarily as an introduction to the tradition of the uncommon commonsense metaphysical wisdom and moral prudence of the Ancient Greeks; and, thereby, hopefully contribute to Adler's work to help establish future global peace; and secondarily to teach readers classical rhetoric, and Adler's understanding of this subject.

Questions for the reader: Was the author totally, partially, or not at all partially successful in achieving these goals? Why or why not? In light of his success or failure to realize these goals, was this book worth the time, trouble, and bother for you to read?

Reason 6): To stand on the shoulders of the metaphysical and moral teachings of Adler, Aristotle, and Saint Thomas Aquinas to convey to readers an understanding of the nature of Aristotle's rhetoric as an essential means for conveying to contemporary readers and to posterity a specific understanding of philosophy as an essential humanistic, cultural and transgenerational enterprise and educational tool.

Questions for the reader: Was the author totally, partially, or not at all partially successful in achieving these goals? Why or why not? In light of his success or failure to realize these goals, was this book worth the time, trouble, and bother for you to read?

Reason 7): To transmit to the reader an understanding that rhetoric is an essential means necessary to use to convey a living tradition of uncommon common sense wisdom from one generation to another.

Questions for the reader: Was the author totally, partially, or not at all partially successful in achieving these goals? Why or why not? In light of his success or failure to realize these goals, was this book worth the time, trouble, and bother for you to read?

Reason 8): To convey to readers how rhetoric helps trans-generationally to transmit uncommon commonsense metaphysical wisdom and moral prudence in the form of a cultural heritage as a traditional enterprise (team effort) that fosters trans-generational improvement of individual and social life, and peaceful and cooperative living together.

Questions for the reader: Was the author totally, partially, or not at all partially successful in achieving these goals? Why or why not? In light of his success or failure to realize these goals, was this book worth the time, trouble, and bother for you to read?

Reason 9): To compose the chapters of the book in the form of lessons usable as part of an academic course of instruction in commonsense wisdom and leadership coaching out of which a future commonsense wisdom academy and post-Enlightenment uncommon commonsense wisdom university will naturally eventually be able to grow.

Questions for the reader: Was the author totally, partially, or not at all partially successful in achieving these goals? Why or why not? In light of his success or failure to realize these goals, was this book worth the time, trouble, and bother for you to read?

Thank you!

Peter Redpath

JACEK WORONIECKI MEMORIAL LECTURES

CLASSICAL RHETORIC
HOW TO SPEAK. HOW TO LISTEN

Prof. Peter A. Redpath

President, International Etienne Gilson Society
CEO Aquinas School of Leadership
Rector, Adler-Aquinas Institute, USA

THE FACULTY OF PHILOSOPHY
THE JOHN PAUL II CATHOLIC UNIVERSITY OF LUBLIN

online

31 MAY - 5 JUNE, 2021 • 30 HOUR-COURSE • 2 ECTS POINTS

Program on www.kul.pl/woroniecki

www.ingramcontent.com/pod-product-compliance
Lightning Source LLC
Chambersburg PA
CBHW050120170426
43197CB00011B/1659